Literary Translation

TOPICS IN TRANSLATION
Series Editors: Susan Bassnett, *University of Warwick, UK* and Edwin Gentzler, *University of Massachusetts, Amherst, USA*
Editor for **Translation in the Commercial Environment:** Geoffrey Samuelsson-Brown, *University of Surrey, UK*

Other Books in the Series
Annotated Texts for Translation: French – English
  Beverly Adab
Annotated Texts for Translation: English – French
  Beverly Adab
Annotated Texts for Translation: English – German
  Christina Schäffner with Uwe Wiesemann
'Behind Inverted Commas' Translation and Anglo-German Cultural Relations in the Nineteenth Century
  Susanne Stark
Constructing Cultures: Essays on Literary Translation
  Susan Bassnett and André Lefevere
Contemporary Translation Theories (2nd Edition)
  Edwin Gentzler
Culture Bumps: An Empirical Approach to the Translation of Allusions
  Ritva Leppihalme
Practical Guide for Translators
  Geoffrey Samuelsson-Brown
The Coming Industry of Teletranslation
  Minako O'Hagan
The Interpreter's Resource
  Mary Phelan
The Pragmatics of Translation
  Leo Hickey (ed.)
The Rewriting of Njáls Saga: Translation, Ideology, and Icelandic Sagas
  Jon Karl Helgason
Translation, Power, Subversion
  Román Alvarez and M. Carmen-Africa Vidal (eds)
Translation and Nation: A Cultural Politics of Englishness
  Roger Ellis and Liz Oakley-Brown (eds)
Time Sharing on Stage: Drama Translation in Theatre and Society
  Sirkku Aaltonen
Words, Words, Words. The Translator and the Language Learner
  Gunilla Anderman and Margaret Rogers
Written in the Language of the Scottish Nation
  John Corbett

Please contact us for the latest book information:
Multilingual Matters, Frankfurt Lodge, Clevedon Hall,
Victoria Road, Clevedon, BS21 7HH, England
http://www.multilingual-matters.com

TOPICS IN TRANSLATION 22
Editor: Geoffrey Samuelsson-Brown, *University of Surrey*

Literary Translation
A Practical Guide

Clifford E. Landers
New Jersey City University

MULTILINGUAL MATTERS LTD
Clevedon • Buffalo • Toronto • Sydney

To my wife Vasda Bonafini Landers, who translated me into a translator

Library of Congress Cataloging in Publication Data
Landers, Clifford, E.
Literary Translation: A Practical Guide/Clifford E. Landers.
Topics in Translation: 22.
Includes many examples, chiefly in Portuguese.
Includes bibliographical references and index.
1. Translating and interpreting. 2. Literature–History and criticism–Theory, etc.
I. Title. II. Series.
PN241.L29 2001
418'.02–dc21   2001041009

British Library Cataloguing in Publication Data
A catalogue entry for this book is available from the British Library.

ISBN 1-85359-520-9 (hbk)
ISBN 1-85359-519-5 (pbk)

Multilingual Matters Ltd
UK: Frankfurt Lodge, Clevedon Hall, Victoria Road, Clevedon BS21 7HH.
USA: UTP, 2250 Military Road, Tonawanda, NY 14150, USA.
Canada: UTP, 5201 Dufferin Street, North York, Ontario M3H 5T8, Canada.
Australia: Footprint Books, Unit 4/92a Mona Vale Road, Mona Vale, NSW 2103, Australia.

Copyright © 2001 Clifford E. Landers.
Some of the material in this book has appeared in modified form in *ATA Chronicle*, *ATA Source*, *Brasil/Brazil*, *Discurso*, *Literary Review*, *Proceedings of the Annual Conference of the American Translators Association*, *Platte Valley Review*, *Prime Crimes* and *Translation Review*.

Printed and bound in Great Britain by the Cromwell Press Ltd.

Contents

The Working Translator

La Dernière Translation

by Millôr Fernandes

When an old translator dies
Does his soul, *alma, anima,*
Free now of its wearisome craft
Of rendering
Go straight to heaven, *ao céu,*
al cielo, au ciel, zum Himmel,
Or to the hell – *Hölle* – of the great
traditori?
Or will a translator be considered
In the minute hierarchy of the divine
(*himmlisch*)
Neither fish, nor water, *ni poisson ni l'eau*
Nem água, nem peixe, nichts, assolutamente
niente?
What of the essential will this
mere intermediary of semantics, broker
of the universal Babel, discover?
Definitive communication, without words?
Once again the first word?
Will he learn, finally!,
Whether HE speaks Hebrew
Or Latin?
Or will he remain infinitely
In the infinite
Until he hears the Voice, *Voz, Voix, Voce,*
Stimme, Vox,
Of the Supreme Mystery
Coming from beyond
Flying like a birdpássarouccelopájarovogel
Addressing him in…
And giving at last
The translation of Amen?

– translated from Brazilian Portuguese by Clifford E. Landers

Preface

As the title states, this is a practical, not a theoretical, guide. While I have no quarrel with theorists, in theory at least, this is a get-your-hands-dirty, wrestle-with-reality type of book. *Literary Translation: A Practical Guide* is based on the following assumptions.

(1) The direction of translation is *from* a given source language (SL) *into* English, the target language (TL). This does not necessarily assume that the translator is a native speaker of English. Though there are powerful arguments that one should always translate into one's mother tongue, there are enough counterexamples, both of authors (Conrad and Nabokov come to mind) and of translators to convince a fair-minded observer that this rule is not inviolable.

(2) The goal of literary translation is publication. Translating for pleasure or as intellectual exercise is well and good, but the dedicated literary translator aims at sharing the final result with TL readers for whom the work would otherwise forever remain inaccessible. A portion of this guide is devoted to the question of how to go about finding an outlet for one's translations.

(3) The translator possesses a working knowledge of a language pair – fluent English and a solid grounding in the SL. Convincing arguments can be made that thoroughgoing command of the TL is by far the more important of the two, and there are instances of translators producing excellent renderings of works, especially in the case of poetry, whose original language is complete terra incognita to them. An instance of the TL's paramount role in literary translation: when Gregory Rabassa was about to begin his exemplary translation of Gabriel García Márquez's monumental *Cien años de soledad*, he was asked if he thought his Spanish was good enough. 'What I wonder,' replied Rabassa, who was born and raised in the United States, 'is whether my *English* is good enough.'

In *Literary Translation: A Practical Guide*, both beginning and experienced translators will find pragmatic techniques for dealing with problems of literary translation, whatever the original language. The specifics of translating, say, Bulgarian, obviously differ from those of rendering French, Chinese, or any other language into English. But certain challenges and certain themes recur in translation, whatever the language pair. This guide proposes to help the translator navigate through them.

Because a book about translation without examples is like a book about photography without pictures, illustrations, mostly from my language of specialty – Portuguese – appear frequently. They are meant not as models but as stimuli to thinking. The same kinds of associations and thought processes that 'solve' problems in one language are usually transferable to another tongue.

The quotation marks around *solve* are a reminder that translation problems are not like math problems that have only one or at most a strictly limited number of right answers. As a subfield of literature – and literature is indisputably an art rather than a science – translation is subjective in essence. Reasonable people may well disagree about which of several proposed alternatives to a particular translation problem best addresses it. Nevertheless, there are guidelines that can help us work our way through, to use a Borgesian metaphor, the seemingly infinite labyrinth of forking paths. That is the purpose of this book.

The Fundamentals

Why Literary Translation?

Why do literary translation? Consider:

NIGHT DRIVE
by Rubem Fonseca

I arrived home with my briefcase bulging with papers, reports, studies, research, proposals, contracts. My wife, who was playing solitaire in bed, a glass of whiskey on the nightstand, said, without looking up from the cards, 'You look tired.' The usual house sounds: my daughter in her room practicing voice modulation, quadraphonic music from my son's room. 'Why don't you put down that suitcase?' my wife asked. 'Take off those clothes, have a nice glass of whiskey. You've got to learn to relax.'

I went to the library, the place in the house I enjoy being by myself, and as usual did nothing. I opened the research volume on the desk but didn't see the letters and numbers. I was merely waiting.

'You never stop working. I'll bet your partners don't work half as hard and they earn the same.' My wife came into the room, a glass in her hand. 'Can I tell her to serve dinner?'

The maid served the meal French style. My children had grown up, my wife and I were fat. 'It's that wine you like,' she said, clicking her tongue with pleasure. My son asked for money during the coffee course, my daughter asked for money during the liqueur. My wife didn't ask for anything; we have a joint checking account.

'Shall we go for a drive?' I asked her. I knew she wouldn't go – it was time for her soap opera.

'I don't see what you get out of going for a drive every night, but the car cost a fortune, it has to be used. I'm just less and less attracted to material things,' she replied.

The children's cars were blocking the garage door, preventing me from removing my car. I moved both cars and parked them in the street, removed my car and parked it in the street, put the other two cars back in the garage, and closed the door. All this maneuvering left me slightly irritated, but when I saw my car's jutting bumpers, the special chrome-plated double reinforcement, I felt my heart race with euphoria.

I turned the ignition key. It was a powerful motor that generated its strength silently beneath the aerodynamic hood. As always, I left without

3

knowing where I would go. It had to be a deserted street, in this city with more people than flies. Not the Avenida Brasil – too busy.

I came to a poorly lighted street, heavy with dark trees, the perfect spot. A man or a woman? It made little difference, really, but no one with the right characteristics appeared. I began to get tense. It always happened that way, and I even liked it – the sense of relief was greater. Then I saw the woman. It could be her, even though a woman was less exciting because she was easier. She was walking quickly, carrying a package wrapped in cheap paper – something from a bakery or the market. She was wearing a skirt and blouse.

There were trees every twenty yards along the sidewalk, an interesting problem demanding a great deal of expertise. I turned off the headlights and accelerated. She only realized I was going for her when she heard the sound of the tires hitting the curb. I caught her above the knees, right in the middle of her legs, a bit more toward the left leg – a perfect hit. I heard the impact break the large bones, veered rapidly to the left, shot narrowly past one of the trees, and, tires squealing, skidded back onto the asphalt. The motor would go from zero to sixty in eight seconds. I could see that the woman's broken body had come to rest, covered with blood, on top of the low wall in front of a house.

Back in the garage, I took a good look at the car. With pride I ran my hand lightly over the unmarked fenders and bumper. Few people in the world could match my skill driving such a car.

The family was watching television. 'Do you feel better after your spin?' my wife asked, lying on the sofa, staring fixedly at the TV screen.

'I'm going to bed,' I answered, 'good night everybody. Tomorrow's going to be a rough day at the office.'

*   *   *

The pleasure of reading such a seemingly simple, brief, yet fully realized short story is something most of us would want to share with others. But if it is written in another language, access is limited to only those who read that tongue.

Its theme, the banality of evil, is delineated concisely and tellingly; no words are wasted – every detail adds to the totality of a setting and a life hurriedly glimpsed yet understood as much as any of us can understand the Other. It is a deceptively uncomplicated work that stays with and haunts us long after the few moments it takes to read. It, and the myriad of other fine pieces of literature appearing in hundreds of the world's languages, are the best argument for doing literary translation.

Why do literary translation? Of all the forms that translation takes – such as commercial, financial, technical, scientific, advertising, etc. – only *literary* translation lets one consistently share in the creative process. Here alone does the translator experience the aesthetic joys of working with great literature, of recreating in a new language a work that would otherwise remain beyond reach, effectively 'in code,' in the metaphor of the celebrated Dutch novelist Cees Nooteboom.

By itself, is this enough to motivate a would-be translator? For the majority of those who do literary translation, the answer is yes. For others, the incentives may be more tangible. To begin with, literary translation eschews the anonymity of other areas of translation; uncredited book-length translations belong to an earlier, less enlightened time. Although glory is unlikely to attach to a translator's name, for better or worse he or she is now recognized as part of the literary world.

The intellectual rewards of translation (which, hereafter will mean literary translation unless otherwise specified) are many. For some, the pleasure of puzzle-solving is an important element. How to find an equivalent for a source-language pun? Can the tone of the original be reproduced in the target language? What to do about slang, nicknames, colloquialisms, proverbs, references to popular culture, metalanguage (when a language becomes self-referential, as for example an allusion to *tú* vs. *usted* in Spanish)? The delight, mental though it be, that a translator feels in cutting through any of these Gordian knots can best be described as somewhere between chocolate and sex – you choose their rank-order.

The literary translator can take heart from having expanded the potential readership of a novel from, say, the five million who read Finnish to the half a billion who read English as a first or second language. By rendering 'Passeio Noturno' into 'Night Drive,' the translator increased over fourfold the potential audience for the work, in the process making it accessible to students and researchers of comparative literature who may not read Portuguese. Finally, the new version may serve as source for translation into third languages (see 'Indirect Translation').

Some translate for the prestige. Seeing one's name on a title page just below that of a Nobel laureate is, well, heady, even if the author is long departed or, if living, far too busy to engage in dialogue with a translator. This is not to imply that major writers look down upon their translators, merely a reminder that English is not the only language into which outstanding literary works are translated.

Still others value translation for the relationships that can develop from it. The very first author I translated, Rubem Fonseca, whose story 'Night Drive' introduced this section, became a close friend, and that friendship has endured some 15 years. In many countries, writers are a small coterie, all of whom know one another. A successful translation of one writer's works may often lead to referrals to other literati in the same circle, some-thing that has happened with me consistently in the last decade. English is a prestige language, especially in developing countries, and writers are very cognizant of the role that translation into English plays in making their works known beyond their own linguistic boundaries.

As superficial as it may seem, some translators report that their activities give them access to a world they would never penetrate in their home coun-tries. An ordinary citizen who would scarcely hope to have tea with literary luminaries of his own nation – John Updike, Joyce Carol Oates, or Norman Mailer – can interact socially and professionally with their equivalents in Denmark, Brazil, Egypt, or Romania. For often underappreciated word-workers like translators, this is a not inconsequential perk.

There are many reasons for doing literary translation, but ultimately only you can decide which ones impel you. As for money, it has been omitted from these deliberations because if it's your primary motivation for doing literary translation, you should choose another field. Much greater monetary compensation can be had in any of the other areas of translation; many people make a respectable living doing nothing but commercial or technical translation. While it's a cliché that literary transla-tion is a labor of love, basically it *is*. Of the scores of literary translators I know, not one is motivated to exercise the craft primarily by bottom-line considerations. (At this writing, even the most prolific of living translators of Spanish- and Portuguese-language literature, Gregory Rabassa, whose output spans more then three decades, has not given up his university day job.) This is not to suggest that literary translation is philanthropic or totally uncompensated volunteer work, just that it should not be counted upon as one's main source of income. Financial aspects of the craft are discussed in a later chapter.

So, why do literary translation? For me, at least, to have the pleasure of introducing English-speaking readers to outstanding works like 'Night Drive.'

The uniqueness of literary translation

Literary translation, at least in the English-speaking world, faces a difficulty that texts originally written in English do not: resistance by the public to reading literature in translation. There is no need to belabor this point, so evident to publishers in England, the United States, and the other Anglo-Saxon nations. As Jorge Iglesias has said, 'To know we are reading a translation implies a loss of innocence.' This imposes a significant burden on the translator to overcome, and to do so means having a firm grasp on principles and techniques.

The anecdote in the Preface about Gregory Rabassa's feelings before he began translating *One Hundred Years of Solitude* illustrates one of the unique qualities that set literary translation apart from all other branches of translation. In addition to a thorough mastery of the source language, the literary translator must possess a profound knowledge of the target language. In reality, being in love with one or both languages, if not an absolute necessity, is a trait frequently found among the best and most successful literary translators. A lifelong love affair with words is one of the qualities that sets logophiles apart from others – e.g., journalists, publicists, copywriters – who may make their living dealing with the written or spoken word but whose attachment is often more utilitarian than the translator's.

One of the most difficult concepts about literary translation to convey to those who have never seriously attempted it – including practitioners in areas such as technical and commercial translation – is that *how* one says something can be as important, sometimes more important, than what one says.

In technical translation, for example, style is not a consideration so long as the informational content makes its way unaltered from SL to TL. The freight-train analogy is a useful one: in technical translation the order of the cars is inconsequential if all the cargo arrives intact. In literary translation, however, the order of the cars – which is to say the style – can make the difference between a lively, highly readable translation and a stilted, rigid, and artificial rendering that strips the original of its artistic and aesthetic essence, even its very soul.

Now that we have established that literary translation is the most demanding type of translation, a short digression. Why, I am often asked, does it pay less than the other branches? Shouldn't it be the other way around?

Let's not mince words. In some cases, rather than pay poorly, literary translation pays not at all. (Unlike novels, most of the short stories I've translated yielded not a cent.) And yet there is no shortage of aspiring translators ready to take the plunge. Literary translators are usually delighted to see their work in print, and for many this is reward enough. No exception to the law of supply and demand, literary translation is underpaid because so many are willing to do it for sheer pleasure. For comparison, think of the vast numbers of people who paint and how few earn a living at it. Yet neither painters nor literary translators are deterred from the pursuit of their art. Many literary translators are academicians, with the language background, necessary free time, and income to devote themselves to the activity. (There's no income in bird-watching either, but the pastime continues to grow.) There are far more people willing, even eager, to do literary translation than there are individuals who will pay them to do so, and outside the publishing world there is virtually no demand for literary translation. The result? As has been said before, if you're in literary translation for the money, you picked the wrong field. End of digression.

Consider some of the capabilities that the literary translator must command: tone, style, flexibility, inventiveness, knowledge of the SL culture, the ability to glean meaning from ambiguity, an ear for sonority, and humility. Why humility? Because even our best efforts will never succeed in capturing in all its grandeur the richness of the original. The description of translation attributed to Cervantes will always haunt us: a tapestry seen from the wrong side. If we produce a translation that approximates the TL text or stands as a literary work in its own right, that is the most that can be expected.

A simple SL phrase like Portuguese *Não vou lá* can be rendered in a variety of ways in English, from the highest grammatical register exemplifying 'refined' speech to the solecisms usually associated in the public mind with incomplete education and lower social status. Restricting ourselves only to subject–verb–complement order (there are other, less common possibilities: I go there not, there go I not, there I do not go, etc.), each variant slightly alters the effect:

I do not go there.
I don't go there.
I am not going there.
I'm not going there.
I shall not go there.
I shan't go there.
I will not go there.

I won't go there.
I am not going to go there.
I'm not going to go there.
I ain't going there.
I ain't goin' there.

The choice from among this wide range of TL choices, any of which can conceivably be the most appropriate rendering of the SL phrase, hinges on a thorough grounding in context. As there is no way to say 'ain't,' for example, in Romance languages (though of course non-standard usages exist that convey similar social and intellectual clues about the speaker) native speakers at every level would fashion an identical phrase indicating unwillingness or lack of intent. But in the context of the work, it would be clear what level of discourse the individual, if speaking in English, would be likely to use.

More than in other branches of the translator's art such as legal, technical/ scientific, financial/commercial, or in interpretation (simultaneous or consecutive), literary translation entails an unending skein of choices. And the same phrase, such as *não vou lá* may actually be translated differently each time it occurs – a cardinal sin in technical translation, where terms must be clear and unambiguous.

One example of the heightened sensitivity to nuance that marks literary translation can be found in the opening sentence of a short story by the Argentine writer Leopoldo Lugones (1874–1938) entitled *'Un fenómeno inexplicable' (An Unexplained Phenomenon)*: *Hace de esto once años*. Selecting only from the high register that characterizes the work, here are some possible renderings of this seemingly straightforward phrase, each with a subtle if perceptible shading.

This happened eleven years ago.
This occurred eleven years ago.
This took place eleven years ago.
Eleven years have passed/gone by since this happened/occurred/ took place.

All these semantically interchangeable sentences convey the same information but differ significantly in aesthetic effect. Each is defensible, and each would have its defenders, but the literary translator must make a choice, and from a succession of such choices emerges the final product. Small wonder that since the Septuagint no two translations of the same literary work have been identical!

The role of choice in literary translation cannot be overemphasized. As seen in the section 'A Day in the Life,' at every turn the translator is faced with choices – of words, fidelity, emphasis, punctuation, register, sometimes even of spelling. (In *A Samba for Sherlock* I debated for days whether to use *clue* or the quainter *clew* before opting for the former.) Breon Mitchell, a noted translator of German literature, devoted an entire article to decisions involved in merely the first two sentences of his retranslation of Franz Kafka's *The Trial*. As he comments:

> The sad fact is that in spite of all the attention paid to the opening sentence, which is indeed rich in complexity, the sentence that follows poses an even greater difficulty for the translator: '*Die Köchin der Frau Grubach, seiner Zimmervermieterin, die ihm jeder Tag gegen acht Uhr früh das Frühstück brachte, kam dismal nicht.*' For it soon becomes clear that including Frau Grubach by name seems incompatible with constructing an acceptable English sentence... When the Muirs [translators of an earlier edition] reached this stumbling block, they simply leaped over it: 'His landlady's cook, who always brought him his breakfast at eight o'clock, failed to appear on this occasion.'

> The possible solutions are all terribly awkward. A literal version has little to recommend it: 'The cook of Frau Grubach, his landlady, who brought him...' Any attempt to smooth over the use of the genitive while retaining Frau Grubach's name only makes matters worse, creating grammatical monstrosities. We can hardly accept 'Frau Grubach's cook, his landlady, who...' or 'His landlady's cook, Frau Grubach, who...' or 'His landlady Frau Grubach's cook, who...' Yet a different approach dissolves into grammatical ambiguity as well: 'Frau Grubach, his landlady, had a cook who usually brought him his breakfast around eight, but this time she failed to arrive.'

In any other branch of translation this problem would not arise; the information would be conveyed irrespective of considerations of style. As John Bester has observed, as related to literature, *translation* denotes 'the attempt to render faithfully into one language (normally, one's own) the meaning, feeling, and, so far as possible, the style of a piece written in another language.' He goes on to add: 'I realize that this can only be an ideal. Translation, like politics, is an art of the possible; compromise is inevitable and universal.'

An ephemeral art

The half-life of a translation, it has been said, is from 30 to 40 years; every 30 years (or 40 or 50 – take your pick) the translation loses half its vitality, its freshness, its ability to communicate to the reader in a contemporary voice. If this is true, it follows that major works of literature must be retranslated periodically if they are to retain their function as a bridge between cultures and eras.

For all its grandeur – and it was truly a fine example of the translator's art, resounding with the masculine vigor of its prose – Thomas Hobbes's 1629 rendering of Thucydides is virtually unreadable to the modern speaker of English, cluttered with *thee* and *thou* and complex, baroque sentences. The R. Crawley 1874 version is much easier to absorb but its slightly obsolescent vocabulary nonetheless gives off the faint scent of mothballs. Only Rex Warner's lively 1952 translation communicates with fluency, precision, and modernity, speaking the contemporary reader's language directly and forcefully. Is it therefore 'better' than the Hobbes or Crawley efforts?

Not necessarily. It is, however, newer and more in touch with the times in which we live. Even when the source text is in a dead language, the target language never remains static. Living languages are *moving* targets, and all we can say with certainty of today's translations is that, however good they may be, they will at some future date become obsolete. In the memorable metaphor of Gregory Rabassa, '[T]here is a kind of continental drift that slowly works on language as words wander away from their original spot in the lexicon and suffer the accretion of subtle new nuances… The choice made by an earlier translator, then, no longer obtains and we must choose again.'

Far from a tragedy monumental enough to daunt a would-be translator, this is as it should be, for it affords every generation the opportunity to discover its own voice in a new translation. The oft-cited observation is apt: the Greeks have only one Homer; we have many.

The same process works both within and between languages. Some of Shakespeare's vocabulary, and many of his allusions, are lost on today's audiences, as David Crystal illustrates in his *Cambridge Encyclopedia of Language* (2nd edition), with the court jester Touchstone's speech in *As You Like It*:

'Tis but an hour ago since it was nine;
And after one hour more 'twill be eleven;
And so, from hour to hour, we ripe and ripe,
And then, from hour to hour, we rot and rot;
And thereby hangs a tale.

In Crystal's words, 'The bawdy pun involved can be appreciated only when we realize that *hour* and *whore* were pronounced alike, at that time.'

Shakespeare wrote 'modern' English, and even so, in the 21st century most readers need a glossary to fully apprehend him. Chaucer borders on a foreign language; *Beowulf* requires serious linguistic study. A poet's chance at immortality, we may conclude, is greatest in a language that changes but little over the centuries.

Look at Andrew Marvell's wonderful poem '*To His Coy Mistress.*' The way the word *thorough* is articulated has changed so much since the 17th century that today's reader must choose between correct meter and correct pronunciation:

> Let us roll all our Strength, and all
> Our sweetness into one Ball:
> And tear our Pleasures with rough strife,
> Thorough the Iron gates of life.
> Thus, though we cannot make our Sun
> Stand still, yet we will make him run.

The poem speaks of the time when '... worms shall try / That long preserved virginity, / And your quaint honour turn to dust, / And into ashes all my lust.' The modern reader loses much of the resonance of the original because *honour*, no longer a euphemism for the female genitalia, cannot do double duty as in Marvell's day. Also, *quaint* was a contemporary term for the female pudenda, while *lust* was by some accounts 17th-century usage for the male organ. All these secondary meanings have become shrouded in time. The poet, though writing in the same language of his modern readers, no longer fully communicates with them.

In the West, the Bible is the most universal example of the phenomenon of the slow decay of semantic integrity. Many of its agrarian allusions from a simpler time convey little to the inhabitants of a complex, modern, urban society. Or take the well-known citation 'Suffer little children ... to come unto me' (Matthew 19:14); lamentably, misunderstanding the word *suffer*, which at the time of the King James Version meant *allow*, some have interpreted this as a call to inflict regular beatings on children so they may 'come to Jesus.'

We neither can nor should rewrite the English of Shakespeare or Marvell. How fortunate, then, that we can retranslate the Spanish of Cervantes, the French of Villon! It matters little that all translations are foreordained to obsolescence. Their value to the future lies in their expression of how we spoke and thought and wrote in our own time. A good translation, like Warner's Thucydides, may well outlive its creator, and with luck our efforts may serve as the standard against which translations of the same work are judged long after we have heard Marvell's wingèd chariot hurrying near.

Now, let's talk about Getting Started.

Getting started

For many readers, perhaps a majority, this section is probably the reason you bought this book in the first place. Still, valuable as this guide hopes to be, it cannot make a translator out of anyone who is unwilling to put forth the effort and endure the frustration, occasionally rising to the level of angst, that comes with the territory known as literary translation.

Because there is no magic that instantly makes a person a translator, as a public service I hereby affirm and declare: *you are a translator*. Granted the assumptions mentioned in the Introduction, especially command of a language pair, you now have all you need to Get Started.

Or, to put it more accurately, you now have everything that the overwhelming majority of literary translators had when *they* got started.

The point to remember is that you get started by, well, getting started. A swimmer swims; a translator translates. As resistant as I am to sports metaphors, I recognize that one becomes a swimmer by plunging into the water, not by reading about it. You must translate something to become a translator; it is the act of translating that makes you a translator.

How many languages?

Before choosing what to translate, the question for some is what language or languages to translate. Although most native speakers of English won't encounter the 'problem,' those fortunate enough to have a multilingual background may possess the ability to translate from two or more languages into English. The question arises, then, whether a literary translator is better off concentrating on a single language or can successfully deal with two or more.

As is often the case, there are two sides to the issue. First, the argument for sticking to a single language.

- *Familiarity*: It is easier to become totally comfortable with one foreign language than with two, four, or more. Beyond the question of fluency in other languages, however, lies the greater issue of cultural familiarity. I believe that the truly bicultural individual is a near impossibility, for reasons too complicated to go into here. (See 'What literary translators really translate.') It takes years and extensive exposure to another culture to become conversant enough with it to translate its literature with confidence and accuracy.

- *Career implications*: With few exceptions, the most noted literary translators today specialize in a single language, even with occasional forays into others. William Weaver (Italian), Edith Grossman (Spanish) and Richard Howard (French) are some examples. A handful of translators – Gregory Rabassa (Spanish and Portuguese) and, in an earlier period, Samuel Putnam (five languages) – are exceptions to the rule. Obviously, a translator gains more standing among his or her peers and achieves greater name recognition with book publishers by concentrating on a single language.
- *Competition*: If you're fortunate enough to be a native speaker of English who also knows Bulgarian, say, or Bengali, it's safe to assume you don't have too many competitors in the literary translation field. There are no reliable statistics to go on, but it's likely that in the US there are at least two or three hundred people who translate Spanish for each one who handles Estonian. On the less exotic side, if your main source language is French, why add Spanish or Italian? Rather, branch out into Catalan, or Haitian Creole, or some other tongue where competitors are fewer.
- *Resources*: Is it feasible to accumulate for more than one language the requisite library of dictionaries and reference materials needed for significant literary translation? (See 'The translator's tools.') And what about the extensive network of resource individuals – native speakers and educated, literate consultants – that takes years to acquire? Can one reasonably expect to have all this for three or four languages?

Now the multilingual view.

- *Flexibility*: If you translate from two or more languages, it adds another string to your bow. You can avail yourself of the wide panoply of, say, Hispanic literature as well as that of Francophone nations. Or, if your combination is Swedish/Norwegian, you double the potential supply of material on which to draw. You alone must decide whether the advantages are outweighed by the time spent learning and maintaining an additional language, not to mention costs of keeping abreast of one more culture.
- *Fallback*: If the bottom drops out of the US market for novels or poetry in Language A, perhaps Language B is enjoying a resurgence.

Whether you end up translating one language or several, the same high standards of professionalism, *ça va de soi*, must apply to each.

So, how to choose a work to translate? There is no easy answer. Choice of what to translate is an exercise in subjectivity. It stands to reason that the more interested you are in the SL text, the more energy and enthusiasm you will put into translating it. For a first translation, the best choice is something that speaks to you personally, something you feel *must* be translated. Many a translator has taken the first steps after reading a particularly moving piece of prose or poetry and being overcome by a powerful urge to share it with others. From a practical point of view, falling in love with an author's writing is a heady feeling, but don't let it cloud your judgment about the appeal of that literature to the TL audience or about other realities of the obligations you're about to assume.

Where do you find these writings? First, by reading widely in the source language. This means keeping up with the literary field in the source-language nation(s). If you have an informant in the SL country or countries, ask that person to send clippings or reviews on acclaimed new works of fiction or poetry, especially if the writer is a newcomer. On any visit to the country, make inquiries about bright new lights in the literary firmament. Second, drop by local universities and see which authors are being read in foreign-language courses. Ask the professors what writings they might like to see available in English. Don't overlook the growing number of courses in literature in translation; sometimes instructors will welcome new translations by established writers or hitherto untranslated gems by relative unknowns. Browse college catalogs to find out what writers are hot at major centers of higher education. Sometimes academics are ahead of the curve; after all, they were the first to discover Borges, Cortázar, and García Márquez. Third, ask any authors you've previously translated if they can recommend talented, deserved, and unpublished writers.

One of the safest approaches is to find an author whose works are already in the public domain. Although international copyright provisions are a complicated matter (see 'The © question'), in general you're safe translating something published in the 19th century. After that, it becomes problematical.

Here are some tips to maximize your chance of success and minimize unpleasant surprises:

- Once you've found someone whose novel clamors for a larger readership in the TL, look for a short story by the same writer. Or pick a self-contained excerpt from the longer work that functions well as a stand-alone passage – all things being equal, shorter texts have a better chance of publication in periodicals.
- Resolve all authorization issues before starting. Don't expose your-

self to the disappointment of sweating away on a translation only to learn that the foreign rights aren't available. (See 'Contracts.')

- Have a game plan before you begin. Where do you foresee publishing the translation? If you can't rattle off at least three periodicals that publish similar translated works (and *The New Yorker* doesn't count!), you haven't done your homework.
- Decide how much time you are willing to invest in the undertaking. How many drafts do you estimate will be necessary? Have you budgeted the time to work on the project in the free hours from parenting and/or your day job?
- Line up qualified readers to give a second opinion before you send the translation to an editor. At least one person proficient in both SL and TL is desirable, but in a pinch TL monolinguals will do, provided they are endowed with a sense of style and a nose for infelicities in English.
- Formulate your backup plan. If the translation doesn't find a publisher, do you persist? Give up? The first *mano a mano* with translation can sometimes make or break the would-be translator, and more than one wannabe has abandoned plans for a second career as translator after a single rejection. For your own emotional health, you should have a contingency plan in case your first try doesn't work out.

How good will your maiden effort be? Not as good, probably, as your later attempts. While practice doesn't necessarily make perfect (it makes permanent), the assumption is that with time one hones techniques, adds skills, and acquires confidence. Let's look at two possible scenarios:

- *Scenario 1.* Your first translation (which, I repeat, should be short) reads well, passes muster with evaluators, and is accepted for publication by a periodical. Congratulations, you're now officially a literary translator. Bully for you, and keep up the good work.
- *Scenario 2.* Despite your best efforts, despite several revisions based on feedback from trusted advisers, the translation is consistently bounced back from editors. Now what?

In the first scenario, you've shown you have what it takes to do translations, or at least one translation. But there are other issues. First and foremost, did you enjoy it? Some neophyte translators find it a chore, even torture, and swear 'never again!' Was it emotionally and intellectually rewarding? Is the game worth the candle? (In most cases payment is minimal or non-existent for short translated fiction, and even more so for translated poetry.) Did the experience generate a desire to take on longer, more arduous texts in the future? If you can answer yes to all of these questions, you've found a calling. How far you go with it is now up to you. Godspeed.

In the second scenario, unfortunately the more usual of the two, it's time to reassess. Remember, unlike an English-language original, a translation has a double obstacle to surmount. First, the translation itself must be good, for a bad translation can make any writer look clumsy. Second, the SL original must also be good – no translation can turn a literary sow's ear into a silk purse. Editors will reject submissions of translations on either or both of these grounds. All things being equal, *only good translations of good writing end up in print*. It may be that your translating skills are more than adequate but your choice of source language texts is uninspired. Give some thought to a more appealing choice of SL materials. Read between the lines: although most rejections come as form letters, if the editor appends a note complimenting the translation, this should tell you something. Cast a wider net in your search for texts to translate and don't lose heart. Every translator has a few rejection letters in his or her files.

To be sure, some rejections are less discouraging than others. Here's what bids fair to be the gentlest letdown ever written. It appeared in the *Financial Times* in the mid-1990s and cited a Chinese economics journal:

'I have read your manuscript with boundless delight. If we were to publish your paper, it would be impossible for us to publish any work of lower standard. And as it is unthinkable that in the next thousand years we shall see its equal, we are, to our regret, compelled to return your divine composition and to beg you a thousand times to overlook our shortsightedness and timidity.'

Submissions: a primer

Assuming a good translation of a good SL original, it should be possible to publish it somewhere. However, if you're not satisfied with anything short of *The New Yorker*, it's time for a reality check. Perhaps one of 500 unsolicited submissions to a periodical of its stature even gets a cursory reading, and the winnowing process continues from that point, leaving a minuscule number of works to make the final cut. Before you prematurely discard the idea of publishing in small journals, remember this admonition, which has become a mantra of mine: *no publication is as obscure as non-publication*.

Every translator faces the problem of getting and staying organized. Even in the computer age it is far too easy to lose track of when and where a particular translation was submitted, and it's embarrassing to be informed none too politely that a periodical has already seen – and rejected – your material.

Though this discussion focuses on literary magazines and journals, the same principles apply, with modifications, to book publication. The information in this section is based on materials first published in *Source* by Alexis Levitin, a noted translator of Portuguese poetry whose works have appeared in close to 200 periodicals. His observations, while mainly dealing with poetry, apply equally well to fiction.

(1)   After the translation is finished, prepare to send it out to magazines. If it's a collection of poems or stories by the same author, or different authors connected thematically (e.g., contemporary women writers of Peru), you can simultaneously start searching for a book publisher. The object is to publish as many of the poems or stories as possible in periodicals before the book appears; it goes without saying that the more extensive the publication record – which proves that some editor somewhere thought your efforts worthy of putting into print – the better your chances of finding a book deal. Levitin, an unusually prolific poetic translator, normally manages to place 'at least 80%' of any collection in periodicals before they appear in book form. Bear in mind that while serious authors, confident that good literature will always find its outlet, supposedly write unconcerned with a specific market, translators are under no such restraint. There is nothing wrong with tailoring submissions to a predetermined market, and the closer the fit the more likely the acceptance.

(2)   Research the market before mailing your manuscript to a periodical. Not all magazines publish translations, and some that do are language-specific. (Don't send your French translations to *Dimension*,[2] a journal for German-language literature.) There are literally thousands of small periodicals in the English-speaking world, most of which pay nothing but still meet the fundamental criterion: *no publication, however obscure, is as obscure as non-publication.* An indispensable guide is *The International Directory of Little Magazines and Small Presses* (order from Dustbooks, Box 100, Paradise, CA 95967, USA), with over 5000 entries that include more than 200 magazines in the Translation index; actually, many more publish translations. Another, smaller-scale guide is *The Directory of Literary Magazines* (666 Broadway, New York, NY 10012), which lists over 400 magazines. You can also get ideas from periodicals like *Poets & Writers* and from bulletins and newsletters to learn where other translators have placed their recent efforts, such as the *ALTA Newsletter*. Obviously, your best bet for acceptance is a periodical that is translation-friendly and receptive to unsolicited manuscripts, but don't restrict yourself to

language-specific publications. Many general-interest magazines will also publish translations if they are of high enough quality. Also, while most periodicals that publish in English are located, naturally, in countries where it is the official language, the near-universality of English as a second language opens possibilities in other nations as well. Don't overlook magazines like *Traffika*, from the Czech Republic, or the English-language version of Spain's *Cuadernos*. And don't limit yourself to periodicals specifically listed under the Translation heading; many magazines publish the occasional translation, and as always, quality is the key factor. The Internet is a good source for discovering lesser known periodicals. Among the multitude of web sites offering information about magazines is

http://www.chateauxshadeaux.com/marketlist3.html

which also provides other useful information about the publications such as payment rates, whether it accepts e-submissions, genres, and maximum word count.

(3)   Send a computer-generated original or a photocopy of your transla-tion with your name and address in the upper-right-hand corner of each sheet. The venerable SASE (self-addressed stamped envelope) for return of rejected manuscripts is still highly desirable, but the computer age offers an alternative. Many editors will honor your request to 'toss' the manuscript if it's 'unsuitable to our needs' (a cliché in the trade), because it's so easy to simply run off another copy on your printer. If you submit fiction, a single story is permissible, or as many as three or four, depending on length. For poetry, four to six poems per submission, to give the editors an idea of the range and abilities of the poet and the translator. In the brief cover letter (no more than two pages) you should include background information on the author, especially if he or she is unknown to the editors. This is no time for false modesty, so mention any earlier successes as a translator, any awards, pending publications – whatever will enhance your bona fides.

(4)   To a greater extent than we recognize, getting published has an element of statistics and, yes, luck to it. Assuming literary merit to begin with, the more often you send out a work, the better the chance it will hit print. Acquire a feel for what a given magazine likes. In Levitin's words, 'The most important thing is to keep the manuscript moving. There is no time for self-pity: the day you get a rejection, sit down and send the manuscript elsewhere.' To cite the example of poetry, if you've translated 50 poems, there should be about 12 submissions circulating around the US, Canada, England, and

Australia at any given time. Keep knocking on doors, Levitin advises, and 'something good will eventually happen.' Remember, an acceptance/submission ratio of 1:10 is not bad, and anything approaching 1:4 means you've arrived! Small magazines being what they are – often a one-person operation – don't get discouraged if months go by without a reply; the beauty of having numerous submissions floating around is that every few weeks there's some news in your mailbox. After a reasonable period with no response, probably six to nine months, it's time to submit the same work somewhere else. Unless your author wins the Nobel Prize, stick to the little magazines, at least at first. Don't expect riches from translating poetry or short stories, but you will experience the pleasure of seeing yourself in print, and others may also. More than one referral for a longer work has resulted from a casual notice of a translator's work in a periodical. Besides which, Levitin says, you'll amuse your friends with the magazines' weird titles: *Crab Creek Review, Hanging Loose, Lips, pod, Kyack, The Dirty Goat, Sackbut, Asylum.*

(5) If you have 12–15 submissions out in various places, you have a book-keeping problem that demands attention. Levitin recommends the following methods:

   (a) Make at least four copies of your completed book-length collection of poems or short stories. Put one aside for potential book publication. Put another in a safe place as a fallback in case, heaven forbid, your hard drive dies and you neglected (shame on you!) to back up your data. The third copy is the one that is sent far and wide in search of a publisher, divided into 10–12 smaller bundles of four or so poems each. Which leaves one copy as your control.

   (b) On the control copy, each time you send out a translation, type the name of the magazine and the mailing date beneath the poem or on the title page of the short story (on the back of the sheet if the poem is a long one). Whenever a poem is accepted or rejected, note that fact plus the date of reply to the right of the original entry. The two-column system looks like this:

```
┌─────────────────────────────────────────────────────────────┐
│                            Poem                               │
│  xxxxxxxxxxxxxxxxxxxxxxxx                                      │
│  xxxxxxxxxxxxxxxx                                              │
│  xxxxxxxxxxxxxxxxxxxxxxxxxxxx                                  │
│  xxxxxxxxxxx                                                   │
│  xxxxxxxxxxxxxxx                                               │
└─────────────────────────────────────────────────────────────┘
```

Submission	Response
Translation 8/22/00	Rejected 1/14/01
Poetry Northwest 1/17/01	Rejected 3/22/01
Confrontation 3/23/01	*Accepted 5/5/01*

This way the entire submission history of each poem or story is visible at a glance, on the same sheet in the control file as the work itself. The main advantage is that you avoid sending the translation twice to the same publication and are immediately alerted to which poems or stories to remove from circulation because they have been accepted. More technically-oriented translators may prefer to computerize the entire process by setting up a data base. Fine, but be absolutely certain to print out a hard copy at intervals, preferably each time a change is made. If your computer goes south, having the information on paper will allow you to reconstruct the lost material.

(c) Keep a complete record of all correspondence, including your cover letters to editors. If you have received a warm and encouraging letter of rejection (yes, there can be such a thing) from an editor, you may want to stay in touch over the years, both professionally and personally. Once an editor has published your work, you increase your chances of getting a careful reading next time. The easiest way to file translation correspondence is alphabetically by the name of the periodical. Letters to and from editors of publishing house should go in a separate file: call it BOOKS.

As for the issue of multiple submissions, there's no simple answer. Though traditionally the practice has been frowned upon – editors have no desire to waste time reading a manuscript that may already have been accepted by a rival publication – if you state in your cover letter that you are sending the same translation to other outlets, your ethics and your honesty can't be challenged. While some editors will automatically reject your submission, others don't mind. Most translators eschew multiple submissions, but some magazines state clearly that they have no objections. When it comes to looking for a book publisher, however, you should first make multiple *queries* and submit multiple samples. Otherwise, too much time is lost in the evaluation process, which can easily span a year or longer. Once a publisher expresses interest in seeing the entire manuscript, standard policy is to then submit it to only that one house until a decision is reached. So-called small presses enjoy more flexibility than in the high-stakes world of the multinational giants like Bertelsmann, so feel free to propose multiple submission; if the publisher says no, you have the option of exclusive submission or looking for a publisher who doesn't mind.

Whatever system you adopt, as a translator you owe it to yourself to get organized. The creative act of translating is demanding enough without having to worry about where the *#@&# you put that acceptance letter from *Artful Dodge*.

Let's assume your SL is German. Here, in roughly descending order of importance, are criteria that would raise the probability of a goodness-of-fit between your translation and the needs of the periodical:

(1) Its focus is German literature and culture.
(2) It frequently publishes translations from German.
(3) It considers submissions in various genres (for example, drama as well as poetry and fiction).
(4) It has a reasonable turnaround time, no more than six months between receipt of manuscript and final decision.
(5) It accepts simultaneous submissions.

Whatever your language, there are some steps you can take to maximize chances of finding a periodical to publish your translation. Here are a few.

- **Look for special (thematic) issues.** The odds of getting published shoot up if you find a special issue that fits linguistically or thematically with work you have done or will do. One periodical that publishes thematic issues exclusively is *Two Lines*. This annual review, which prints only translations, chooses a single broad-based topic (to date, Battlefields, Tracks, Waves, Possession, Ages, Fires, Crossings, Cells), to which all submissions must somehow relate, albeit in some cases tenuously. More general magazines often devote issues entirely or in part to a given theme or language. For example, *Beacons*, published by the Literary Division of the American Translators Association, had a section on Francophone Canadian literature. The best way to find out about upcoming special issues, some of which are announced as much as two years ahead of publication, is by sending a brief query letter to the editor. It may be that you already have a translation ready to go that fits in nicely with the focus of a thematic issue.

- **Read the ad pages.** Often, small magazines will trade display ads with other periodicals, and in these advertisements you can frequently become aware of a magazine that seems tailor-made for your work. This is also a good way to find out about special issues.

- **Browse the local library.** Its periodical shelves may feature a magazine you'd never come across otherwise. Where else would you stumble across *Glas* (Russian) or *Calaloo* (Afro-Caribbean)? When you do get published, remember that small magazines operate on a shoestring, and sometimes a frayed shoestring at that. I have made it a practice over the years to take out a one-year subscription to any magazine that publishes my translations. You may want to do the same.

Finally, all translators need a bookkeeping system, both as a means of keeping track of submissions and as a gauge of their batting average. A visual record in the form of a table is one good method, with as many columns and rows as desired. Feel free to adopt or adapt my version, a portion of which is reproduced on the following page.

Notice that even a cursory glance shows that my record as translator of poetry poses no threat to anyone.

Coping with bad reviews

Into all translators' lives, if they continue long enough in the field, comes negative notice from a literary critic. So what, you may say, the important thing is to get published, and let the reviews fall where they may.

Well, yes and no. It's true that without publication there is nothing to review, favorably or otherwise, but translators understandably prefer their efforts to be lauded rather than lambasted. For the sake of emotional equilibrium, a translator's attitude toward criticism must be significantly different from an author's.

When a source-language work is reviewed, presumably every word in the critique is a reference to the text in question – good, bad, or mixed. The author can take solace from being the focus of attention even in a negative review. Not so with translators.

As the invisible men and women of literature, literary translators learn to accept the notion that a 'good' review of a translated work may expend thousands of words without once alluding to the quality of the translator's effort, as if the English text had somehow sprung into existence by spontaneous generation. In other words, the reviewer, unburdened by any in-depth knowledge of the SL, treats the text like an English-language original. Frequently, translators are obligated to find a perverse kind of satisfaction in being ignored; a good translation 'disappears' into the thoughts and style of the author, while a bad translation draws attention to itself even as it diminishes the artistic impact of the original.

If a non-review is a 'good' review for the translator, what constitutes a bad review? A personal example: the first review of my 1992 translation of *The Golden Harvest* to hit print, from *Publisher's Weekly*, was short but far

TALLY SHEET

Title (genre, author)	Submitted to, date	Returned/ Accepted (P)	Submitted to, date	Returned/ Accepted (✓)	Submitted to, date	Returned/ Accepted(✓)
The Ship Catrineta (s: Fonseca)	Latin Amer. Lit. Review, 2/19/85	6/6/85 ✓				
Way of St. Joana Carolina (s: Osman Lins)	Brasil/ Brazil, 8/18/89	4/14/90 ✓				
Suave mari magno (p: Machado)	Grand Street, 10/14/90	11/8/90	Seneca Review, 11/21/90	3/1/91	Kenyon Review, 3/6/91	9/24/91
A mosca azul (p: Machado)	Grand Street, 10/14/90	11/8/90	Seneca Review, 11/21/90	3/1/91	Kenyon Review, 3/6/91	9/24/91
No alto (p: Machado)	Grand Street, 10/14/90	11/8/90	Seneca Review, 11/21/90	3/1/91	Kenyon Review, 3/6/91	9/24/91
The Center of Summer (s: Godoy)	Fiction, 9/11/91	11/12/91	Literary Review, 11/17/91	2/2/92	Prairie Schooner, 2/14/92	5/5/92
La dernière translation (p: Fernandes)	Platte Valley Rev., 9/3/94	11/7/94 ✓				
The New California (s: Lima Barreto)	Two Lines, 11/9/96	3/18/97 ✓				
Chocolate Mousse (s: E.T. Ribeiro)	Urban Voices, 6/21/97	1/27/99 ✓				
Vigil for the Dead (s: Maupassant)	Two Lines, 9/11/00	11/14/00	Beacons, 11/16/00	1/13/01 ✓		
Barbara (s: Varella)	Cuadernos, 3/22/01	3/31/01 ✓				

key: p: poem; s: short story; n: non-fiction; o: other

from sweet, and generally dismissive. It read in part: 'Landers's translation
... renders rural Brazilian Portuguese in idioms of the southern US – "I'll
learn you some respect" – with awkward effects.'
Piercing, that terse 'awkward.' A year's effort discarded in less than a
sentence, tossed off as a parenthetical phrase. All the translator's subtlety
and sweat, ingenuity and insight dwindle down to a single citation of an
anonymous reviewer's quarrel with one of the thousands of choices that go
into a book-length translation.

Sure, later there would be other reviews, all favorable, from *The Washington Post*, *News from Brazil*, *Booklist*, and *Américas*. But the sting of that first
negative review lingers. Face it – the reviewer always has the last word, and
any attempt at rebuttal by author or translator is futile at best. (For example,
I forgo the temptation to point out here that *PW*'s reviewer was mistaken in
claiming that *learn* used for *teach* is exclusively southern American.) Unfair
perhaps, but it comes with the territory. Translators, like authors, must be
able to roll with the punch.

Gregory Rabassa has helped popularize a creature invented by Sara
Blackburn known as Professor Horrendo, the nemesis of literary
translators:

> In his anality he fetches his dictionary and finds that on page twenty the
> translation reads 'chair' where the true meaning of the original was
> 'stool.' This is usually done in defense of the integrity of the author, but
> often ... not knowing that the author, who knows English quite well, has
> checked and approved the translation. Professor Horrendo has long been
> our bane, and we should be thankful when a far-sighted editor gives a
> translation to a writer rather than to a scholar for review.

Ideally, the translator should be able to avoid ego-involvement in a way
the author cannot. The novel is, after all, the author's baby in every aspect –
plot, characterization, structure, dialogue – and only an emotional autom-
aton could be expected to escape close identification with his or her
creation. The translator, on the other hand, is responsible 'only' for the
words themselves as they appear in the TL version. Nevertheless, this
charge is so all-encompassing that the final product is in every sense a
collaborative effort. Small wonder that translators also writhe under the
lash of criticism.

As for 'constructive' criticism, *there is no such thing*. At least not once the
translation is in print, when it's too late for anything but second-guessing.
The time for constructive suggestions was before the work was published.
A fiction writer may conceivably learn something from a scathing review to
use in a future work, but it's improbable that a translator will. First, a

skilled translator seldom perpetrates errors of the kind discernible to a reviewer unfamiliar with the SL (the usual case). Second, translators confront a wide range of styles and subject matter, with each project characterized by its own imperatives, which precludes 'keeping at it till you get it right.'

Few would consider the following example constructive. A review by John H.R. Polt of Manuel Vázquez Montalbán's novel *Galíndez*, it appeared August 23, 1992, in *The New York Times Book Review*. The translators' names have been omitted.

> Whatever one may think of *Galíndez*, it does not deserve what the translators ... have done to it. They fall into every linguistic trap (thus *conferencia*, 'lecture,' is translated as 'conference'); they have a shaky command of Spanish syntax, vocabulary, and even geography ('at Aragon' and 'at Ebro' as though these were towns). Would any American talk about 'North American poetry'? About 'Cordell Hull's woman'? Since when is a prosecutor a 'fiscal attorney'? Or a bookworm a 'library rat'? The list of blunders could go on and on. Even the translators' English is substandard. Do we 'pull one over on people,' feel 'nauseous,' step 'off of' a sidewalk, send things 'to whomever remains'? Can you imagine, in 1988, calling your cleaning woman 'a very conscientious negress'? It is incomprehensible that a respectable publisher should accept this scandalous translation and print it unedited without consulting someone who knows Spanish.

This is the type of review that can cause a translator to seek another line of work. May the gods of criticism deliver us from being on the receiving end of any such excoriation.

Preparing to translate

At least since Matthew Arnold's seminal 1861 work *On Translating Homer*, the majority view among translators has been that a translation should affect its readers in the same way that the original affected its first readers (or listeners, in the case of Homer). The American author John Irving has the makings of a literary translator. In discussing how he wrote the screenplay for the 1999 film adaptation of his 560-page novel *The Cider House Rules*, he said, 'What I tried to ask myself was this: Do the characters have the same emotional effect on the audience that they have on readers?' (Quoted by Brett Kelly, *New York*, December 13, 1999, p. 96.) This is precisely what the literary translator attempts to achieve. Not only characters but all facets of the work, ideally, are reproduced in such a manner as to create in the TL reader the same emotional and psychological effect experienced by the *original* SL reader.

This principle addresses some of the issues that confront neophyte and veteran translators alike. First, it is important to understand that by the SL reader we mean the *original* source-language reader, which eliminates many questions when dealing with other than contemporary texts. For example, the translator of a new English version of *Don Quixote* might wonder whether the title character and his faithful squire should speak modern or 17th-century English, whether to translate dialogue into today's English or to retain the supposedly 'quaint' nature of early 17th-century Spanish. A red herring if there ever was one. In Cervantes's time, 17th-century Spanish was not quaint, it was the everyday language. The original readers of *Quixote* in no way perceived the speech of the characters as archaic or antiquated, even if today's native in Madrid or Santiago may. Therefore, translate *Don Quixote* into a contemporary, albeit not slangy or faddish, English.

Similarly, if the speech patterns in the SL text struck the reader as deliberately old-fashioned, stilted, facetious, jargon-ridden, sub-standard, or in any other way a departure from expected modes of expression, that too should be reflected in the translation. An example of this occurred in *A Samba for Sherlock*. (See 'English with a restricted vocabulary: a case study.') The author, Jô Soares, used no Portuguese word or expression that was not current in Brazil in 1886, the period in which this delightful pastiche is set. I honored this convention in the translation, finding in the process the *Oxford*

English Dictionary to be a translator's best friend, for its citations list the earliest printed appearance of a word or phrase. In one or two instances, the absence of parallel evolution in Portuguese and English obliged me to eschew a perfectly good word that had not entered the English vocabulary by 1886. *Hangover* is one example; *ressaca* (literally, 'undertow') was already in use at least a decade and a half before its English equivalent would emerge.

The question is often raised about formal training to become a translator. It is unfortunate that there is no mentorship program for literary translators, and precious little training is available for would-be literary translators in the handful of translation programs at American colleges and universities. Even in Europe, where the importance of mastery of other languages is much more ingrained in the public consciousness, the bulk of university-level training is devoted to interpretation and areas of translation other than literary. As a result, most literary translators have to be self-taught; making mistakes along the way, they gradually evolve a *Fingerspitzengefühl* that serves them well once they have surmounted the initial barriers that may deter all but the most dedicated or tenacious.

The good news is that very few successful literary translators learned their craft through courses of formal study. Which leads to the question of whether literary translators are made or born. The following is merely one translator's opinion, but will perhaps yield some insight.

In any field of human endeavor, nature imposes certain limitations: a speech impediment probably rules out a career as television anchorperson, and a genetic propensity toward obesity obviates hopes of winning a decathlon medal at the Olympics or making it to prima ballerina. Similarly, intrinsic factors can militate against becoming a literary translator.

It is true that no one is born a literary translator any more than he or she is born speaking English or Chinese. These are learned skills. Obviously, without command of a language pair no one is destined to become a translator (*pace* Nabokov), but equally obviously this is only a necessary, not a sufficient condition. The issue boils down to whether the requisite skills are teachable. If so, theoretically anyone with the proper linguistic background could acquire them.

The problem lies in defining what a 'proper' background is. It is far easier to specify what it is not. It goes without saying that the semi-literate, the grammatically challenged, the rigid and inflexible linear thinkers are less than optimal candidates for the job. A kind of self-selection process filters out such candidates.

But what about the legions of well educated, linguistically qualified individuals who function perfectly well in scientific, technical, or commercial translation but find themselves stymied when attempting literature? Can technique be of help? Within limits, yes. All professions have tricks of the trade; translation is no exception. In art, be it painting, music, or writing, techniques can be taught, but not talent. Expensive cameras do not make a photographer, nor do shelves of dictionaries and piles of reference books make a translator.

Perhaps the most distinctive characteristic of good translators is their sense of dedication. They do translation because they *enjoy* it and perceive it as making a contribution, however small, to greater understanding between cultures. I have yet to meet a successful literary translator who does it for the money, but I have met any number of would-be literary translators whose first question was 'How much does it pay?' In this case, the familiar price-of-yachts answer applies: if you have to ask, you can't afford it. For all but those fortunate enough to translate a blockbuster best seller, income from literary translation is not even secondary but tertiary. Even at the minimum wage, on an hourly basis you stand to make more money flipping burgers at a McJob than by translating Proust.

But, in art, is dedication enough? Unfortunately, no. For every Van Gogh who strives a lifetime only to be lionized posthumously, there are thousands whose lifelong efforts remain unsung even postmortem. So what *are* the traits that make a literary translator? The poet Gary Snyder (Pantheon Books, 1992), in a slightly different context, gives us a hint:

What You Should Know to Be a Poet

all you can about animals as persons.
the names of trees and flowers and weeds.
names of stars, and the movements of the planets
and the moon.

your own six senses, with a watchful and elegant mind.

at least one kind of traditional magic;
divination, astrology, the book of changes, the tarot;

dreams.
the illusory demons and illusory shining gods;

kiss the ass of the devil and eat shit;
fuck his horny barbed cock;
fuck the hag;
and all the celestial angels and maidens perfum'd and golden –

& then love the human: wives husbands and friends.

children's games, comic books, bubble gum,
the weirdness of television and advertising.

work, long dry hours of dull work swallowed and accepted
and livd with and finally lovd. exhaustion,
hunger, rest.

the wild freedom of the dance, *extasy*
silent solitary illumination, *entasy*

real danger. gambles. and the edge of death.

Or, more prosaically, like Terence (c. 186–159 BC), the literary translator believes that 'nothing human is foreign to me.' In its good and its evil, its most elevated flights of beauty and its basest profanities, humanity is both subject and object, and the translator's role is to capture its often contradictory impulses as first given voice in another language.

Can we mold ourselves into translators if we lack the innate talent? We must first be honest with ourselves and ask at what level we are aiming. If only the best and the brightest are tapped to translate Nobel laureates, there is still great value in introducing to the English-speaking public new talents from Nicaragua, Japan, or Sweden. The perfect should never be allowed to smother the good.

Literary translation is pleasurable and can be intellectually and emotionally rewarding, but there is no denying that it can also be hard work. In our own language we may skip over words, phrases, even entire paragraphs that we don't understand; the translator enjoys no such luxury.

Do you have talent, and if so, how much? No amount of schooling can tell you if you do or provide it if you don't. No certificate or diploma is going to make a literary translator. The only way to find out is by trying.

Down to work

Okay, you're convinced you have the calling. Good for you. What next?

Every translation is different, yet in some respect every translation is the same. If each translation is unlike any that has gone before or will come later, can one reasonably hope to learn from another translator's efforts, or even from one's own? Yes, for however different their content, all translations incorporate lessons that can be applied to other projects by other translators. I use 'lessons' in its most general sense. It is self-evident that the cracking of a particularly thorny problem of rendering a French or Japanese pun into English is of little direct relevance to someone translating Czech or

Arabic. But the experience gained in translating one novel, for example, can yield valuable insights for the next.

Success builds on success. Whoever translates one novel well can translate a second novel. (Notice I'd didn't say 'translate *any* novel.') The methods mastered in an initial effort often carry over to subsequent projects, especially the more mechanical elements: time management, research techniques, efficient use of dictionaries and references, and correspondence with publisher and author. Equally important, the self-confidence born from completing one's first book-length translation is an incomparable morale-booster for the inevitable moments of doubt and frustration entailed in any major translation undertaking.

Permissions

Beginners often ask me, 'Do I have to get permission to translate X?' The surprising answer is that *anyone can translate anything*. If you decide to do a retranslation of the complete short stories of Jorge Luis Borges, *mazel tov*. If you think you can do a better job than William Weaver's towering translation *The Name of the Rose*, don't let me be the one to stop you.

As I said, anyone can *translate* anything; the problem comes in trying to *publish* it. Translating for its own sake may be a fine intellectual exercise, but few of us would be content to have the fruits of our labor moldering away in a drawer. We translate, after all, to make one person's thoughts and one's nation's culture, through our intermediation, known to another. Thus the overriding necessity to get clearance before starting a translation. This has the added advantage of ascertaining that the right to publish an English-language translation has not already been granted to someone else.

The more lackadaisical (or ethically challenged) among us might argue, 'What difference does it make to publish a translation of one poem in a magazine with a circulation of 500? It doesn't reduce the poet's reputation or deprive him of income because they don't pay anything, and besides, he lives in the remote reaches of Terciomundo beyond the reach of phone, fax, or e-mail. Not to mention the fact that I'm helping him gain recognition overseas…' Okay, in all candor, any harm done is probably trifling. And in the worst-case scenario, a small payment could be made if any remonstration is forthcoming. But that's not the issue. A decent consideration for the intellectual property of others, even a property transformed by your intervention as translator into a different artistic entity, dictates that every reasonable effort be made to secure permission from the possessor of the rights. Presumably you desire to be respected as a literary creator and would take umbrage if someone used your translation without your knowledge; put yourself in the author's place.

If you make a conscientious effort to secure rights – which would include at least three unanswered letters or other bootless contacts with the presumed holder of the rights – and if you are willing to compensate the rights holder in case the issue ever arises, then you may wish to go ahead anyway. In a court of law you would probably be able to show your good faith, but things are unlikely to come to that head. In mentioning this expedient I am not counseling flouting copyright laws, simply recognizing the reality that it has been known to happen.

Another copyright-related question has to do with whose name the copyright is in. You might want to specify in the contract that on the copyright page the notice © [DATE] BY [YOUR NAME] appear. A quick check reveals that of the 14 novels I have translated to date, about half are copyrighted in my name, the others in the publisher's. For what it is worth, I can state that it has never made the slightest difference in royalties, recognition, or in any discernible way. It may be an ego boost to 'own' the copyright, but it's certainly no deal-breaker if the request is turned down. (See 'Contracts.')

Most of the common obstacles facing first-time literary translators, which include selecting a work to translate; obtaining translation rights from the author, the author's estate, or the publisher; finding an outlet – book or periodical – for the final product; and of course the time-honored 'How do I get started?', are dealt with in other sections of this guide. The present focus is on preparatory steps once a text has been chosen.

For all but the most experienced translators, the first step in a translation does not mean starting at page 1 and slogging away until reaching the final page of the text. Yes, some seasoned practitioners can pull off the feat of 'sight translating' – i.e., translating as they read the text for the first time – but most of us mere mortals need to gird our loins for the task at hand. Here's how.

- *Read the entire text at least once.* An admonition seemingly so elementary as to preclude mention, but one that in their eagerness to plunge into the work neophytes often overlook. And 'reading the text' means doing so as a translator, not as a casual reader. Underlying everything else, the translator is a *very careful reader*; only through a close reading of the text is it apperceived beyond the superficial level of the casual reader. As Ilan Stavans has remarked, 'The best reader is the translator, and second best, the critic' (quoted by Marjorie Agosín, *Américas*, July–August 1996). Reading the work as a whole, especially in the case of fiction, is vital to firmly establish the authorial voice, which will affect the translation throughout. In this way you begin with several advantages: a preview of the translational challenges in the more difficult passages; a firmer idea of the time the project is likely to require; appreciation of any fore-shadowing in the original, which lets you begin searching for TL equivalents earlier; avoidance of misjudging the scope of a project from a possibly unrepresentative sample – very important in fiction, which unlike non-fiction may show marked variation in style and difficulty from one section to another.

- *Do any necessary research first.* Even with the Internet, some texts will require significant amounts of legwork; some will need none at all. But where research is called for, put it behind you at the outset. Check those dates. Consult with the author about apparent discrepancies in the text. (In a work I recently translated, the author had at one spot inadvertently substituted the name of the killer for that of his victim; an e-mail exchange was enough to clear up the confusion.) See if English-language titles exist of books cited in footnotes and/or bibliography; this need may arise even in fiction, as was the case in Jô Soares's two novels, *A Samba for Sherlock* and *Twelve Fingers*, which were accompanied by extensive bibliographies. What is Saint Jacinto called in English and where do I go to find out? Rather than allow these problems to stop you dead in the water later on, clear them away before tackling the body of the text.
- *Deal with possible roadblocks at an early stage.* On your second or third reading (of whose desirability I hope you're convinced by now), you underlined words, phrases, and even entire sentences that present problems. Some of these will be of the kind only you can solve (e.g., an item that you understand perfectly in the SL but for which you can't quite find *le mot juste* in English), others will yield to consultation with native informants, and still others will require the intervention of the author (to resolve ambiguities, to vet your adaptation choices, and to eradicate possible factual errors.). Overcoming your impatience to get down to actual translating is not easy, but removing such sticking points before beginning will pay dividends later on.
- *Negotiate a reasonable deadline.* Publishers have one thing in common: they all want a manuscript ASAP, preferably by yesterday. Don't let the possibility of losing an assignment cow you into accepting an unrealistic deadline. Beginners especially must allow themselves some leeway; there is always some slippage between intention and realization. One of the prevalent causes of translator's

equivalent of writer's block – those long stretches of time when you produce nothing – is pressure. Time pressure is in a class by itself; the calendar is inexorable, and the closer the deadline the more the stress builds up, compounding the problem. So give yourself some wiggle room. If you should happen to finish ahead of time, well, no publisher has ever complained.

A real-world illustration of what it means to prepare for a translation appeared in *Source*, Spring 1999. Consider the steps that veteran translator John Felstiner reports having gone through as he geared up to translate the poet Paul Celan:

Preliminary

- Listen to Celan's voice (multiple recordings).
- Check draft versions.
- Employ word index to Celan's oeuvre.
- Develop word index to Celan's translations of other poets.
- Peruse Celan's libraries.
- Search Luther and King James Bibles, plus German literature.
- Consult earlier German–German and German–English dictionaries.
- Read the secondary criticism.
- Compare translations into other languages.
- Get help from native speakers plus Celan's friends and relatives.

Qualities peculiar to Celan

- Ambiguity, obscurity, contradictions, etc.
- Syntactic ruptures, warping, ellipses, etc.
- Puns and other plays on language.
- Neologisms.
- Allusions and citations (religion, history, myth, private experience).
- Foreign language terms.
- Archaic, obsolete, and rare usages.
- Technical nomenclature (geology, botany, mineralogy, etc.).
- New Germanic compounds.
- Self-citations and recurrence of key words throughout his oeuvre.

While not all the above items would be appropriate or even possible in every translation, the list demonstrates the thoroughness of a world-class translator at work.

Staying on track

Any full-length translation project has phases. Now that you've gotten started, which if not half the battle is certainly a significant fraction of it, there are still dangers to beware of. Consider this admonition a signpost pointing to a possibly bumpy road ahead. To extend the metaphor, some translation tasks speed along smoothly on the *autobahn*; others seem to crawl along pothole-ridden, one-lane roads through inhospitable countryside.

Not the least of the risks is the tendency to come to hate the project midway through, or sooner. As anyone who's ever done an MA thesis or doctoral dissertation can testify, you usually arrive at a point where you loathe the work and wonder why you ever started. In a much more sedentary guise, this is the famous Wall that marathon runners encounter 15, 20, sometimes 24 miles into the race. Be aware that a degree of self-doubt is inherent in long-range undertakings and in no way reflects on your fitness as a translator.

On the other hand, there *are* signs that should alert wannabe translators that perhaps they've set out on the wrong path. While any one of them by itself is not grounds for rethinking one's commitment, three or more should send up a warning flag.

Frequent and/or lengthy periods without translating. On the whole, translation should be enjoyable, not something we look upon as a chore. If you find yourself spending weeks at a time without working on the translation, if you're easily distracted from translating, or if you constantly find excuses to keep from returning to the task, consider it a possible wake-up call.

False starts and excessive rewrites. While editing one's work is a *sine qua non* for anyone in the world of letters, starting and restarting the same project numerous times could be a signal from our subconscious that our heart isn't really in this endeavor. By the same token, a large number of rewrites could be an indication of a fear of failure, or a penchant for perfectionism. Either way, there are problems ahead. The story is told that when James Thurber was writing *The Thirteen Clocks* he kept tinkering with the manuscript long after it had become more than polished, apparently for the sheer joy of putting it through its paces. Finally, in what today would be called an intervention, a group of friends went to his apartment, literally wrested the pages from his grasp, and delivered the work to his publisher… In literary translation as in everything else, the perfect forever remains the enemy of the good.

Slowing of production. In any translation there will be stretches of more difficult passages that, perforce, require more time and effort than others. If, however, you find that progressively (if that's the word) you're taking more and more time to produce less and less, that's a danger sign. Normally we translate a novel faster after familiarizing ourselves with its characters, style, and vocabulary; words that we had to look up on page 15 – and maybe again on page 42 – are old friends by page 123. If the opposite occurs, bells should sound. Disenchantment with a project can become a vicious circle: we spend time away from the translation, so we forget vocabulary items that should be familiar, or we inadvertently translate a character's nickname differently from its first appearance some hundred pages back. When we discover our lapses, it undermines our confidence even further. And the downward spiral continues.

Writer's block. Theoretically, this shouldn't occur with translators. After all, we have plot, characterization, description, style, and dialogue handed to us ready-made; we 'merely' have to render them from language A into language B in a graceful, literate manner. But translators too suffer their version of writer's block. It doesn't entail staring at a blank sheet of paper in a typewriter (or, these days, at a blinking cursor on a computer monitor), because we can always translate a few lines of easier text here and there. It manifests itself in more subtle ways, some of which have been noted above. Words just don't seem to flow. Phrases emerge jejune. Inspiration is non-existent. The flashes of brilliance that make translation so rewarding are absent. The entire undertaking seems flat and mundane. Words may continue to emerge, but the level of creativity plummets. You're blocked. What now?

First, is your blockage the result of a particularly difficult passage and do you spend hours on a couple of intractable sentences? If so, don't let these hurdles derail you. One tactic is simplicity itself: skip over them, marking them in some distinctive way (I use ####, making it easier to use search-and-replace to locate them later). Then proceed with the easier part of the translation. When you finish, preferably after the entire remainder of the text is done, go back and put your neurons to work on the task. This approach has two psychological advantages: the growing stack of pages successfully translated reinforces your assurance that you're up to the job, plus you give your subconscious time to noodle out a solution, which may magically pop into your head three days or three weeks later.

Some translators, perhaps because of personal idiosyncrasies, find themselves incapable of plowing ahead until they discover a way around each and every trouble spot. For them it is even more essential to adopt pre-emptive tactics by reading the text carefully and in full before beginning. This way, notwithstanding the stop-and-go nature of their work, they are at least forewarned of what's in store for them, which may be of some comfort. Or not.

Unrealistic expectations. Once the translation is in print, do you expect the publishing world to beat a path to your door with lucrative offers to translate Nobel laureates? Are you disappointed, even disillusioned when this fails to materialize? Are you upset by the meager royalties, by the fact that some reviewers don't even mention that it *is* a translation? These are all-too-common characteristics of our profession, and a dedicated translator learns to live with them. Grudgingly, perhaps, but realistically. If neither fame nor fortune is normally the translator's lot, there are still compensations, as has been seen.

That you may momentarily detest your material is no reason to abandon it. Finish the project, wait for it to appear in print, read the reviews, then reassess your feelings. Just as, allegedly, mothers forget the pains of childbirth, so too do translators banish from memory the anguish of the process itself. For some of us, the greater reward comes not from translating but from *having translated.*

A day in the life of a literary translator

It may be useful to get inside the head of a literary translator as he thinks aloud, or at least grapples with the moment-to-moment problems attendant to translating a work of fiction. Many of the stumbling blocks encountered here will be dealt with at greater length subsequently in this guide. What follows is a highly compressed but all-too-typical day in the life of this literary translator as he squared off against the challenges of bringing Rubem Fonseca's *Bufo & Spallanzani* from Portuguese into English.

Breakfast behind me, so *mãos à obra*, as they say: down to work.

Gustavo Flávio, the narrator/protagonist, quotes Flaubert in French: *Reserve ton priapisme pour le style, foutre ton encrier, calme-toi sur la viande... une once de sperme perdue fatigue plus que trois litres de sang*. It's only page 2 and there's already a problem. The passage is crucial because it helps establish the main character's almost pathological obsession with women. Nevertheless, it will be lost on TL readers who don't know French. Leave it in the original or translate it? Let's see: how close to Portuguese is the excerpt? Could the average Brazilian reader make sense of it without knowledge of French? I'll try it on a couple of educated Brazilians with limited mastery of the language of Hugo... Just as I thought: they can pick out words (as can the American reader – *reserve, style, sperme, fatigue*, maybe even *litres*) but can't discern the overall meaning. So it stays in French.

Vernissage: The narrator, whose pseudonym is an homage to Flaubert, enjoys flaunting his erudition by using phrases in French, English, even Latin. *Vernissage*, though more familiar to the Brazilian readers than to their English-speaking counterparts, contributes to Fonseca's deliberately pedantic effect; no reason to change it.

Gustavo's work in progress is also the name of the novel itself. But he consistently refers to it without italics: Bufo & Spallanzani. Fonseca presumably had his reasons for this departure from Portuguese (and English) standards, so let's honor them and leave it for the editors to thrash out.

Contractions. Might as well resolve this matter once and for all by making a decision and sticking to it. In dialogue virtually always, of course. Brazilian Portuguese has few contractions compared to English, but there are other, often subtle indications of colloquial discourse. And the conversations must sound natural. Fonseca has a marvelous facility for reproducing the way Brazilians of all social levels speak, and it would be catastrophic to make him sound as if he had a tin ear... What about contractions in narration and description, in the authorial voice? The novel is first-person, which allows some latitude, and much of it is actually related orally to his long-time lover Minolta (yes, she was named for the camera – wouldn't dream of changing that). So I'll go with contractions unless trumped by considerations of emphasis, euphony, or some other constraint. In other words, play it by ear.

The police detective Guedes, who suspects Gustavo of having murdered his latest lover, Delfina Delamare, wife of a millionaire playboy, practiced *'o princípio da Singeleza, de Ferguson.'* Who? The principle of what? Ah, the text has an explanation, of sorts: 'If there are two or more theories to explain a mystery, the simpler one is correct.' So Ferguson must be a philosopher, or maybe a logician. Pop the Encyclopaedia Britannica into the CD-ROM drive and... Hmm. FERGUSON, ADAM (1732–1816), of the so-called Scottish 'common sense' school of philosophy... No mention of a 'Simplicity' Principle or any other principle. Time to bother the reference librarian, who after a short wait informs me that Ferguson originated something called the Perfection Principle. Can *singeleza* also mean perfection? Let's see... Not according to *Aurélio*, who should know, or *Caldas Aulete* or *Melhoramentos* or any of the other Portuguese-to-Portuguese dictionaries on my shelf. Well, lest I confuse a knowledgeable reader who unlike ignorant me is familiar with Ferguson, I'll stick with Principle of Perfection, which is how the doctrine is known. [Later I would learn that this was a subtle maneuver by Fonseca to demonstrate that the narrator wasn't as smart as he thought; unfortunately, by then the translation was already in print, tangible proof that the translator wasn't as smart as he thought.]

I call a different library to check on progress for my request last week for help in locating an article by Wade Davis, author of *The Serpent and the Rainbow*, quoted in Portuguese by Fonseca: 'The toad is a laboratory and chemical mill...' But since back-translation is so dicey I want to cite the original article, which appeared (no date given) in *The Journal of Ethnopharmacology*. The public library drew a blank, so I called a university research library. Given the vagueness of the request (no title, no date, only author and journal), they told me it would take several days. Good news: they mailed the article two days ago.

'Dona Delfina' – here's that problem again. Will English-speaking readers recognize Dona as an honorific and not a variant of the name Donna? Guess I'll stick to my previous approach and leave it as is, trusting the reader to get it. 'Miss Delfina' sounds overly servile, something servants might use but not others.

Should I leave Avenida Brasil, easily understood, or change it to Brasil Avenue (or even Brazil Avenue)? Well, if Anglophones can fathom Rue Voltaire or Piazza Vecchia, why not Rua Paula Freitas? Okay, street names and such remain in Portuguese. Let's educate the reader a little.

The old profanity issue, again. Why doesn't English have a scatological word halfway between *crap* and *shit*? Portuguese *merda*, like French *merde*, is stronger than the former but carries less impact than the latter. Well, can't euphemize the author, so I'll go with the s-word and hope it doesn't get me in deep doo-doo.

Guedes had investigated an armed robbery 'during a *feijoada* with over a hundred people present.' Should I explain what the Brazilian national dish consists of? No, because this is a novel, not a cookbook. So, 'during a dinner...' is good enough.

The police title *delegado* has no exact American or British equivalent. He's college-trained, often an attorney, doesn't pound a beat, and investigates serious crimes like homicide and assault. Let's see what the *Dicionário Jurídico* has to say: (1) DELEGATE; scratch that. (2) PUBLIC AGENT; meaningless to the TL audience; (3) POLICE OFFICER (CHEFE DE UM DISTRITO POLICIAL); more like it but still not quite on target. I decide to go with 'detective,' a slight distortion but one that contextually English-speaking readers will relate to and find totally acceptable. Also, *delegado titular* can be rendered satisfactorily, if somewhat inexactly, as 'precinct captain' without undue violence to the concept.

Time for a break. As they say in Brazil, *ninguém é de ferro* (nobody's made of iron).

The library called. The *lex Oppiana* is the law proposed by Cato the Elder (234–149 BC) that attempted to regulate how women displayed themselves on the street. Fonseca's phrase *lei opiana* was a toughie. Ah, the difficulties of translating a polymath.

Should *Ministro de Segurança Pública* be Minister or *Secretary* of Public Safety? American usage calls for the latter, but the office has no true US counterpart, so perhaps I ought to leave it Minister as a subtle concession to the foreignness of the concept. (A point for Lawrence Venuti!) To further complicate things, in Brazil national cabinet-level officials are ministers, while at the state level they're secretaries... My seat-of-the-pants feeling says go with minister, but I'd have no quarrel with a colleague who translated it the other way.

Is there a term in English, *livor mortis*? Can he possibly mean 'rigor mortis'? It's not like Rubem Fonseca to make mistakes in such matters, so I'll double check... Not in the unabridged; let's try *Taber's Cyclopedic*

Medical Dictionary. Ah, here it is: 'dark spot on a cadaver due to gravitational pooling of blood.' You learn a lot reading Fonseca.

Delfina's body was found in her late-model Mercedes on Diamantina, a dead-end street in Rio's Jardim Botânico district. Not likely that TL readers will call me on place names in Rio de Janeiro, but to be on the safe side I'll dig out my street map of Rio and follow the author's detailed description of the scene of the crime... Yes, it all checks out. One less thing to worry about.

Time for lunch, if I still feel like eating after reading about the autopsy on Delfina Delamare.

Back to work. Which looks better in print – sonofabitch or son of a bitch? As a rendering of *filho da puta* the former appeals to my aesthetic sense. I add it to my spell check so the software won't hiccough every time it comes across it.

The normally reliable *Taylor* lists *assaltante* as assailant, aggressor, housebreaker; *Michaelis* adds burglar and waylayer, but none of these reflects the current use: mugger. (Going English-to-Portuguese, *Houaiss* correctly shows mugger as *assaltante.*) But there's a problem: since Delfina was killed in her car, mugger seems wrong; muggers work on foot.) Tentatively I settle for the somewhat puerile 'robber'; maybe something better will turn up later.

As promised, the mail brings a photocopy of the *Journal of Ethnopharmacology* article. Suspicions confirmed: the actual wording is 'a veritable chemical factory,' significantly different from 'a laboratory and chemical mill.' After reading Davis's *The Serpent and the Rainbow* I'm building a minor expertise on the subject of toad venom as applied to induced suspended animation. The same mail delivery brings a flyer for a new software package designed for translators in 12 languages, including Danish, Dutch, Swedish, and Norwegian – the four of which total just over 40 million speakers. No Portuguese, with its 180 million or so native speakers. Sigh... Also in the mail, courtesy of Rubem Fonseca, is the recently published French translation of *Bufo & Spallanzani.* A quick glance reveals a problem that hadn't occurred to me and that fortunately I don't have to confront: what to do with the French phrases in the original. The translator, Philippe Billé, faced not only with the Flaubert quote but also terms like *tour en l'air, entrechat dix,* and *grande jeté en tournant* has taken what strikes me as an odd tack: an asterisk by each, with the notation *en français dans le texte.* The result is a rather star-studded manuscript, and, as if *le pauvre* didn't have trouble enough, it means the French edition opens with the word *foutre*! Well, it's not my place to second-guess my Gallic colleague. *Chacun à son goût.*

Do I need to explain that *Jornal do Brasil* and *O Globo* are newspapers? Don't think so.

Manicômio Judiciário? I toy with Asylum for the Criminally Insane – too melodramatic – and go with the more prosaic Psychiatric Hospital.

On the subject of pseudonyms, Gustavo Flávio remarks that 'Stendhal was named Henry Beyle.' *Was* he – Henry, with a *y*? Nope, *Bénet's Reader's Encyclopedia* says 'Marie Henri Beyle, 1783–1842.' To Brazilians Henry may be as exotic as Henri, but not to Anglophones. Henri it is.

Here's a page-long letter from a girl friend of Delfina's. Italicize it, as is common English-language practice, or leave it plain as in the original? Long passages in italics are harder to read, but on the other hand it'll occupy only a third of a page when set in type. Let's try the italics for now, run off a copy on the laser printer, and see how it looks before committing to a final decision.

Um tira de merda: When you've translated as much Fonseca as I have, you've probably encountered every scatological and erotic term in the Portuguese language at least once. But *de merda* remains a thorny construction, calling for variant wording depending on context. For example, *país de merda* would be something on the order of 'shithole of a country.' *Tira* is of course 'cop.' So, shitty cop? Shit of a cop? That piece of shit the cop? After prolonged rumination I opt for 'a shitheel cop.' Less than poetic, perhaps, but it gets the job done.

Should I use a non-standard contraction like 'why'd' meaning 'why did'? Do people talk that way in informal American English? Certainly, but could it be misread as 'why would'? Solution: use it where appropriate if there's no possibility of misinterpretation and only if it doesn't call attention to itself.

I don't care what the dictionaries say. I refuse to write 'good-bye,' which to me seems as archaic as 'to-morrow.' I'll strike my small blow for modernity with 'goodbye,' and let the proofreaders overrule me if they will.

Gustavo decides to go for a rest to a resort in the mountains called *O Retiro do Pico do Falcão*. The first word is fine as 'retreat,' but what about *Pico do Falcão*? Should the bird be translated as 'falcon' or 'hawk'? Is the other term best as 'peak' or something else? Finally, what about the phrase as a whole? I reject 'Hawk's Peak' and 'Falconridge' and am left with 'Falconcrest,' which has a nice ring to it. It must, since it was the name of a long-running American television series. Will readers automatically make the association? I have to trust they won't.

'Tractor' in English has several meanings, but the primary image is one related to agricultural machinery. So to say a *trator* took him up the steep mountainside to the Retreat conveys the wrong idea. Maybe 'all-terrain vehicle'? But it's hauling a wagon full of passengers behind it, which wipes out that possibility. Whether I like it or not, I'm stuck with tractor, in the sense of a tractor-trailer, and must count on the reader's discernment to fill in the gaps.

Brazilians subdivide classification of certain reptiles into *lagarto* 'lizard' and *lagartixa* 'small lizard'. Preserving the separation in English, in a term that appears only once in the book, would be awkward, so I lump them together as 'lizards.' If the distinction were critical to the story – it isn't – I might have to do some rethinking.

In a long flashback to the time before he became a writer, the narrator talks about his 'dark past' some 20 years earlier as an investigator for an insurance company. Suspecting fraud in a million-dollar claim, he undertakes to prove that the deceased party feigned death using a tetrodotoxin derived from toads, the method using for creating zombies – or is that zombis? – in Haiti. (No, it's zombies.) While researching tetrodotoxins at the National Library, he meets the young hippie Minolta, who is wont to say things like '*Os livros são um bom astral.*' Am I on solid ground trying to capture her hip lingo with 'Books are a good trip'? I realize it sounds slightly obsolescent, but the setting *is* the sixties.

What television character is Xerife Lobo (Sheriff Wolf, literally)? The context makes it clear that he's dubbed, whoever he is, so it's a safe bet it's a program imported from the United States. For one of the few times in my life, I wish I watched more TV. I call a friend who has young children and ask if there's some carton character who plays a sheriff. He suggests Deputy Dog. There are no contextual clues, so this one goes in my SOS letter to Rubem himself. (Later I am apprised of a defunct TV series 'The Misadventures of Sheriff Lobo,' starring Claude Akins.)

More TV: Brazilian *novelas*. I'll call them soaps and leave it at that. Close enough as makes no difference. Hey, this is a novel, not a sociological treatise, and footnotes are anathema.

One of the protagonist's colleagues at the insurance company learned his questioning techniques 'from the American manual *Interrogation – Probing and Evaluation.*' Is this a real book or the author's flight of fancy? If real, I have to get the title exactly right. A call to the library: no similar title found in *Books in Print*. Another one for the SOS file.

Minolta moves in with the narrator and does the cooking, after a macrobiotic fashion. Can *bife de soja* be 'soy loaf'? Sounds unpalatable enough, so let's go for it.

Exame do corpo de delito: Mello's *Dicionário Jurídico Português–Inglês, Inglês–Português* lists *corpus delicti* as a synonym, so in this case it's equivalent to a judicial hearing.

Minolta uses a mixture of current and old-fashioned slang. (*Não vem que não tem. Comigo o buraco é mais embaixo.*) How to convey this in the TL? First let's check for exact meaning; it'd be a nice fillip if I can preserve both denotation and tone. Viotti doesn't have either expression, so they're probably not *that* old. Ah, Chamberlain's *Dictionary of Informal Brazilian Portuguese* – why didn't I check there first? As I thought, the latter phrase means 'I don't buy that, you can't fool me.' Something semi-archaic along the lines of 'I wasn't born yesterday' should do. For the former, 'No way José' is new enough to pass muster for the period in question and carries roughly the same message.

Rio's *Zona Sul* (South Zone) comprises, *inter alia*, Copacabana, Ipanema, and Leblon. Though some parts are less elegant than formerly, in Brazil it is still largely synonymous with the better part of town and middle- to upper-class status. Obviously, 'South Zone' or 'South Side' has no such connotation for non-Brazilians, so in the phrase *classe média da Zona Sul*, 'middle-class types' is adequate, if just barely. Something of a distortion, but short of providing a sociological lecture it's the best I can do.

At last an easy one! *Feira Hippie* equals Hippie Fair. Not flea market, which downplays the arts-and-crafts aspect, but plain old Hippie Fair.

That's a good one to end the session with. It's been a full day. My hair grew 0.0082", my fingernails 0.0027", my heart beat 4320 times, I expended 659 calories, breathed 10,450 times, and translated 10 pages, making 4289 decisions in the process. I'm tired.

Stages of translation

There are several typologies of the steps through which the translator and the translation itself pass before taking on its definitive form. One of the best known of these, Robert Bly's '*The Eight Stages of Translation*,' is seemingly more geared toward poetry translation than prose. A more recent one by Di Jin, reduces these to three stages. John Felstiner's approach, obviously particularistic, seen earlier in this guide, demonstrates one way of readying oneself for the strenuous job ahead. For what it's worth, my own typology – admittedly aimed more at prose translation than poetry and based primarily on my personal way of working – comprises the following steps.

(1) Read the entire work at least twice. For those who might contend that this is not actually a step in the translation process, I argue that no translation can succeed without a thorough grounding in the SL text. An unaware translation is *ipso facto* a bad translation, and 'unaware' means failing to have a firm grasp on the meaning of the work, both at the surface level (words, phrases, idioms, culture) and at the underlying level of deeper significance. (See the section on Subtext.)

(2) Determine the authorial voice. This will affect virtually every choice in the thousands of words to be translated. Note any shifts in tone from one part of text to another.

(3) Do the first draft, marking troublesome areas in square brackets and/or bold face for further attention. At this stage there is relatively less emphasis on smoothness and fluency and more on capturing the semantic gist of the text.

(4) Consult with an educated native speaker to clarify any points that are still vague. For especially vexing items, consult the author.

(5) Revise the manuscript, with emphasis on phraseology, fluency, and naturalness. At this stage it should come as close as possible to reading as if it had been written originally in English.

(6) Have a highly literate native speaker of English, preferably one with no knowledge of the SL, go over the manuscript and indicate any rough spots – i.e., parts that are awkward, stilted, 'translationese,' or that make no sense. Make any necessary changes.

(7) Go over the manuscript line by line with a native speaker of the SL who is also fluent in English. Read it aloud while the other person follows in the SL text. This catches mistranslations as well as inadvertent omis-

sions – it is incredibly easy to skip words, sentences, even entire paragraphs without realizing it – *and* it focuses your attention on questions of sonority. Unwitting homonyms, undesirable connotations, puerile constructions ('I see the sea'), unintentional repetitions of a word, and other infelicities are more likely to make their presence felt here than at any other stage of the process. (I concede this step will not possible for many translators, but it adds immeasurably to the final product. If no such listener is available, read the text aloud to yourself.)

(8) Make the final changes, run it through a spell-check, and let it rest for a few days. Then give it one last reading (typos may have been introduced in the revision phase) and send it off.

The literary translator's brain (right and left hemispheres)

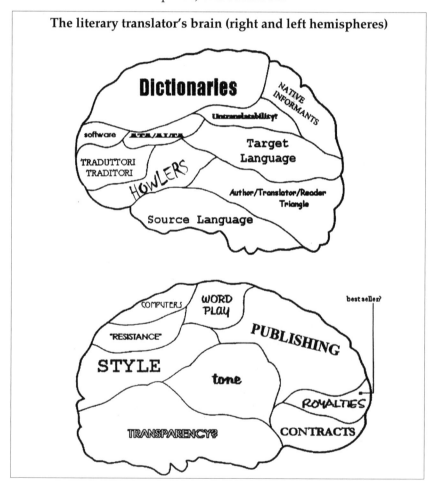

Techniques of Translation

Decisions at the outset

Even before beginning to tackle a text, the translator faces several crucial decisions of great importance to the final product. Awareness of these pivot points is fundamental to adopting a strategy for the project, and each translation requires an approach that takes into account the specific challenges of the SL text. What works for one writer may not function well for another. Some texts will call for adaptation rather than straightforward translation. Should the author be encouraged to participate, and if so, at what stage?

Fluency and transparency

The prevailing view among most, though not all, literary translators is that a translation should reproduce in the TL reader the same emotional and psychological reaction produced in the original SL reader. Thus, if the SL reader felt horror or curiosity or amusement, so should the TL reader. This approach is not without its hazards, for the question arises as to whether a translator is obligated to reproduce boredom, incoherence, unintentional grammatical lapses, factual errors, etc.

Most translators judge the success of a translation largely on the degree to which it 'doesn't read like a translation.' The object is to render Language A into Language B in a way that leaves as little evidence as possible of the process. In this view, a reader might be unaware he/she was reading a translation unless alerted to the fact. Whether adopting this perspective or not, upon beginning a project the translator must decide to what point transparency is a desideratum. Although the majority of readers hold it to be perhaps the single most important aspect of a 'good' translation, the view among translators, especially academics, is less unanimous. Scholars are more receptive to a visible role for theory in the production of a translation, and this raises the question of how much translation theory you need to be a translator.

How much understanding of the theory of the internal combustion engine do you need to drive a car? Theory and practice are two different entities, though there comes to mind the hoary definition of an economist as a person who sees something work in practice and wonders if it will work in theory. While I have no quarrel with theorists, they work a different side of the street; I am first and foremost a practitioner and have yet to meet a working translator who places theory above experience, flexi-bility, a sense of style, and an appreciation for nuance.

There is no inherent problem with theory *per se*, but when it interferes with translational output, either by reducing productivity of negatively impacting the final result, we are on shakier ground. No one complains that the many translators who work without a conscious theoretical basis are thereby somehow impugning theory; contrariwise, overly zealous applica-tion of theoretical guides can wreak havoc with a translation. One example, discussed later in this section, is the doctrine known as 'resistance,' whose best known advocate is Lawrence Venuti of Temple University.

In the time-honored author/translator/reader triangle, many would interpret this *modus operandi* as placing consideration for the author (as representative of the source culture) above that of the reader. The question naturally arises: who other than scholars would want to read prose that bears the heavy imprint of foreign grammar, idiom, or syntax? Examples of this literalistic approach might be 'a seven-headed beast' (Portuguese for a daunting or difficult task) or 'from the same field a berry' (Russian for six of one, a half dozen of the other). Well, it might work in theory…

The author–translator–reader triangle

It is almost a cliché for the relationship between author, translator, and reader to be represented graphically by an isosceles triangle:

author

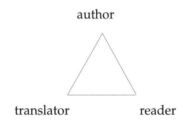

translator   reader

The underlying concept is that ideally the translator maintains equal proximity to the author (or the SL text) and to the reader (the final product, the TL text). Fine in theory but, as will be seen, the reality of in-the-trenches translating usually results in a lopsided triangle at best. Moreover, real-world translating means there is an irregular swing, sometimes in a single paragraph, between favoring the author and favoring the reader. If the translator must 'privilege' (appalling piece of jargon!) either the author or the reader, how is a balance struck?

Perhaps a more accurate depiction of the author–translator–reader relationship might be a simple linear one:

author ———— translator ———— reader

This has the advantage of placing the translator more realistically in an intermediate position between SL author and TL reader, for without the intervention of the translator the author would be unable to reach the TL audience. At the risk of straining the analogy, we could think of the lines joining the three as elastic, at times bringing the translator closer to the author, at times narrowing the distance between translator and reader. Let's examine how this works in practice.

'Targeteers' and 'sourcerers'

The two approaches boil down to what the always sound Peter Newmark calls 'targeteers' and 'sourcerers.' Targeteers, obviously, are TL-oriented, while sourcerers are SL-oriented. As Umberto Eco has said:

> A source-oriented translation must do everything possible to make the B-language reader understand what the author has thought or said in Language A... If Homer seems to repeat 'rosy-fingered dawn' too frequently, the translator must not try to vary the epithet just because today's manuals of style insist [otherwise]. The reader has to understand that in those days dawn had rosy fingers whenever it was mentioned, just as these days Washington always has DC.

In other instances, Eco continues, translation is rightfully target-oriented. In *Foucault's Pendulum*, one of the characters cites a phrase from a poem by Giacomo Leopardi, '*al di la della stepe*,' literally 'beyond the hedge.' Eco's purpose was 'to show how Diottallevi could experience the landscape only by linking it to his experience of the poem. I told my translators the hedge was not important, nor the reference to Leopardi, but it was important to have a literary reference at any cost.' The ensuing English translation by William Weaver reads, 'We glimpsed endless vistas. "Like Darien," Diottallevi remarked...'

But how does a translator discover whether he or she is one or the other, or perhaps a hybrid of both? Complicating the issue is the fact that what Newmark calls 'authoritative' texts, because of the literary or political importance of their author, demand a close translation, even when the result may sound a bit eccentric. As Andrew Hurley, who retranslated the complete short story oeuvre of Jorge Luis Borges, has intimated, one proceeds with extreme caution before opting to, say, rearrange word order in Borges.

Academicians tend more toward the sourcerer approach, surely a reflection of their rigorous research orientation stressing the primacy of meaning. With no intention of offending my professorial colleagues, candor compels me to concede that a lifetime of reading reams of scholarly articles is hardly the best preparation for producing smooth, transparent prose. This is an unfortunate fact of life, because college faculties tend to be over-represented among literary translators, for reasons mentioned elsewhere in this guide. While a significant number of the most accomplished translators have come from the halls of ivy, other academicians have foisted upon the reading public some of the driest, most awkward, most impenetrable prose imaginable, all in the interest of being 'faithful' to the original.

Resistance

Then there is the problem of 'resistance.' At the risk of oversimplifying, resistance is the concept that a translation should patently demonstrate that it *is* a translation. A less-than-perfect fit (the argument goes) is the 'resistance' of the SL culture and SL language to being shoehorned into a dissimilar cultural-linguistic frame. Translators who follow resistance theory deliberately avoid excluding any elements that betray the 'otherness' of the text's origin and may even consciously seek them out. Smoothness and transparency are therefore undesirable and even marks of a colonizing mentality. The reduced readability of the final product is an indication of its fidelity to the source language and the culture in which it originated. Advocates of resistance might be termed the radical fringe of literary translation.

Murat Nemet Nejat has put it this way: 'A successful translation must sound somewhat alien, strange, not because it is awkward or unaware of the resources of the second language, but because it expresses something new in it.'

My opinion is that there is little to be gained from skewing a translation to make it sound odd. Oh, a confirmed sourcerer might answer, what if the original itself sounds odd? What about your obligation to the author?

I acknowledge the translator's duty to the author just as I recognize that same translator's accountability to the TL reader. But I believe that of the two, the targeteer better meets both responsibilities. Here's my reasoning:

Authors' interest in being translated is related to their desire to achieve exposure in a foreign culture by appearing in another language. For writers from languages of limited diffusion, breaking into print in English – and to a lesser extent in any of the major European languages like French or German – can mean the difference between being known only in their native land and becoming the next Umberto Eco or Gabriel García

Márquez. Monetary rewards for the author, not so incidentally, are also proportional to the total number of readers in the TL, if the book is lucky enough to catch on. Whatever your feelings about the movie version of *The Name of the Rose*, it is a virtual certainty the film would not have been made had the novel never appeared in English.

But publication in translation is only the first step. If the author appears to the TL public as inaccessible or esoteric, the end product may be merely a *succès d'estime*. Further, while SL readers may be forgiving of, or even oblivious to, small idiosyncrasies in the author's style, TL readers are less tolerant. Worse, any deviation from 'normal' usage is likely to be chalked up as a shortcoming of the author, poor work by the translator, or both, when in reality it is an artifact of the structure of the SL culture.

Did Pushkin, Baudelaire, or Ibsen sound strange in the original? Lofty, certainly; inspired, absolutely; but not odd. A literal rendering of any world-class writer invariably makes that individual sound tongue-tied, as if he or she were speaking a foreign language, and poorly at that. 'Resistance' of this kind, I contend, often places cultural and academic considerations so far ahead of literary and aesthetic concerns as to distort the TL reader's perception of the author. Why bother with a masterpiece from another language if it reads like a trot?

Here, from an insightful article by Margaret Sayers Peden, one of the finest translators of Spanish and Latin American literature, is an excellent example of a trot:

'A su retrato' is one of Sor Juana's most widely anthologized poems and pursues themes common to her writing and to the writing of her age: the treachery of illusion and the inevitability of disillusion.

Este, que ves, engaño colorido,
que del arte ostentando los primores,
con falsos silogismos de colores
es cauteloso engaño del sentido:
    este, en quien la lisonja ha pretendido
excusar de los años los horrores,
y venciendo del tiempo los rigores,
triunfar de la vejez y del olvido,
    es un vano artificio del cuidado,
es una flor al viento delicada,
es un resguardo inútil para el hado:
    es una necia diligencia errada,
es un afán caduco y, bien mirado,
es cadáver, es polvo, es sombra, es nada.

This, that you see, colored (false appearance) fraud (hoax, deception),
which of art showing (exhibiting, bragging) the beauty (exquisiteness),
with false (treacherous, deceitful) syllogisms of colors
is cautious (wary, prudent) fraud (hoax, deception) of the sense (reason):
   this, on which flattery (adulation) has attempted (claimed, sought)
to excuse (avoid, prevent, exempt) from years the horrors (fright, dread),
and conquering (defeating, subduing) from time the rigors (severity,
cruelty)
   triumph from (over) old age (decay) and forgetfulness (oversight,
oblivion),
   is a vain (empty, futile) artifice (trick, cunning) of care (fear, anxiety),
   is a flower on the wind (air, gale, breeze) delicate (refined, tender),
   is a useless (fruitless, frivolous) guard (defense) for fate (destiny):
      is a foolish (stupid, injudicious) diligence (activity, affair) erring
(mistaken),
   is a worn out (senile, perishable) anxiety (trouble, eagerness), and, well
considered
   is a cadaver (dead body), is dust (powder), is shadow (shade, ghost,
spirit),
      is nothing (nothingness, naught, nonentity, very little).

… [T]he trot is an act of pure violence performed on a literary work. It
destroys the integrity of the sonnet, reducing it an assemblage of words
and lines that may convey minimal meaning, but no artistry.

In my view, in all too many cases what seems to be 'resisted' is the beauty of
the author's mode of expression.

All in all, it's in the author's *and* the reader's interest for the translator to
lean toward the latter in case of doubt. I remember Theodore Savory's
aphorism in *The Art of Translation*: 'The original reads like an original: hence
it is only right that a translation of it should too.' Or, as Eugene Eoyang has
put it, 'Something simple and inevitable in one language may be difficult in
another language with the same simplicity, yet there is no reason for that
difficulty in the *process* of translation to be reflected in the *text* of the translation. Art in translation is that which hides art.' Thus my identification with
the targeteers. In short, I resist resistance; literary translation is hard
enough without intentionally introducing elements of obfuscation.

Word by word or thought by thought?

Independent of the ongoing debate about the optimal approach to translation, the practitioner must establish certain principles when beginning a

project. One of these is to determine what the *translation unit* is to be. Is it the word, the sentence, the paragraph, or none of the above? Whatever strategy is adopted, it must be flexible enough to adapt to changing conditions in the text.

Among the most common mistakes of inexperienced translators is that of trying to squeeze every last kernel of meaning from the SL text. This is usually the result of an overly zealous concern for 'fidelity' to the original, but more often than not the effect is to produce an odd-sounding TL version that is a far cry from the author's intent. This phenomenon frequently results from the absence of a one-to-one relationship between a particular word or phrase in the source language and its counterpart, or lack of counterpart in the target language. For example, Portuguese *menino* means 'little boy,' and the word may occur every time the narration refers to the character in question. In English, however, it would seem strange to keep repeating 'little boy' after the initial mention; an author writing in English would be inclined to call him simply 'the boy' in subsequent references. Repetition of 'little boy' would qualify as an *error of frequency (q.v.)* and stems from a word-by-word orientation to the task of translation.

Thought-by-thought normally yields more fluent or transparent translations. The question is, how would the speaker have said this if he/she were saying it in English? This is especially important in translating profanity and other highly emotional discourse. With the exception of the foreign equivalents of the f- and s-words, most expletives sound downright silly if literally translated into English: imagine someone exclaiming 'Sperm!' (To be fair, the Brazilian vulgarism *porra* is much closer to 'come,' used nominally, than its scientific alternative. Still…) Thought-by-thought also lends itself to the translation of emotional outbursts such as profanity (about which I'll have more to say later).In Brazil, *buraco na água* is literally 'hole in the water,' but the meaning is 'banging your head against a stone wall' or attempting a futile task, and a competent translation will find an equivalent phrase in the TL.

In summary, the goal is not to translate what the SL author wrote but what he or she *meant*, and thought-by-thought is usually the superior vehicle for accomplishing this.

Adaptation or translation?

What is an adaptation and how does it differ from a translation?

Normally, in an adaptation the SL text is less sacrosanct than in a traditional translation. An adaptation, while taking as its point of departure the information content of the original, is less 'faithful' than a translation. (The quotation marks around _faithful_ are to hint that a close rendering of literal meaning is only one way to demonstrate fidelity to a text.)

What kind of situations call for adaptation rather than 'straight' translation? One obvious case is drama, in which dialogue must be not only intelligible but also 'speakable.' (See 'Translating for the theater.') Many lines that look good on paper sound forced, or worse, when uttered on stage. We are all familiar with so-called Tom Swifties from _The New Yorker_, whose filler items often gleefully ridiculed the stilted speech characteristic of the Tom Swift books. One (fictitious) example:

> EXCLAMATIONS WE SERIOUSLY DOUBT EVER GOT EXCLAIMED:
> 'We must flee at once before the nitroglycerin explodes into a raging inferno, destroying our escape route and leaving this entire building a charred ember!' Tom exclaimed.

Another occasion for adaptation rather than translation on stage comes about in frothy works like farce. Often, current references are added to the translated play to enhance appeal and topicality for a local audience. While one would never do this when translating Shakespeare or Goethe (or probably not even Tom Stoppard), it is normally considered no violation of propriety to inject such new material into lesser works like insubstantial comedies. Note that even Shakespeare is frequently adapted by changing not the dialogue but the setting, as seen in 1990s film versions of _Titus Andronicus_ (with Anthony Hopkins) and _Romeo and Juliet_ (with Leonardo DiCaprio).

A third motive for adaptation often occurs when a language is self-referential – that is, discusses its own grammatical structure or involves puns or other word-play. (See 'Puns and word play.') For instance, try translating into English (the problem is trivial in Romance languages and several others) the phrase 'No, in German one says _das_ Kind, not _der_ Kind.' To convey the situation – rather than the meaning of the specific phrase itself – to an English-speaking audience an adaptation would be necessary.

Jô Soares's _Twelve Fingers_ presented several challenging play on words that demanded adaptation, all of them with the author's compliance.

> Aparício Torelli – Aporelly – the famous humorist who wrote under the pen name Baron of Itararé ... The baron, after [the police] invaded the newspaper and cowardly beat his fellow workers, hung on the door to the editorial offices a sign that read ENTRE SEM BATER.

How to handle this? The surface meaning of the phrase is 'Enter without knocking'; the humor lies in a secondary sense of _bater_, which is 'to beat (up).' After mulling it over for days, I finally settled for THE BEATEN PATH.

Later in the novel, for reasons too complicated to relate here, Dimitri, the protagonist, becomes known as the Roach Man of Grande Island, a hellish compound for political prisoners.

> [T]he duty sergeant ... orders a private: 'Go get the Roach.'
> 'Captain La Roche?' asks the private, referring to Antônio La Roche, who was also confined on the island.
> 'No, idiot. The Roach Man. He's got a visitor.'

Here I adapted the name of an unseen character to make the jest work. In the SL text his name is Barata, which means 'roach' in Portuguese. A final example occurs when Dimitri tries to convince his lover that by acting as a banker for the illegal lottery he is serving a 'social function,' which elicits the rejoinder, 'The only thing social about the animal lottery is the social diseases a lot of the bookies have!' In the original, her words were 'the social elevators in the bookies' buildings.' (In the Brazilian context, *social* means 'private,' derived from *sócio*, member.) How effective any of these solutions is left to the judgment of the readers.

I resorted to adaptation in tackling a hilarious but seemingly 'untranslatable' short story by the Brazilian novelist and essayist José Bento Monteiro Lobato (1882 – 1948). Its original title, 'O Colocador de Pronomes,' literally 'The Pronoun Placer,' alludes to the difficulty even well educated Portuguese speakers have in deciding where to put the object pronoun in relation to the verb.

The first adaptation was to change the title to 'The Grammarian.' Next I had to find a series of English grammatical miscues similar to the TL. One that immediately came to mind was the slippery *who/whom* dichotomy, which causes even college graduates to sometimes go astray, as in the egregious 'The trophy will go to *whomever* wins the race.' Another area of confusion is the apostrophe, an endangered species in English that fewer and fewer seem to master with each generation.

Armed with these and other weapons, I sallied forth to do justice to the tale of Aldrovando Cantagalo, who 'came into the world by virtue of a grammatical error [and] died, in the end, the victim of another grammatical error.'

In his quest to correct his countrymen's slovenly use of language, Aldrovando points out to a blacksmith that his sign *'Ferra-se Cavalos'* should be *'Ferram-se Cavalos,'* in keeping with subject/verb agreement. I chose a similar error, 'We shoe horse's,' thus preserving the humor in the smithy's rejoinder: 'What I shoe here is a horse's hoof. Hoof was left out to save space. That's what the sign painter explained to me, and I understood him real good.'

Comedy may demand adaptation more than any other feature in a text. Jo Soares, author of *A Samba for Sherlock* and *Twelve Fingers*, is a well known late-night television talk-show host and comedian in Brazil, and his books reflect his penchant for humor. Knowing as he does how even an excess syllable can vitiate the comedic impact, he was very understanding in allowing me to adapt where necessary the otherwise untranslatable passages in his two novels.

In *Samba*, set in 1886 Rio de Janeiro, when the redoubtable English detective arrives to pay a visit, a house slave's ignorance of English surnames is reflected in her failure to understand Sherlock's 'I'm Holmes,' which she hears as '*"Eu sou homem, eu sou homem." "Que ele é homem eu já sei"* ('"I'm a man, I'm a man." I already *know* he's a man'). Can the humor be salvaged in translation? 'I'm homo' was rejected immediately, not for reasons of prudery but because the slang term for a homosexual wasn't registered until the third decade of the 20th century. Then the inspiration (?) 'I'm home' struck, which allows the slave to say, 'Does he think he lives here?' The meaning goes, the humor (hopefully) stays.

In *Twelve Fingers*, adaptation based on sound was necessary to convey the effect of delirium when Dimitri, the 'hero,' lay racked with fever aboard a transatlantic ship:

> [T]he ignoble seaman who commands this ship ... avoids me as if the cough ... were a harbinger of hemoptysis. Shitty seaman. I piss in the pestilent sea. On the waves the boat wavers and wanders. I'm thirsty, very thirsty, but they try to give me sea water. See slaughter. A mass moves over the mast. It's the pelican. I must suck its wet beak to quench this fire that blurs my sight... Somewhere on the ship someone is murmuring my name... Is it night? It must surely be night. Or else it's day dressed in darkness...The gangway! Why don't they lower the gangway? I never had a bilboquet...Never had a bilboquet. Beside me, a dying old man keeps muttering a prayer all the time. What time is it?

One of the first decisions the translator must make: does the text call for a more or less 'normal' translation or is an adaptation in order? Only a careful perusal of the entire work can answer this question. As in the above examples, most of the task will customarily be straightforward but some points may require adaptation.

Adaptations are not inferior to translations. They merely apply a different set of methods to the selfsame problem of recreating as closely as possible for the TL reader the effect experienced by the SL reader. In some ways, adaptations are even more challenging than more conventional translations, for they demand even greater flexibility and an unfailing sense for what the TL audience will find humorous, scary, or persuasive.

Beginning translators are better off sticking to more straightforward translation until they acquire the experience and confidence to take on adaptations, which are certain to test their mettle.

Register and tone

In English as in all other languages, virtually every word falls into a *register*. (As will be seen, depending on context, many words may belong to more than one register.) In *The Cambridge Encyclopedia of Language* David Crystal defines register as a 'socially defined variety of language, e.g., scientific, legal, etc.' But we must flesh out this definition with examples to understand the uses of register in translations.

There are various categories of register – e.g., non-technical/technical, informal/formal, urban/rural, standard/regional, jargon/non-jargon, vulgarity/propriety. Words may fall into more than a single category; 'reckoning,' for example, would be high on the technical or jargon scales if used in the maritime context of 'dead reckoning' but low on the urban scale, at least in North America, where *reckon* is a word associated with unsophisticated country folk.

Register can be thought of as a continuum, ranging from informal to formal, 'lowest' to 'highest.' The quotation marks are to emphasize that such designations are culturally determined rather than any inherent linguistic given – so-called high prestige dialects of a language such as 'BBC English' or Received Pronunciation merely happened to be the dialect of English spoken by the dominant political and economic class at an earlier historical period. (For an excellent discussion of this issue, see Lars Andersson and Peter Trudgill, *Bad English*.)

The late André Lefevere, in *Translating Literature*, offers an instance of technical register, which the would-be translator (from English in this case) would miss at his or her peril. The narrator in Conrad's *'Youth'* says, 'When the ship was fast we went to tea.' As Lefevere points out, the author 'does not mean that the ship is traveling at top speed while the characters … are daintily sipping the celebrated brew from fine china cups.' The present discussion, however, focuses on non-technical aspects of register.

In any language virtually every utterance, and often a word in isolation, conveys a set of associations that go beyond the literal denotation of the words themselves. Consciously and unconsciously, human beings equate words and expressions, grammatical constructions, even intonation patterns, with socially-defined non-linguistic characteristics such as class, status, and educational level. The same underlying meaning can be expressed various ways, normally along a spectrum of register. Some words – and not necessarily so-called ten-dollar words – are perceived as having more prestige, or demonstrating a firmer command of expression, than others. For an elementary example, substitute 'when' for 'as' in this phrase and see the effect: 'As I was coming over here today…'

Thus, an extremely simple Spanish phrase like *No tengo nada* would be used by native speakers of that language at all levels of education and social status. (The only variation likely to be encountered among certain lower socioeconomic groups might be *No tengo na'*.) But this same idea could be translated into English in a surprising number of ways. Here, in roughly descending order of register, are some:

Naught have I (archaic).
Nothing have I (stately, poetic).
I have nothing ('standard' or formal, more usual in writing).
I don't have anything ('standard' or colloquial, more usual in speech).
I don't have nothing ('substandard,' almost always spoken).
I ain't got nothing ('substandard,' spoken).
I don't got nothing ('substandard,' often dialect).

Each of these, depending on the source material, could conceivably be the preferred rendering from Spanish. Notice that in isolation *No tengo nada* provides almost no clue to the social status, background, or educational level of the speaker. There is no way for a native speaker to commit a sole-cism in its use; the double negative is correct in Spanish. It is only in combi-nation with other internal clues in the text that the appropriate register can be chosen. In Portuguese, no native speaker would confuse the adverb *bem* with the adjective *bom*; *Ele fala bem* 'He speaks well' is heard at every level of society, while in English the use of the adverb *well* typically marks the speaker as educated.

One implication of this is that you may be called upon to translate a grammatically 'correct' utterance in a less-than-standard manner. In the above example, if the person saying *Ele fala bem* is, based on internal evidence, the type who in English would say 'He talks good,' then so be it. That is, the translation unit to be considered here is not the word, or even the sentence, but the speaker's entire idiolect. Often, there will be no way to reproduce a specific substandard usage in the TL (you can't say *ain't* in Dutch), but the shortcoming can be compensated for by transferring the solecism to another utterance by the same individual.

In translating Patrícia Melo's *Inferno* (*Ascent into Hell*), I encountered a sentence, *Um rapaz armado tentou evitar que ela entrasse na boca-de-fumo*: An armed youth tried to – – – her from entering the drug site. Should it be 'to keep her from…'? 'to prevent her from…'? Or perhaps the sentence ought to be recast: 'tried to prevent her entering…' Which is best? In a vacuum, the question is an imponderable, for like most things in literary translation the sentence cannot be dealt with in isolation. We must know the context. In this case, we must first establish the authorial voice. Is the novelist using an omniscient point of view or speaking through one of the characters? Does the point of view shift? Where does the overall tone fall on the informality/formality spectrum? Only after determining these variables can the translator decide the correct register for a given phrase.

Register also applies to individual words. A single word can be jarring if it resonates in the wrong register. Switching to German, *Natürlich!* might be translated along a continuum ranging from 'Most assuredly!' through 'Of course!' to 'You betcha!' (among the many possibilities). We would expect a diplomat or a university docent to use the first or second but would be nonplussed to encounter the third.

I faced an unusual problem of register when translating a phrase from José de Alencar's 1865 romantic classic *Iracema*. The work, still widely read in Brazilian schools, is a prose poem noted for its elevated use of language in recounting the tragic tale of a doomed love between an early 16th-century Portuguese explorer and the title character, an Indian maiden. I came across the phrase *morder o pó*, literally 'to bite the dust.' What to do? The register seemed wrong, given the apparent Americanness of the phrase and its inevitable associations with countless western films. Yet there it was, staring me in the face. I finally opted to translate the phrase literally, for two reasons. First, it occurs in dialogue (an Indian speaking of the fate of an enemy from another tribe); second, it is highly probable that such a picturesque but obvious metaphor has arisen independently in any number of languages. There are times when register must yield to other considerations.

What the reader unconsciously perceives as the 'correctness' of a translation hinges on many elements, including the crucial choice of the appropriate word, both denotatively and connotatively. Register matters.

A few examples:

Lower register	*Higher register*
afterwards (similar: backwards, towards)	afterward (backward, toward)
anybody (nobody, somebody)	anyone (no one, someone)
brought up (reared)	raised
by oneself	alone
can't	cannot (and other non-contractions)

Lower register	*Higher register*
crazy	insane, mad
fast, quick	swift
for good	forever, permanently
get	[almost any alternative]
guy	man, individual
have to	must
jerk	idiot
just (adv.)	merely
kid	child
like (conj.)	as
maybe	perhaps
only (adj.)	sole, lone
only (adv.)	merely
ought to	should
reckon*	suppose
real (adv.)	really, very, quite
sure (adv.)	surely
very	quite
weird*	strange, odd, bizarre
whole	entire

* Other considerations (dialect, regional, substandard, slang connotations, etc.) may apply.

As can be deduced from this list, a given word may have multiple classifi-cations. Let's examine *kidding*. On the informal/formal scale it's near the bottom; one ascending progression on that spectrum might be *kidding/ joking/jesting/japing*. But the vulgarity/propriety spectrum might start with *bullshitting* at one extreme and *kidding* at the other. Similarly, a word like *die* may well pass through permutations ranging from *kick the bucket, buy the farm*, and *cash in your chips* to such solemn constructions as *pass away, go to one's reward*, and Machado de Assis's strikingly metaphoric *study the geology of holy ground*. Even the most frequently used words in English may coexist in several forms: simple negation can encompass *nah, nope, nay* (dialect) *uh-uh*, and *no*, while affirmation comprises *yep, yeah, uh-huh*, the dialectical *aye*, and *yes*. The translator must think about in which segment of the register-continuum a speaker's utterances fall and translate accordingly.

Iracema, the twelfth novel that I translated from Brazilian Portuguese, represented a departure for me in several ways, as well as a formidable translational undertaking. I had never before translated a book by a deceased author (which short of contracting a medium obviated any possibility of enlisting his or her help), nor had I taken on a project as historically far removed as this classic work of mid-19th-century Brazilian romanticism. The challenges I confronted, and the lessons I learned, constitute a case study of the application of register that may be of interest to other translators.

José de Alencar's novel, first published in 1865, is considered one of the high points of Brazilian literature of the period and is read even today, in part or in its entirety, by virtually all Brazilian secondary school students. A prose poem, it combines a strong narrative sense thematically reminiscent of James Fenimore Cooper with an elevated use of language that seamlessly blends the elegant Portuguese of its day with numerous Tupi words to create a heightened effect of lyricism.

Iracema had been translated into English only once before, by Isabel Burton, the wife of the famous explorer and linguist Sir Richard Burton. (It is not known whether he played any role in the translation.) Based on internal evidence – Alencar died in 1877 and the translation would not appear until 1886 – the project apparently took close to a decade to complete and included a trip by the translator to the Brazilian town of Santos. That the undertaking had the author's blessing and participation is clear from Burton's preface:

> I cannot allow my readers to remain ignorant of the name of Senhor J. de Alencar, the author of this and several other works; for he deserves to be as well known in England as in Brazil, ...
>
> He is their first prose and romance writer. His style, written in the best Portuguese of the present day – one to be learnt and copied – is in thorough good taste and feeling. It contains poetic and delicate touches, and beauty in similes, yet it is real and true to life.
>
> ... I have endeavored to be as literal as possible, but I cannot pretend to do him justice, for our harsh Northern tongue only tells coarsely a tale full of grace and music in the Portuguese language; but I have done my best, and if he permits me to translate all his works, I hope to do better as I go on, especially if he will again – as he has already done – give me instructions in Tupy, the language of the aborigines.

In 1997 I was selected to do a retranslation of *Iracema* for the Oxford University Press *Nineteenth Century Brazilian Classics* series, under the direction of Professor Richard Graham of the University of Texas at Austin. A century and a third after its first publication and light years away in terms of the evolution of literary styles, the novel offered an opportunity to convey to a late-20th-century audience some notion of its appeal. Unlike my predecessor, I could not avail myself of Alencar's invaluable assistance in clearing up doubts or elucidating obscure references. And I made a point of not reading Burton's translation until after I had finished my own, lest I suffer unconscious influences. Unlike the earlier rendering, which incorporated Alencar's copious etymological observations as footnotes on the respective pages, it was the decision of the editors that all such information would be contained in a glossary to follow the main text – an approach I favored because of the marked tendency of footnotes to interfere with mimesis.

As I said in the Translator's Introduction to *Iracema*:

> To a contemporary audience Alencar's prose can seem florid, even purple. A balance had to be found between literalism, which would make the text all but unreadable to today's audiences, and an overzealous modernization that would vitiate the exoticism and richness of vocabulary of the original.
>
> Where there are no common equivalents to native animals and plants, or where a literal translation would introduce erroneous associations – such as 'parakeet' for *jandaia* – they have been left in the original, provided the context makes the meaning clear. In other cases, they were either rendered into English or an explanatory word or phrase was interpolated. For example, in Chapter XIII, 'warriors who crept along the ground like toads' conveys more meaning than 'crept along the ground like the *intanha*.' Nevertheless, because of the decision to include Alencar's Notes, it was necessary to leave many words – those for which he analyzes their etymology – in the original, even where they are unclear in context. Such words are italicized, and any vagueness can be resolved by referring to the author's notes that follow the novel. Animal and plant names sufficiently anglicized to appear in the *Oxford English Dictionary*, such as agouti and carapa, are treated as English words and are not italicized, despite their strangeness to many readers.
>
> Because the present version is aimed at a readership on the eve of the 21st century, the second-person pronoun has been translated as *you* rather than *thou/thee* except when the speaker is addressing inanimate objects. Similarly, the author's use of the historical present, which occurs frequently but not consistently throughout the text, has been translated uniformly into the past tense.
>
> In the final draft, a balance was sought between what the translator deemed as excessive reliance on either the archaic or the hypermodern. Some constructions have been rendered so as to suggest, without slavishly imitating, Alencar's sometimes idiosyncratic syntax – always

correct and grammatical but often far removed from the common parlance of his own time.

The difference a century makes can be seen in these two versions of the same description of the Indian maiden. First, the Burton rendering (her footnote numbers have been omitted):

> The comb of the Játy-bee was less sweet than her smile, and her breath excelled the perfume exhaled by the vanilla of the woods.
>
> Fleeter than the wild roe, the dark virgin wandered freely through the plains and forests of Ipú, where her warlike tribe, a part of the great Tabajára nation, lay wigwamed. Her subtle, naked foot scarcely pressed to earth the thin green garment with which the early rains clothe the ground.
>
> One day, when the sun was in mid-day height, she was reposing in a forest-clearing. The shade of the Oitycíca, more refreshing than the dew of night, bathed her form. The arms of the wild acacia dropped their blossoms upon her wet hair. The birds hidden in the foliage sang for her their sweetest songs.

In the current version, the passage reads:

> The *jati's* honeycomb was not as sweet as her smile; nor did the vanilla sending forth its fragrance in the forest match the perfume of her breath.
>
> Swifter than the wild ema, the tawny maiden traversed the interior and the woodlands of Ipu, where dwelled her warrior tribe, of the great Tabajara nation. Her graceful, naked feet, scarcely touching the ground, merely smoothed the green plush that carpeted the earth with the first rains.
>
> One day, when the sun was at its height, she was resting in a clearing in the forest. The shade of an oiticica, cooler than the dew of night, bathed her body. The branches of the wild acacia scattered flowers on her damp hair. Hidden in the foliage, the birds coaxed forth their singing.

Certainly the latter translation makes no claim to superiority over the earlier one; any value it may possess lies in its ability to speak to a modern audience, even when couched in speech intended to invoke the gentle phrases of a bygone era without lapsing into artificiality or mere mimicry.

Probably the word occurring most frequently in the SL text is *doce* (sweet, gentle), followed closely by *murmúrio* (murmur) and its verb-form equivalents. Both present problems for a translator wishing to avoid mawkishness and to make his rendering accessible and appealing to a contemporary readership.

Other challenges abound in the novel. Let's take an example, from Chapter XI. The difficult words are underlined. *Como* trota *o* guará *pela orla da mata, quando vai seguindo o rasto da presa* escápula, *assim* estrugava *o passo o* sanhudo *guerreiro.* First, before dealing with *trota*, we have to decide what a *guará* is. The Tupi word means both the scarlet ibis and a kind of wild dog. *Orla* introduces some confusion, because it can mean 'edge' as well as 'shore.' On balance, however, it seems Alencar is speaking of the mammal rather the bird. Even so, does 'trot' sound right? True, animals other than horses can be said to trot, but the equine association is very strong; I opted for 'moves quickly' to avoid jarring the reader's eye (or ear). Though *escápula* clearly seems to derive from *escapar*, no dictionary lists it in that sense. Nor does the possibility of an extraneous accent mark (*escápula* for *escapula*) resolve the impasse. *Estrugar*, albeit an unfamiliar term, means 'to quicken one's step.' *Sanhudo*, an archaic form of *sanhoso*, poses a problem: it can mean either 'enraged' or 'terrible,' in the sense of 'formidable.' The final version of the passage emerged as 'As the *guará*, the wild dog, moves quickly along the edge of the woods, when following the spoor of its escaping prey, so did the enraged warrior quicken his step.'

In deciding which animal names (there is a veritable menagerie of birds) to translate, euphony was a major consideration. For example, does *alcíone* become 'halcyon,' 'kingfisher,' or merely the generic 'water bird'? *Inhuma* (or *anhuma*) sounded better left in the original than 'horned screamer.' There is probably sufficient exoticism in the unfamiliar names – albeit accepted English terminology – of tropical plants and animals to make unnecessary the use of the foreign originals. Thus, *genipap, jabiru, carapa, granadilla, angico* from the vegetable kingdom and *cavy* and *coati* from the animal kingdom. To an English-speaking reader, is 'wine palm' any less exotic than *muriti*? Euphony was more important in this translation than in most, since *Iracema* is a prose poem. Although it was impossible to capture Alencar's rhythms in English, I attempted to avoid cacophonous constructions and jarring juxtapositions. Target-language homonyms sometimes created problems in this respect: *sea* and *see*, as in *volvia os olhos ao mar, para ver se…* Obviously, it is less than poetic to say 'He turned his eyes to sea, to see if…' It became necessary to substitute 'ocean,' a less obtrusive change than would have been 'to spy' or 'to descry' for the ordinary word 'see.' By the same token, *grande avô* had to be translated as 'mighty grandfather,' because 'great grandfather' – well… Or take the case of *os seios, onde se forma o primeiro licor da vida*: what's wrong with 'the breasts, where the first liquor of life forms'? Call me finicky, but that phrase 'life forms' sounds like something out of *Star Trek*; I prefer 'is formed.'

How much precision is necessary? For *folha da taioba*, can I say simply 'taro leaf' or must it be 'leaf of the elephant's ear taro'? A check of the *American Horticultural Society Encyclopedia of Gardening* yielded a photo of taro under cultivation, and the leaves are clearly large enough for the purpose mentioned in the novel (carrying a bit of honeycomb).

Some passages were especially challenging. From a description of drug-induced dreams: *O velho renasce na prole numerosa, e como o seco tronco, donde rebenta nova e robusta sebe, ainda cobre-se de flores.* Just who or what covers himself (or itself) with flowers? Logically, it would be the vegetation (*sebe*), and such a translation would surely have passed unnoticed. Grammatically, however, it would appear to be the old man: *O velho* [subject] *renasce* [verb] ... *e* [coordinating conjunction] ... *cobre-se* [verb]. And since this is a hallucinogenic state, it could well be that the old man dreams of covering himself in flowers. At least that's how I translated it: 'The old man was reborn in his numerous offspring, and like the dry trunk from which bursts forth a hardy new hedge, still covered himself in flowers.'

Another puzzler: 'Iracema also avoided her husband's eyes, for she had come to know that those beloved eyes were troubled at the sight of her, and instead of filling themselves with her beauty as before, dismissed it from themselves. *Mas seus olhos dela não se cansam de acompanhar à parte e de longe o guerreiro senhor que os fez cativos.*' The difficulty lies in that *dela*; is it *seus olhos dela* (admittedly, an unusual construction, as the normal way would be *os olhos dela*) meaning 'her eyes,' with *dela* used to distinguish it from *os olhos do esposo*, 'her husband's eyes'? Or is the meaning that her eyes never tire of accompanying him? I opted for the latter: 'But her eyes did not weary of accompanying, secretly and from afar, the warrior her master, who had made captives of them.'

Some of Alencar's words were not to be found in any dictionary I consulted, whether contemporary (Aurélio) or 19th century (Caldas Aulete from *c.* 1876). One such term was *marugem*, which in context cannot mean a type of plant (*o cão fiel ...lambendo ainda nos pelos do focinho a marugem do sangue tabajara*). I finally had to omit it, the translator's admission of defeat: 'the faithful dog ... still licking from the hair of its snout the Tabajara blood.' Fortunately, it did not affect the overall meaning of the phrase.

Using tone in translation

One of the most useful tools a translator can possess is the apperception of tone. By assigning a high priority to tone, the translator avoids such traps as a slavish fealty to literal meaning that distorts the author's intent. Tone can also help in dealing with puns, indirect allusions, solecisms, and slang. Obviously, tone also provides an important clue to register as well.

By tone I mean the overall feeling conveyed by an utterance, a passage, or an entire work, including both conscious and unconscious resonance. Tone is more than just style, although the two are often interrelated. Without changing style, a writer may within the space of a few lines vary greatly in tone. Fidelity to tone accommodates such flexibility while remaining faithful to style.

Tone can comprise humor, irony, sincerity, earnestness, naïveté, or virtually any sentiment. Just as after Poe the short story traditionally strove to achieve a single mood such as horror or amusement, tone has its own unity. This, however, does not prevent the author from shifting tone in mid-paragraph, as sometimes happens, but there is integrity of tone within what I call the *tone-unit* – the text between changes in tone. Normally encompassing at least a complete utterance, they may characterize an entire work, which is usually the case in non-fiction.

Tone violation occurs when the translator ignores requirements of tone, whether in dialogue, description, or narration. The most conspicuous examples are usually found in dialogue, as in this passage from Samuel Putnam's 1945 translation of Jorge Amado's *Terras do Sem Fim* (called *The Violent Land* in English):

> You will pardon me, colonel, but we would like to know when we may have the deed to the land... [D]on't you remember that you sold *us* that piece of forest? In place of money on the cacao contract?

Just who is speaking? A well-educated individual, surely: note the use of *may* rather than *can*. In reality, however, the original text shows the speaker to be an illiterate agricultural laborer in the Brazilian backlands whose speech abounds with such provincialisms as *'arrecordar'* for *'recordar'* ('remember') and grammatical errors like *'nós queria'* (incorrect subject/verb agreement, on the level of 'I is'). In short, precisely the kind who would say 'ain't' if the construction existed in Portuguese. But judging by the tone, he could be a lawyer or college professor.

A tonally accurate rendering might go something like this:

> Beggin' the colonel's pardon, but we'd like to know when we can have the deed to the land... Don't the colonel recollect sellin' that piece of forest to *us*? Instead of the cacao contract?

Nothing overstated, no hillbilly dialect, just a few implied indicators of the speaker's educational level and probable social standing *vis-à-vis* his listener.

Now for a more subtle instance of tone. Marcos Rey's novel *Esta Noite ou Nunca* (*Tonight or Never*) is a comic treatment, with serious implications, of a once-dedicated writer reduced to cranking out cheap formula detective novels for a two-bit pirate press. Writing under the pseudonym William Ken Taylor, he appears on the title page only as the 'translator' of the putative author. Gradually he comes to identify with the more celebrated and successful American, for whom he has created a fanciful if strangely plausible biography:

> WILLIAM KEN TAYLOR was born in one of the poorest areas of Chicago. In his youth he worked at a wide range of professions: hotel elevator operator, errand boy for gangsters during Prohibition, waiter in a brothel, slot machine repairman, aquatic clown, drugstore detective, amusement park magician, dubber for animated films (he was the voice of the fox in Walt Disney's *Pinocchio*), and dog racing promoter. During World War II, disguised as a Nazi general, he single-handedly captured the crew of a German tank. He can be seen entering liberated Paris at the side of Charles de Gaulle (he's the shorter of the two). When the war ended he returned to the United States, where at the advice of a seasoned detective he dedicated himself to crime literature. With the appearance of the book we now publish he won instant fame and fortune. Today William Ken Taylor lives in a veritable palace in Malibu and is married to the fascinating television actress Gloria Stevens.
> The back cover reads: TEN MILLION COPIES SOLD!!!
> 'This young man takes up where I left off.' – Hemingway.

He fantasizes about luxuriating in William Ken Taylor's Olympic-sized swimming pool in Southern California:

> I dived in, and when I came up I saw who had just arrived, and smiled at her: Gloria Stevens. Straight out of a Hollywood script, she slipped off her dress, removed her shoes, and within a few frames merged her actress's fame with her husband's, in the water. There followed a long aquatic kiss as we sank to the bottom of the tiled surface... That was when I remembered I can't swim and woke up to keep from drowning.

Here's where tone comes in. Literally translated, the passage ends 'to keep from dying.' But that isn't funny, and the tone of both passages is clearly intended to evoke laughter. I changed the literal meaning of a single word to preserve the tone of the original. 'To keep from drowning' is funny, as side-by-side comparison shows. Though we are hard pressed to explain why the latter rendering is funny while the former is not, we *can* recognize the difference and appreciate the author's tonal design.

In the same author's *Memoirs of a Gigolo* there are two recurring leitmotifs, and tone was important in reproducing both. Throughout his life Mariano, the narrator, identifies real people with the figures on playing cards: Lu, the beautiful young prostitute with whom he falls hopelessly in love, is the Queen of Hearts; a lifelong nemesis becomes the Jack of Spades; his benefactress Madame Iara, proprietor of a high-class bordello, is the Queen of Diamonds. While many of the allusions and secondary meanings defied translation, it was possible to unobtrusively introduce others that legitimately compensated for the loss by recreating the original tone – e.g., *shuffle, pack, deal, hand*, and *suit*. (It's always a bonus when a translator succeeds in retaining the quasi-subliminal elements of a text.) The second theme running through the novel is nautical, related to the deep impression made on the 12-year-old Mariano by his arrival at the large old house where Madame Iara lives with her 'nieces':

> My eyes came upon a large old colonial house with green windows, sunny, ample, open and well lighted. On the ground floor was a general store, and above, so far above on that morning, lived my protectress, ... surrounded by her nieces – young, wearing makeup, sportive, sinful, and happy.... It was a transatlantic liner in a sea of buildings, embarking on a luxury cruise, its captain my Queen of Diamonds. The captain waved to me... Her crew swayed in the air, their hands fluttering and wanton.

Maritime terminology is central to this pivotal incident, which marks the beginning of his new life and, under the influence of his environment, his adult emergence at a full-fledged gigolo. It was therefore crucial to find the psychologically exact word to capture the tone of *maruja*, which is what he calls the girls (they are never referred to as prostitutes). *Marujo* means sailor or seaman, but in addition to being male-oriented, neither term conveyed the affection and warmth experienced by the young boy. As often happens, I left the choice of words open for a few days, and the answer suddenly burst from my subconscious: 'mariners.' Years later, Mariano and Lu are down to their last pennies, and she decides to work the streets again. When he asks what she plans to do, she answers '*Viração.*' Less pun than untranslatable allusion, the primary contextual connotation of *viração* is slang: 'hooking.' But there is a lovely second sense, a more traditional usage: a sea breeze. Given the impossibility of retaining both, I opted for denotation. My disappointment at my inability to preserve the exquisite turn of phrase was somewhat mitigated by the fact that English offered at least one instance – the word '*deck*' – that was a fortuitous confluence of leitmotifs unavailable to the original.

Similarly, the title of Rubem Fonseca's story 'Dia dos Namorados' is literally 'Valentine's Day.' As far from sentimental as any work I have read, it depicts the misadventures of a wealthy, middle-aged, married banker who picks up a beautiful young girl in Ipanema and takes her to a motel, only to discover that 'she' is a transvestite. The ironic, hard-edged tone was better served by the sardonic title '*Be My Valentine.*'

Consistency of tone is not a panacea, even if fidelity to overall tone trumps any single lexeme in the text. Armed with the primacy of tone, however, the translator can face with some degree of equanimity the inescapable allotment of untranslatable items that are certain to arise. Rubem Fonseca's dour story 'Onze de Maio' (The Eleventh of May), about the abbreviated and unhappy lives in a futuristic asylum for the aged, contains the phrase '*Edmundo o imundo*' (Edmund the filthy). After much lucubration I was forced to the conclusion that, short of changing the character's name, no TL equivalent replicated the SL sound and rhythm. Nevertheless, I took consolation in knowing that this setback would be balanced by opportunities yet to come, in which I could use tone to surmount limitations and preserve for an English-speaking audience the essential genius of the Brazilian creator.

What literary translators really translate

It is commonly thought that translators deal with words, but this is only partly true. Whatever their branch of translation, they also deal with ideas. And literary translators deal with *cultures*. In a very real sense, *Time* magazine was right when over a decade ago it called literary translators 'couriers of culture.'

E. Annie Proulx, upon receiving a PEN/Faulkner award in 1994, decried the notion that books have had their day and that we live in a post-literate era. 'To some [this] means sluggish book sales, ... to others that *the old gray novel ain't what it used to be*' (emphasis added). Take a close look at that italicized phrase – especially if you're not a native speaker of American English. Did it resonate? Was the allusion (not the fundamental meaning) clear?

If not, imagine how an Argentine translator might interpret it. Novel – *novela*; no problem there. But *old gray*? Is the author referring to fiction from an earlier century, now gray with age? Is there in English a genre of 'gray' novels, perhaps on the order of black comedy or film noir? And why did Proulx choose the ungrammatical *ain't*? Is the gray novel only sold on the gray market, mostly to the semiliterate?

Given the cultural gulf, except for one who has lived in the United States for some years, the most likely Spanish translation of *old gray novel* – and a defensible one under the circumstances – might be something on the order of *novela tradicional* or *venerable novela*. But in that case neither the translator nor the TL reader would appreciate the cultural colloquialism in Proulx's choice of words. Indeed, it is all but impossible for a person outside a given culture to marshal the depth and scope that natives assimilate automatically and unconsciously; that is why it's critical for a translator to establish reliable and authoritative native-speaker contacts (aka informants) in the SL culture. Undeniable as it is that not all cultural allusions are gracefully translatable, *an unrecognized allusion cannot be properly translated*.

In order to appreciate the extreme importance of understanding the SL culture, let's take a short test. We all pride ourselves on our command of language, so see how you do with the following terms, all of them genuine contemporary English-language usage.

What is *wanking*? How about a *higgler*? Just what does a *monkey's wedding* refer to? *Mickle*? Finally, *esky*?

Before you begin doubting your knowledge of English, you should know that none of these terms is normally used in the United States. 'Wanking' is British, 'higgler' is Jamaican for an itinerant peddler; 'monkey's wedding' is a South African term for rain with sunshine; 'mickle' is Scottish for large, as in a mickle lad; 'esky' is Australian for a portable cooler for beer, from 'Eskimo.'

I use these English-to-English examples to demonstrate the difficulty in understanding in all its complexity even our mother tongue, however familiar we may be with it. To illustrate, let's look at the word 'wanking.'

It is a current British term for masturbation ('to wank,' 'wanker,' etc.). Suppose we wanted to translate *wanking* into another language, French, say. Even though we now understand the basic meaning, we must still know what level of discourse it represents before we can choose an appropriate TL equivalent. Is *wanking* slang or merely colloquial? (We can safely judge that it is neither scientific nor technical.) Is it vulgar, to be avoided in polite society? If so, is it evolving toward wider acceptance? For example, the word 'screw' was once verboten in America in any context except a metal fastener with helical thread, or perhaps to screw up one's face in concentration or one's courage when facing a challenge. Now it is commonly found as synonymous with 'to botch' ('You really screwed up that contract, Johnson') and can even be seen and heard increasingly in American national media as a substitute for its earthier four-letter sexual counterpart. Finally, is *wank* jocose, on the model of the cutesy 'tinkle,' to urinate? All these factors must be taken into account before selecting a TL substitute.

This is precisely the type of information too seldom found in even the best dictionaries. It is *cultural* knowledge coming from a thorough familiarity with the culture in which a language is spoken rather than mere – if that is the word – mastery of the language.

Any literary translator frequently encounters reminders of the difference between knowing the language and knowing the culture. When I translated Marcos Rey's *Esta Noite ou Nunca* (*Tonight or Never*), I came across the phrase 'trashy detective stories to sell at newsstands on the outskirts and in the ABC.' The ABC? Recourse to dictionaries proved fruitless. Finally, a *paulista* enlightened me: in São Paulo, ABC refers to the three working-class districts of Santo André, São Bernardo do Campo, and São Caetano do Sul.

It is tempting to assume that a profound acquaintance with the grammar, syntax, and vocabulary of a foreign language suffices to qualify one as literary translator. Equally essential, perhaps more essential, is a comprehensive appreciation of the culture that produced the work. Language has a locus – it is spoken in and reflects a specific setting and will vary from place to place even within comparatively small distances. Proof of this can be seen in the plethora of European regional dialects, evident in even such geographically circumscribed countries as the Netherlands.

Culture shapes and changes a language, sometimes separating rather than uniting. Instances of a single word having opposite meanings in two countries that share a language are rare, but differences in usage are common. In my own country, I once inadvertently offended some Oregonians by inviting them to dinner and adding, 'You'll have to take pot luck.' In some areas, I discovered to my chagrin, 'pot luck' does not have the meaning I had always attributed to it – namely, whatever we happen to be eating – but that each guest brings prepared food, a practice known in the South as a 'covered dish supper.' In Britain, as a further example, 'bonnet' and 'boot' are as likely to refer to an automobile (motorcar, that is) as to clothing.

Admittedly, it is sometimes difficult to distinguish between incomplete proficiency in the SL and insufficient knowledge of that language's culture. I recall reading a Portuguese translation of a J.D. Salinger story, 'A Perfect Day for Bananafish,' which takes place on a beach, and coming across the phrase 'his blue trunk' (*seu tronco azul*). Perplexed, I sifted through various hypotheses: a sudden cold snap had turned the upper portion of the protagonist's body blue; a follower of ancient Druidic rites, he had painted his torso the color of the sky; for some reason he had lugged a blue steamer trunk to the seashore; or maybe – You, of course, are way ahead of me. In actuality, as a check of the original proved, the English words were 'blue trunks'; Salinger hadn't gone surreal on us.

Because even the latest dictionary is out of date before it is printed – neology always outpaces lexicography – a deep immersion in the SL culture, if not indispensable, is highly desirable. To be sure, scholars have produced excellent translations without ever setting foot in Homeric Greece or Virgilian Rome, but they were nonetheless steeped in the nuances of the culture through reading, research, and other substitutes for firsthand experience.

Fortunately, in dealing with living languages the translator faces no such constraints. Limited only by resources of interest, energy, time, and money, today's translator can stalk the wild allusion till he or she bags it. The translator working with Albanian in Spokane may have some justification for less than exhaustive pursuit of denotation, but his counterpart translating Spanish in New York City does not.

For example, a Brazilian short story contained the phrase *'Fumamos. Esvaziamos uma pitu'* ('We smoked. We emptied a *pitu*.'). As the tale deals with a gang of criminals sitting around a rundown apartment on December 31, smoking marijuana and drinking while they plan the first bank robbery of the new year, the context should be of some help. The root meaning of *pitu* is a large freshwater shrimp (*Bithynus acanthurus*). But 'We emptied a shrimp' is cryptic at best.

There's a further clue: *pitu*, the crustacean, is masculine, but the text reads *'uma pitu,'* feminine. Here, awareness of the culture would have saved the translator from a gaffe. Since even the *Aurélio*, considered the 'industry standard' among Brazilian dictionaries, lists no secondary meaning for the word, the translator rendered it as 'We finished a stash.' As guesses go, a fairly nice try, coming on the heels of the phrase 'We smoked.'

However, a call to any Brazilian would have yielded the answer in seconds, a cultural referent familiar to almost anyone in the country. *Pitu*, it turns out, is the brand name of an inexpensive sugar cane rum (*cachaça*) that has become generic for cheap booze. The correct translation, therefore, is 'We emptied a bottle.' A small difference, perhaps, but a significant one.

Our first lesson, then, in the importance of cultural familiarity and the ways of overcoming the lack of it: assuming you don't live in the SL country, try to establish contacts to call on when necessary to resolve doubts about a particularly obscure reference. Even if you don't know the native speaker personally, most educated individuals in an academic community will be willing to offer assistance. I once had occasion to seek out the original version of an unidentified quote from Curzio Malaparte cited in *Esta Noite ou Nunca*. Rather than retranslate Italian into English via Portuguese, I opted to locate the English version, assuming the novel had been translated. First, however, it was necessary to discover where the passage had originally appeared. Knowing nothing about contemporary modern Italian literature, I called the Italian department at Columbia University, introduced myself and asked to speak to a professor of Italian. Within minutes I had the answer: it was from *La Pelle* (*The Skin*), published in English in 1952; the rest was simple. Nowadays, of course, my first recourse would be the Internet.

Except for those fortunate enough to be born into an environment where more than one language is spoken, becoming bilingual – as opposed to merely extremely fluent in a second language – is quite difficult. Becoming bicultural is even more of a challenge. What does true biculturalism entail? To begin with, it means that the individual is equally at home in two cultures, adapted to both, and able to change from one to the other without experiencing culture shock or psychological dislocation. For the vast majority of bicultural persons, this means having lived in both societies, usually during the formative years.

Even so, problems may arise. We are all familiar with individuals who, though bilingual after a fashion, are not truly bicultural. For example, someone who left Colombia at the age of eleven to come to the United States is likely to speak perfect English and may be culturally American. Even though he or she may speak grammatically correct, unaccented Spanish, it is often the Spanish of an eleven-year-old, innocent of the richness of vocabulary and breadth of expression that characterizes the adult native speaker. This is because the immigrant's first-language development was arrested at the age at which he or she left the birth culture. Even those who have received a college education in the new culture may find themselves ill prepared to discuss technical or philosophical matters in their native language, while easily doing so in their 'adopted' tongue.

But it must be understood that bilingualism encompasses more than just range and depth of vocabulary and mastery of the structure of the language. Given a solid bilingual base, the lacunae in one's command of a language can be surmounted – through study, vocabulary expansion, frequent dialogue with native speakers – and in essence amounts to little more than filling in the gaps. After all, no one argues that an illiterate American with a vocabulary of less than 10,000 words is not a native speaker of English.

The problem arises in trying to achieve *a posteriori* biculturalism. By definition, it is virtually impossible. To fully understand a culture, not in a sociological or anthropological sense but as a functioning member thereof, means living it. A Greek, say, who comes to the United States with the idea of becoming part of a new nation will, after some years, understand the American way of doing things, the English language, and most of the tacit cultural cues by which Americans interact with one another and with their society. Although he will retain his command of the Greek language, his knowledge of his native culture begins to ossify the moment he boards the plane or boat.

A personal example: I arrived in Rio de Janeiro in 1965, for research that would keep me in Brazil for a year and a half. Three months later, I saw mention in the international edition of *Time* of 'flower children.' What on earth, I asked myself, are flower children? In a few short months I had become a stranger to at least one part of my own culture... Multiplied a thousandfold, this is what, subtly and incrementally, takes place for the individual who lives abroad. It is one of the reasons that the US State Department insists on yearly thirty-day home stays for Foreign Service personnel overseas.

For the translator, the implications can be disquieting. Take the matter of slang. Nothing in language changes more rapidly, yet it is only exposure to the culture that alerts us to the shift in such speech patterns. While we may pick up the latest SL slang terms by reading, nothing except living in the culture can inform us of which terms have fallen into disuse. The foreign devotee of American literature whose comprehension of English leads him to read Fitzgerald, for instance, may think that people in the States actually still say 'swell!' Those raised on John O'Hara might use 'in a jiffy' in cocktail conversation. Not to put too fine a point on it, learning slang is far easier than unlearning it, and the literary translator must be aware of times when the SL text is deliberately using an antiquated term for effect.

To be truly bicultural means to perceive in a unique way the signs, symbols, and even taboos of both cultures; to pick up signals even at a subconscious level; and to share in the collective unconscious. The bicultural person reacts to cues not merely intellectually but with affect. For example, in Spanish the word *coño* can be anything from an extremely crude interjection in Cuba to a rather mild exclamation used by eight-year-olds in the neighboring Dominican Republic. The bilingual 'knows' it to be a coarse vulgarism and translates it accordingly; the bicultural may, depending on circumstances, opt for a much softer rendering.

Another point separating the bicultural from the bilingual individual is that the former has internalized certain elements of the two cultures to which the merely bilingual are unlikely to ever be exposed. I refer to those stimuli that we reserve specifically for childhood and that not only contribute to our formation but also may serve as referent in later life: fairy tales, nursery rhymes, children's games, riddles, tongue twisters, infantile jokes. These are things we will never study as adults yet are as much a part of the culture as universities, cocktail parties, and skyscrapers. For example, only cultural familiarity alerted Suzanne Jill Levine to avoid literalism and translate the title of Cabrera Infante's *Tres tigres tristes*, a tongue twister, as *Three Trapped Tigers*. In similar fashion, any American instantly understands what is meant by a Dagwood sandwich or that a couple fights like Tom and Jerry. (Dagwood is Lorenzo in Spanish, so even if the comic strip is reproduced in Latin America, the allusion would probably be lost on anyone unfamiliar with American culture.)

Given that we are either bicultural or not, how do the 99.9% of us who are not bicultural work toward minimizing our cultural ignorance to become better translators? Can the bilingual or the merely fluent close the cultural gap sufficiently? With dedication and effort, the answer is yes. Some concrete suggestions:

(1)   The first and most desirable method, of course, is to live in the SL
      culture for as long as possible – a minimum of six months, preferably a
      year or more – and to take 'refresher' trips at frequent intervals. While
      there, immerse yourself in every conceivable aspect of your surround-
      ings, but especially in the popular culture. After all, so-called high
      culture – e.g., literature, art, and music – tends to be universal and
      needs little if any cross-cultural interpretation. Learn something about
      cockfights, go to the bullring, attend a soccer game. Talk to children
      and elementary school teachers. For the literary translator there are no
      boundaries. He or she may have to translate a passage dealing with
      chess or drug addiction one day, with lotteries or ballet the next.
      Nothing is off limits.
(2)   Next best is to read as much as possible from the SL culture – not only
      the material to be translated, which normally meets high literary stan-
      dards, but newspapers and magazines as well. Don't overlook films,
      especially those produced in the SL culture. Movies and television
      have the added advantage of providing a visual dimension to what
      might otherwise be an ambiguous referent.
(3)   As mentioned earlier, cultivate contacts with members of the SL
      culture, both in your home country and abroad, to consult when
      doubts emerge. It is self-evident that the absolute best source is the
      author of the SL text – admittedly difficult if you're translating a writer
      who's no longer living. Rubem Fonseca's stories often incorporate
      underground argot and slang, and he sometimes provides his transla-
      tors with a glossary of some of the more esoteric terms. I submit my
      translations of Fonseca's stories to the author, and his suggestions
      have been invaluable, though ultimately the responsibility for the
      accuracy of the final product is mine alone. However, even the author
      or those closest to him or her cannot be expected to know everything.
      When I translated Osman Lins's classic story 'Retábulo de Santa Joana
      Carolina,' I journeyed to São Paulo, where his widow, Julieta de
      Godoy Ladeira, lives, to confer on certain rural vocabulary items used
      in the narrative. A lifelong city dweller, she was uncertain in a couple
      of instances but placed a phone call to the son of Graciliano Ramos,
      himself from the rural state of Alagoas, who resolved the impasse.
      More commonly, questions like that of *pitu* will arise that virtually any
      member of the SL culture can answer.

          These observations are in no way intended to discourage the
      non-bicultural from attempting translations; if the field depended solely on
      the handful of biculturals, even Jorge Amado and García Márquez might

well be unknown in the US. My intent is to call attention to the cultural traps and pitfalls confronting the would-be translator. My hope is that all literary translators will immerse themselves in both the source language and the culture that engenders it, lest they repeat the experience of the non-English speaking Brazilian on his first trip to New York City. Sitting in his hotel room, he hears a knock on the door. Hastily looking up the word *entre* (come in) in his pocket Portuguese–English dictionary, he shouts 'Between!'

When not to translate cultural cues

Except in perhaps the most cosmopolitan of writings, a text produced in another language and culture makes reference to persons, objects, and institutions not readily understood by another culture. Presumably familiar to the SL reader, they are often meaningless to the TL reader. How should the problem be handled?

Surprisingly, there are times when the best way of dealing with seemingly opaque items in the source culture is not to translate them at all. This does not mean omitting them; rather it speaks to the self-defining capacity of words in context. Elsewhere in this guide I explain my customary approach to translating money: allowing internal clues to inform the reader of approximate values in the time and place in which the narrative is set. This *modus operandi* can also be applied to other SL artifacts – always, of course, with a judicious appraisal of how far the TL audience's powers of interpretation stretch.

Notorious among literary translators is the issue of food terminology. Except for dishes so international that they need no translation – like goulash, paella, sushi, and a staggering array of French creations – translating food can be dicey. My suggestion is to perform a triage. Divide food items into those that must be explained, those that should not be explained, and those that will provide their own explanation through context. Take this example of a Brazilian buffet by Josephine Humphreys in *The New York Times Magazine* of March 4, 2001:

> *abará* and *acarajé*, bite-size concoctions of manioc, *dendê* oil, shrimp, hot peppers, onions, peanuts, cashews, ginger and coconut,... and *moquecas*, stews of shrimps, fish, crab, mussels or octopus, all dribbled with red *dendê* oil... and *caruru*, an amazing okra-and-shrimp dish (italics added).

I'll understand if the reader wishes to break for lunch at this point. If not, let's dig in. Each of the italicized terms would require the translator's scrutiny. If a similar list were to appear in fiction, the translator would have to assign priorities. Cookbook or novel? Completeness or intimation? Exactness or approximation?

In the list above, a brief interpolation would work in some cases: 'dendê palm oil,' 'a fish stew called *moqueca*,' 'a *caruru* of okra and shrimp.' But rather than go into a lengthy explanation of the ingredients in *abará* and *acarajé* ('bite-size concoctions,' etc.), the translator is better off glossing, even at the risk of slight misunderstanding: 'manioc fritters.'

Whatever the source language, whatever the specialized topic, the principle applies: *provide only as much information as can be conveyed without resort to artificiality.* Surely it is desirable to distinguish whether *manjar* is a dessert or a main dish and to establish that *caldo verde* is a soup and not a salad, but specifications beyond that are odds-on to seem awkward.

The care and feeding of authors

One of the most crucial aspects of literary translation can be the translator's relationship with the SL author.

A decision to involve the author actively in the translation process is not one to be taken lightly, and his or her offer to 'help out' or to 'take a look at the manuscript' should not be accepted merely out of courtesy. Authors are as individual in temperament and personality as other human beings, if not more so, and there are 'easy' authors and, so to speak, 'high maintenance' authors. More than one translation project has foundered because of excessive authorial input (read interference).

In some instances the author's role will be dictated by the publisher, who will insist on the writer's active involvement in every stage of the translation. Even here, however, there is room for maneuvering. Rather than a chapter at a time, larger batches can be submitted. And many authors will defer to the translator's superior TL knowledge in case of doubt. (Prose writers are generally more amenable in this respect than poets, for obvious reasons.)

Some authors simply wash their hands of a work once it's sold for translation, much as writers are advised to do when Hollywood buys a property. Especially if the translation is into a language they don't read – Hungarian or Japanese are good examples – they are forced to rely on the word of others to judge the success of the translation. This is seldom the case with English, with which most intellectuals have at least some acquaintance. It's fairly rare to find a monolingual author completely ignorant of English and therefore totally unattuned to the difficulties the translator faces.

In the other direction, unfortunately, in monolingual North America some writers are notorious for their insensitivity to the plight of their overseas translator. Mordecai Richler, one of Canada's better writers, recounts being 'poleaxed by a long and far-from-reassuring questionnaire' from an unspecified European translator of his novel *Solomon Gursky Was Here*. Here are some of the items the translator wished to clarify: *cloakworkers, Clean for Gene, the Slo-Ball League, a half-trunk, Bergdorf Goodman, 'a wet T-shirt girls' basketball league in which he held the rights to the Miami Jigglers,' Howard Cosell, the Cliveden set, Denys Finch Hatton, the Sherry-Netherland, Wiccans.*

So how did you do? Since I drew a blank on most of them, I guess it means by Richler's standards that I'm unqualified to translate his works into English. Richler holds the translator – who for the sake of argument we'll assume was Danish – up to ridicule for unfamiliarity with such quintessentially North American terms as 'Miss B.C. Lion,' 'Adams House,' 'Life Savers,' and 'Saks Fifth Avenue.' To be fair, 'Corgi' can be found in any good English dictionary, 'tree house' shouldn't stump anyone conversant with English, and 'Windsor-Detroit Tunnel' does seem pretty self-explanatory. But to expect even a seasoned traveler from across the Atlantic to know the names of American hotels and chichi Gotham shops is a bit much. And it's doubtful they've ever heard of David Letterman in Denmark, much less Howard Cosell. Still, the translator, however ignorant of North American cultural artifacts, at least made an effort to find the answers, and from the most unimpeachable of sources, the author himself. Would Richler have preferred that he or she wing it, slapping onto paper whatever seemed contextually plausible, or simply omit the unintelligible references, thus rendering the carefully crafted prose into choppy border-line incoherence? Richler's testy 'How did you get the job of translating my novel? Are you related to the publisher?' seems rather harsh for some poor devil trying to make a few extra *kroner* after a day of teaching English-as-foreign-language to high school kids.

It's surprising that a writer of the cosmopolitan sophistication of Mordecai Richler missed the distinction between knowledge of a language (there were no grammatical errors in the translator's letter of inquiry) and knowledge of a culture. Or perhaps Richler could identify Roberto Carlos, Elis Regina, and Maria Bethânia. (All are icons of Brazilian pop culture.) Richler should be grateful he doesn't have a translator who assume the Plains of Abraham are in Israel or confuse Prince Hal with Prince Valiant.

Luckily, cases of this type are the exception; most SL writers are happy to cooperate with their translators. Perhaps it speaks to the openness of Brazilians, but I have yet to encounter an author who was disinclined to supply the meanings of ambiguous or obscure terms in the text, usually by return e-mail.

There are authors like Kurt Vonnegut, Jr., who display a commendable awareness of the formidable tasks inherent in literary translation and have only good things to say about those who labor to reproduce their works in other languages. (In fact, he argues, 'Translators should be paid the same royalties as authors.') In Vonnegut's words, 'All I require of a translator is that he or she be a more gifted writer than I am, and in at least two languages, one of them mine.'

The potential problem arises when an author thinks he or she is sufficiently fluent in the TL to judge the translation and even to propose changes in it. This is a situation fraught with danger for the translator, who must proceed with tact.

A cautionary tale: a certain Continental author, convinced despite never having written directly in English that his command of the language was beyond reproach, insisted in his contract on having final cut on the translation. Notwithstanding his unavailability for consultation during the actual translation process, which lasted almost a year, he nevertheless minutely pored over the finished manuscript, finally declaring it 'amateurish and unacceptable.' To the consternation of publisher and translator alike, he demanded either a completely new draft or a different version by another translator. The publisher, faced with an unexpected doubling of translation costs and an inevitable delay in bringing the project to fruition, opted to cut his losses; the book was never published in English.

Could this tragedy have been avoided? Probably, if it had been made clear from the beginning that in case of disagreement the translator would have the last word. If possible, this should be specified in the contract. Otherwise, it is best to make it clear with the editors that you will be consulted before any final changes are made. This is another reason it's essential to take part in proofreading – both galleys and page proofs – before the final product goes to press.

Writers feel more deeply than most people, and their involvement with their works is often that of parent–child: any criticism can be taken as hostile and mean-spirited. The time for critical analysis of a work is *before* you take it on to translate. Once committed to the project, for better or worse, your responsibility is to produce the best possible translation, whatever your feelings of the literary merit of the original.

Remember that many (not all) authors, in addition to being blessed and cursed with deep sensibilities, are also fundamentally insecure individuals. With each new work they in effect stand naked before the public, exposing themselves to a critical scrutiny that can all too quickly turn to derision and ridicule. This is true even of successful literary figures. With the rare exception of authors who enjoy both popular *and* critical acclaim, writers who regularly produce popular best sellers often crave acceptance from the academy (e.g., Sidney Sheldon, Jacqueline Suzanne), while many whose works are well received in intellectual circles bemoan their limited appeal to the public. Writing is a profession tailor-made for engendering self-doubt.

If asked directly by the author for your opinion of a given text, tact and diplomacy are called for. Am I recommending hypocrisy? No, because once published, the work is already on record, and nothing you say will change that. Why contribute to further diminishing the author's self-esteem? Besides the obvious negative repercussions for you as translator, would you want to be even partially responsible for an author deciding to abandon the profession?

My recommendation is to profess ignorance – obviously not of the work, but of its deeper meaning. Admitting that you're uncertain about what the author was trying to say in a given text is both self-effacing and allows for the possibility that you and the critics have overlooked some of the subtleties. No writer will take offense in such a situation, and your good author–translator relations remain intact.

Which raises the question of loyalty to one's authors. It ill suits the translator to badmouth any of his or her authors. Even – one might say *especially* – if the work in question or the author's overall oeuvre has come under intense critical fire, you should refrain from lending your weight to the attack, however indirectly. If inquiries are made, as in an interview, into your opinion of an author, try to be noncommittal if you can't be positive. Here's a hypothetical instance.

Q. Having translated him, what do you think of the work of —— ?
A. He's a pleasure to translate because of his clean, straightforward prose. Not only that, he's a most congenial and helpful individual.
Q. Yes, but what is his literary value?
A. While, like all his contemporaries, no one will confuse him with Victor Hugo, he has a forceful narrative style that captures and holds the reader's attention.
Q. So you disagree with the critics who think he's a bad writer?
A. The people have to be the final judge of a writer's worth, and I think his consistent acceptance by the reading public speaks for itself.

(At this point the interviewer gives up and changes the subject.)

The translator has a moral obligation to protect his or her author, a responsibility that includes safeguarding the writer from looking silly in the new language. In one novel I translated, two of the characters were from a neighboring South America country. Unfortunately, the 'Spanish' they were quoted as using was rife with errors. Without the slightest vacillation, I put the utterances into correct Spanish when I did the translation. My reasoning was that I was recreating the author's intent – and his intent was not to appear foolish. If my action can be construed as 'improving' the original, I believe I was responding to a higher mandate, that of what the writer *meant to say*.

Being loyal to authors, besides being the right thing ethically, can lead to mutual benefits, foremost among them an enduring friendship and trust between writer and translator. The author gains from the assurance that his or her works will receive a thoughtful, even loving translation into English. The translator gains from being the first considered to translate the author's subsequent work; it is not unknown for the same person to translate a writer's entire oeuvre. In addition, because in many countries the circle of writers and intellectuals is rather circumscribed and most authors know one another, an informal 'old boys' network' exists. A satisfied author is more likely to suggest his translator to others – a fact from which I myself have benefited, having been recommended in this way for at least five of the 14 novels I've translated to date.

The dubious project

No matter how good the relationship with the author, there may come a time when the translator is asked to translate a text that causes discomfort. The following personal account may shed some light on one way – which I concede is less than ideal – of dealing with the dilemma. The events are true, but some details have been changed to disguise the specifics.

At the author's request I translated, or tried to translate, one of his short stories. The work, which was apparently a favorite of his because of its rela-tion to his novel dealing with the same thematic material, was not an easy one. As I translated, I was bothered by my inability to find satisfactory English equivalents for certain SL terms. Was it me, or did the original abound with rather strange constructions? Do people really talk in the manner the author depicted them? Was my knowledge of the source culture inadequate to the task or was I failing to grasp some less common aspect of the way of life described?

After several drafts, I was still grappling with unresolved areas of diffi-culty. *Item*: non-existent words in the SL text. *Item*: distinctly non-native syntactical constructions and vocabulary, seemingly influenced by a second language. *Item*: symbols and metaphors suddenly dropped into the narrative without referent or discernible connection to the main thrust of the story.

Finally, stumped, I consulted a close friend with unique qualifications to advise me on this thorny question. Himself a renowned writer and coun-tryman of the author, he scrutinized the translation (he is fluent in English), reread the original, and shook his head. 'If you publish this translation you'll damage your reputation. I suggest you tell the author you couldn't do justice to the work and ask him to propose some other story for you to translate.'

And that's what I did.

A somewhat similar problem arises when one is asked to translate a work he or she finds morally or ethically offensive, like hate literature or pornography. Here the quandary is less personal – one is not apt to lose a friend or cause resentment simply by refusing – than professional, in the larger sense of the word.

What does the profession of translation do? Obviously, it translates. If a translator allows ideology to color anything he or she translates, the profession suffers. And when translation is stifled either by repression or self-censorship entire nations are deprived of a glimpse into the mind of the Other. It could mean there would be no one to translate *Mein Kampf* or, in the Muslim world, *The Satanic Verses*. One doesn't have to be a communist to profit from an acquaintance with Marx.

Face time with the author

Though not always feasible for reasons of time, distance, and expense, a face-to-face meeting – preferably a series of encounters – with the SL author is probably the most fruitful activity a translator can undertake. More than any dictionary, native informant, or Internet search, direct contact with the author can prove invaluable in an often arduous task. Perhaps the best known example of the personal element in a writer/translator collaboration is that of Jorge Luis Borges and Thomas di Giovanni. Di Giovanni, who translated many of the Argentine master's works, moved to Buenos Aires to be near Borges and became his amanuensis for four years, all but living under the same roof for part of that time. While opinions of the quality of di Giovanni's translations may vary, his was undeniably an example of making fullest use of author/translator contacts.

Why, it may be asked, couldn't the translator achieve the same benefits by telephone conversations or through e-mail? Wouldn't he or she have available the same factual information without going to the trouble and expense of traveling to the author's home country?

Normally, the answer is no. Reasons for truly *being there* are numerous:

*   To establish a personal and intimate relationship with the author, who can be of inestimable help to a translator he or she esteems both as a professional of the word and as a person. Referrals and other secondary emoluments may come about from this good will.
*   To brainstorm. In a one-on-one setting in which the author ponders alongside the translator which of several possible meanings to assign to a certain word, oftentimes felicitous, even serendipitous, insights emerge from one or both. And, it should be noted, it isn't necessary for the author to know English for this synergy to occur. The manu-

script that emerges is almost invariably a translation superior to what
would have been produced solo.

* To acquire a feeling for the author as human being. Seeing the writer
  en famille can provide a glimpse into character and behavior that casts
  a revelatory light on his or her works.

* To carry out delicate negotiations about the translation. Authors are
  more likely to lend a sympathetic ear to a translator known personally than one with whom they are acquainted only through letters or
  e-mail. This fact can be central to achieving their cooperation in the
  sometimes touchy process of demarcation of the lines between the
  translator's responsibility for the final TL text and the author's. If all
  goes well, the author will agree that ties go to the translator – i.e., that
  in case of dispute the translator's option will prevail.

No contract between publisher and translator provides funds for travel
to discuss the translation with the author, which can entail considerable
expense when, as is usually the case, the writer lives in another country.
Nevertheless, every translator I have spoken with agrees that conferring
with the author is one of the most rewarding aspects of our profession.
Even on those rare occasions when the writer in question turns out to be
aloof or unresponsive, he or she is nonetheless now a more three-dimen-
sional figure after an in-person encounter. And when creator and re-creator
hit it off on the human level, lasting and mutually rewarding lifelong
friendships can result.

An interesting case of translator/author cooperation involved Lia
Purpura, herself a poet, and Grzegorz Musial, an internationally acclaimed
Polish poet. Her account of the year she spent in Poland working with two
collections of his poetry reinforces the value of personal interaction
between author and translator:

Our working method was something like writing a poem in reverse,
starting with a knowledge of the end, and looping back over the beginning until the whole gave way to a point of entry and we could move
freely in any direction. It was important, early on, to get the cadence of
thought in my ear, so Grzegorz would read the poem aloud in Polish a
few times and I'd note down strong phrasings that I heard or similar
metrical beats that might satisfy in English. Next, we looked at the text
together and roughed out a transliteration, faithful to stanza- and
line-breaks. Then we read the new English poem aloud for glaring errors
and to refine our syntax. I'd take it home and work on it for a long time,
comparing and altering. Let it brew. Go to a movie. Work some more.
Go to the opera, the park, a friend's farm. Then we'd approach the poem

again, almost from scratch. In the end, we were both mystified, as if the poem had grown beyond the reach of either language, either interpreter. Grzegorz would nod solemnly and say, 'Sounds good to me.' And then we'd abandon it entirely, for a few weeks.

Authors can be the translator's greatest aid or biggest hindrance. In either case, it pays to cultivate the relationship. A dash of humility can come in handy here: you need the author more than he or she needs you.

The hijacked author

Regrettably, authors' and translators' interests may not always coincide. Look at the matter from the author's point of view. Obviously, it is in writers' interest to see as many of their works in translation as possible – assuming, of course, a competent translator; some translations are worse than not being translated at all. Authors may therefore, unwittingly or not, give the go-ahead to more than one aspirant, even in writing, and sometimes later forget having done so.

This happened to me over a decade ago. When my translation of a well-known Brazilian novella was published, a fellow academician and translator was upset because he was working on the same text. The explanation was that the author's widow, who owned the rights, had forgotten I had been ceded the rights and even that I had spent an entire day with her in Brazil to resolve vocabulary problems.

An added complication is that authors are well aware that a high percentage of translations are begun and never finished, and others never see the light of day, so they may causally 'grant' rights they don't have, or give several translators the rights to the same work. Call it playing the averages.

Even if you have a written statement giving you exclusive translation rights to an author's writings, it sometimes happens that another translator publishes a work by that author. What now?

Realistically, are you prepared to go to court, involving citizens of two countries in litigation, to enforce your rights? Your creative energies would be better spent on a different project, and perhaps a different author. Only in the case of a major investment like three years of translating the writer's 600-page magnum opus would recourse to legal remedies make sense. And even then it would likely be your publisher and not you who would pursue the matter. In such a circumstance, your contract with the US publisher would continue in force (meaning you'd get paid), for you acted in good faith, and ascertaining the availability of translation rights is reasonably the publisher's responsibility. As always, when in doubt consult an attorney.

Legal considerations aside, try not to get ego-involved. Not easy, I know. To some extent we come to feel about a writer, especially one we have discovered, as we might feel about our children. In the hands of another translator – who 'obviously' can't care as much as we do about doing justice to the task – it's almost as if he or she had been kidnapped.

Get over it! As hard as it may be to accept, no one has proprietary rights to any author; a writer's work becomes part of the cultural patrimony, something to which we may all lay claim, aesthetically if not legally. Rather than feel somehow betrayed if 'our' author appears in print in someone else's translation, we should take satisfaction from knowing that others share our recognition of literary excellence and that, if nothing else, at least a greater number of readers will now be able to partake of the author's unique contributions.

Style in translation

Style is a multifaceted topic on which countless treatises continue to be written. Hemingway's style was, among other things, terse; the Spanish poet Góngora's style was elaborate, baroque. In many instances, there are elements of style that transcend the specific words used by the author – e.g., the ratio of long sentences to shorter ones, paragraph division, figures of speech, 'loose' or 'periodic' sentences, along with many others. This discussion will deal only with the translator's choice of words, inasmuch as most of the remaining elements of style are preset by the SL text.

In theory at least, 'style' in a translator is an oxymoron. Ideally, the translator strives to have no style at all and attempts to disappear into and become indistinguishable from the style of the SL author. The translator should adapt to the style of each author translated – now terse, now rambling, sometimes abstruse, but always as faithful to the original as circumstances permit.

Having said this, I should point out that in practice individual translators do have styles, which are as impossible for them to avoid as for the SL author. Style, after all, can be defined as a characteristic mode of expression, and consciously or unconsciously the translator displays one. In this respect, style is inextricably intertwined with one's idiolect, the way an individual normally speaks. Do you say 'for example' or 'for instance'? 'Pardon me' or 'excuse me'? 'Pleaded' or 'pled'? From the accumulation of countless such judgments emerges an idiolect.

David Crystal's discussion of idiolect in *The Cambridge Encyclopedia of Language* is helpful:

> Probably no two people are identical in the way they use language or react to the usage of others. Minor differences in phonology, grammar, and vocabulary are normal, so that everyone has, to a limited extent, a 'personal dialect.' [T]he linguistic system as found in a single speaker ... is known as an idiolect.

Try as you might, you probably won't be able to avoid it, and any attempt to do so risks making you sound artificial, stilted, and, well – not you.

This guarantees that any two translations of a non-trivial nature exceeding a few sentences in length will never be identical. Your idiolect may prefer 'couch' to 'sofa,' 'curtains' to 'drapes,' or 'soda' to any of the alternatives ('pop,' 'soda pop,' 'coke,' 'cold drink'). Semantically, is there any real difference between 'unavoidable' and 'inevitable'? Numerous subtleties influence word-choice, such as connotation – for example, 'gay' is no longer synonymous with 'happy' – but the essence of an idiolect is how it guides you unconsciously to prefer one word to another equally acceptable one.

My own idiolect, I recognize, favors 'nevertheless' to 'nonetheless,' 'sewage' to 'sewerage' for the contents of a sewer, 'SF' for science fiction and not 'sci-fi.' (This latter preference, I acknowledge, is probably a lost cause, dealt a death blow by the advent of the Sci Fi channel.) There are countless other examples of which I am unaware on a conscious level but which instinctively find their way into my translations.

Does this mean that each literary translator has a personal style? Hopefully [*sic*] not! Ideally, the translator should invisibly transmit the author's style. (The current metaphor is that of translation as a pane of glass.) Flaubert and Camus, in the hands of the same translator, should retain their individual styles and idiosyncrasies. As translators we have neither the right to 'improve' the original nor to impose our style – as opposed to our idiolect, which is at the very heart of our being – on the authors we translate.

A book-length translation is made up of literally thousands of decisions, some as tiny as the choice between a comma and a semicolon, others as momentous as whether to render proper names into the TL or leave them in the SL. Over time, an experienced translator will tend to make similar decisions when facing decision points; the result, for better or worse, is a style.

This is not to imply, of course, that a given translator will invariably make the same choices each and every time. I have caught myself translating a term one way on page 15 and differently on page 248. And most of the time it was not only the correct thing to do but clearly necessary under the circumstances.

For a simple instance of translator's style, consider a passage in a Romance language characterized by commas separating half a dozen of what in English would be clauses (the dreaded 'comma splice,' formerly known as a run-on sentence, that our teachers warned us about). There are several ways of approaching the problem:

- Break the passage into discrete sentences. The result, however, might well be a staccato stop-and-go effect that is just the opposite of the breathless, hurry-hurry-hurry pace the author intended. In short, it would change the author's style.
- Use semicolons instead of commas. Unfortunately, this runs the risk

of giving the text a bookish, academic look, possibly not the desired effect.

- Introduce a dash here and there, or even recast the passage.
- Leave the passage as is, hoping for an exotic flavor.

Which alternative is best? Impossible to say in the abstract, because every case is unique. But it is true that translators who frequently encounter such recurring challenges develop a *modus operandi* that, along with other tics and traits, constitutes a style.

For example, my own approach tackles translation of money in the following way. When faced with *pesos* or *cruzeiros* or other currency meaningless to English-speaking readers, I allow the quantities to be self-leveling. That is, I let the reader infer from context how much 50 *contos* or 50 *mil-réis* must have been worth at that place at that time. Isn't this precisely what we as readers do when come across an American novel published in, say, 1930? We don't know exactly how much half a dollar was worth then, but from internal clues we can work out a rough approximation.

Other translators might prefer to append a footnote explaining the sum now or at the time of the novel's setting; some might see fit to convert the amount into its American equivalent. While I have some strong ideas on the topic, I recognize that others may differ; it's a matter of style.

Fiction and footnotes

Often, difficulties arise not only from vocabulary but also from cultural artifacts not found in the target culture. The greater the cultural distance between the source culture and the target culture, the more the translator will need to bridge that gap. How much explanation does the TL reader need to make sense of the text – a great deal, not much, none at all? Any wide gap between the SL and the TL cultures will introduce the problem of whether to attempt to provide sufficient background to approximate the SL reader's response to that word or phrase.

There are three basic ways to cope with lacunae in the TL reader's knowledge of the SL culture: footnotes, interpolations, and omission. (This discussion, it should be noted, deals only with fiction; inclusion of explanatory notes in non-fiction works is a non-issue.)

Footnotes

Some translators adopt this approach routinely, especially academicians, who tend to dominate literary translation in the United States. Based on rigorous training in their disciplines, they desire to convey the maximum possible amount of information and thereby uphold scholarly standards of objectivity and comprehensiveness while affording the opportunity for others to verify their work.

Worthy goals, to be sure, but are they consistent with the ends of literature? In the absence of footnotes in the original, the translation that includes them is a warped reflection. Why? Because they destroy the *mimetic effect*, the attempt by (most) fiction writers to create the illusion that the reader is actually witnessing, if not experiencing, the events described. Footnotes break the flow, disturbing the continuity by drawing the eye, albeit briefly, away from the text to a piece of information that, however useful, is still a disrupter of the 'willing suspension of disbelief.'

The penchant for footnotes in translation seems to follow national lines. The French, for example, use them regularly, even including asterisks to designate phrases as *'en français dans l'original'*; my French friends will forgive me if I fail to see what it adds to the reader's pleasure to know that the SL author wrote *pas de deux* or *plus ça change*. In the United States, practice varies, and your decision to use or eschew footnotes must, like so many aspects of translation, be a personal one.

In making it, you must decide for yourself what the book's primary purpose is. For example, in translating *Dona Flor and Her Two Husbands*, Harriet de Onís wisely refrained from explaining the function and makeup of the various spices and other exotic ingredients described as Flor gave her cooking classes. The North American reader did not need to know what *dendê*, *vatapá*, or *caruru* were, as long as the context made their culinary association clear. In short, despite the several recipes that occur in the book, Amado's purpose was not to write a cookbook but to depict in rollicking, ribald prose a passion that literally transcended death.

Interpolation

Another way to impart essential information already known to the SL reader is interpolation. In its basic form it is nothing more than adding a parenthetical word or phrase, as unobtrusively as possible, as in this example from Jorge Amado's *The Golden Harvest* (original title: *São Jorge dos Ilhéus*), relating to the *candomblé* religion practiced by many black Brazilians. In it, terms unfamiliar to virtually all English-speaking readers appear:

> [The celebration] was in Olivença, on Pontal Island, home of Salu, the *pai-de-santo*, or priest, of the blacks' fetishistic religion brought from Africa… Rosa, Martins' lover, also came. She is an *aiô*, a priestess, and dances in the middle of the site.

Everything following *pai-de-santo* in the first sentence is an accretion, as is the explanatory phrase 'a priestess.' Both are examples of interpolation. If done carefully and with consideration for the rhythmic flow of language, interpolation can be imperceptible.

Few authors will take umbrage at such minor modifications of their text. Their wish is, after all, to find an audience outside their own language boundaries and to be as intelligible to that public as they are to readers in their homeland. If in doubt, you should consult with the author to obtain his or her consent for this cosmetic operation. In reality, judicious interpolation neither adds to or subtracts from the text; it merely makes it more accessible to the TL reader while respecting the unique demands of mimesis.

Interpolations should always be short (remember, you're not rewriting the book), never more than a few words. And avoid the temptation to overdo it. A reference in a Brazilian novel to Dom Pedro II might be expanded to 'Emperor Dom Pedro II' for foreign readers, but there's no need to put 'deposed in 1889,' the dates of his birth and death, or similar biographical information.

A rule of thumb in deciding whether to interpolate: how important is the information? Is it a one-time mention, or does it play a central part in understanding the story? A passing reference to Benedict Arnold in an American novel might very well be replaced in a Swedish translation by the word 'traitor,' for outside America Arnold's name does not resonate as it does in the United States. Or, if used in a generic sense, reference to 'a Benedict Arnold' (if not anachronistic in the context) might be rendered in Norwegian as Quisling.

The big advantage of interpolation is that after the term is explained the first time, it frees you to use the SL term, which is likely to be more concise and certainly more denotative than its translation. For example, in translating *Cidade de Deus*, by Paulo Lins, at its first mention of the word favela I interpolated a short phrase: '*favela*, or shantytown.' This tactic allowed me to use the Brazilian term in the remaining 500-plus pages of the book.

Omission

This option does not refer to cutting out a portion of the work that presents difficulties – deleting any part of the original text is the equivalent of unconditional surrender, an admission that a certain word, phrase, or construction is beyond the translator's ability to render. Rather, what is omitted is the explanation, leaving the reader to his own devices.

In the case of money references this is probably the best alternative. Efforts to transfer monetary units into TL equivalents run into manifold obstacles. And even if the translator appends a note such as 'about $500,' this leaves unresolved the problem of how much that sum represents in today's money. As any consumer can attest, it's extremely difficult to recall the relative price of things in the past, and all of us have an unconscious idea of the 'right' price of, say, a loaf of bread – usually based on what it cost in our childhood.

When dealing with translation of money, I tend toward one of two approaches. The first – always with the author's consent – is to substitute a dollar amount that makes sense in the context. Or the number can be mentioned without specifying the currency: 'fifty thousand' sounds like a significant sum in most countries. Unless money is the focal point of the story, the reader's perception of specific amounts will probably not make a real difference. In any case, even within a single culture the passage of time tends to render prices all but meaningless; we laugh nowadays when we read in a novel from the 1930s that $10,000 was a fortune.

The other approach is 'self-leveling': leave the sums in the original and let the context demonstrate the approximate value of the currency. The setting is removed in space (and probably in time) from 21st-century America in any case, so little harm is done if the reader's estimate is off by 50 or even 75%. This was the option I adopted in *The Golden Harvest*, and it apparently worked.

Which of the three approaches you select – footnote, interpolation, or omission – is your call. Though there are no surveys on the subject, anecdotal evidence indicates that most translators prefer to avoid footnotes in fiction. In cases of absolute necessity, they may decide on endnotes or, better yet, a glossary at the conclusion of the book. By doing so, they leave the reader to decide whether to break the mimetic flow. In an ideal world the reader would peruse the glossary *before* beginning the book. In such a world, of course, translators would be accorded equal footing with authors, and champagne would be as cheap as beer.

Some notes on translating poetry

This is a subject for an entire book, and entire books have been devoted to it, but in the interest of keeping this guide to manageable lengths I'll try to give here the executive summary. And as a translator primarily of fiction, I must defer to more expert minds in the poetry genre. More extensive hints can be found in many sources, including the works mentioned in the Bibliography.

Translating poetry well is so difficult as to be called impossible by most experts; the late John Ciardi referred to translation as 'the art of failure.' And yet we go on trying, sometimes with remarkably reduced degrees of non-success. If literary translation itself is a leap of faith, poetic translation puts that faith to the severest of all tests. As one who has seldom had the temerity to venture into the poetic arena, I do not conceal my admiration for the brave men and women who specialize in bringing into English the loftiest thoughts expressed in languages other than our own.

Poetry has been defined in many ways: by the *Random House Unabridged Dictionary* as 'the art of rhythmical composition, written or spoken, for exciting pleasure by beautiful, imaginative, or elevated thoughts'; as 'memorable speech'; as 'what is lost in translation' (Robert Frost's famous put-down of our art). Whatever the definition, the soul of poetry lies in the use of language in a figurative, metaphorical mode of expression that transcends traditional semantic limitations of language. The embracing of ambiguity and polysemy is one of the hallmarks of literature, and it is here, more than any problems of scansion or rhyme, that the challenge of translating poetry manifests itself in the most unmistakable fashion.

Clement Wood, editor of *The Complete Rhyming Dictionary*, has stated flatly, 'Poetry cannot be translated; it can only be recreated in the new language.' He gives as illustration two lines from Keats's 'Ode to a Nightingale':

Charmed magic casements, opening on the foam
Of perilous seas, in faery lands forlorn.

It is hard to argue with his contention: 'These two lines cannot be said differently in English without wrecking the magic.' A trot might read: 'Enchanted supernatural windows, unclosing on the bubbles / Of dangerous oceans, in unreal romantic countries dejected.' The result, says

Wood, is that 'There is no poetry here now. Translate it with absolute fidelity into another language, and the poetry is dead. It must be recreated by a poet of like emotional power in the other language, if it is to survive as poetry.' Small wonder, then, that before attempting translation of poetry a proper attitude of humility is called for.

An issue that must be considered before beginning to translate poetry is: what does the target audience regard as a 'poem'? Must it be rhymed? What metrical pattern best conveys the feel of the original and can an English perceptual equivalent be found? English-speaking readers usually consider iambic pentameter as the most 'poetic' versification (see Shakespeare, among others), but unrhymed iambic pentameter, known as blank verse, is an acceptable alternative for many. The trend these days is to unrhymed but metric verse in various metrical schemes. Go with whatever works, provided that the final product stands as an English-language poem in its own right. Always, though, bear in mind this admonition by Jorge Iglesias: 'A translator isn't more important than the poem he's translating.'

To rhyme or not to rhyme?

Like the rest of this guide, the following discussion assumes translation into English, which immediately poses special difficulties. English is a notoriously rhyme-poor language. In Romance languages it's almost a challenge *not* to rhyme, and it's no exaggeration to say that in Romance the poet's problem is not one of finding a rhyme but rather of avoiding hackneyed rhymes. For all its versatility and inventiveness, English boasts few rhymes for some of the most crucial words around which much of human experience, and therefore poetry, revolves. *Love* – four rhymes, one of which (*shove*) is a non-starter. *Children. Happiness. Friendship. Have. Mortality. Woman.* True, we encounter the occasional lucky happenstance – *death/breath, youth/truth, life/strife* – but these can quickly wear out their welcome. In English there are few such fortunate coincidences of rhyme as the Spanish *padre/madre* (father/mother), the Italian *amare/odiare* (to love/to hate), the French *âme/dame* (soul/lady), the Portuguese *sorte/morte* (fate/death). To cite only a few examples, the English verbs *hope, sin, desire, kill, sing, find, save, help,* and *transgress* all rhyme in several Romance languages, in both the infinitive and in most of their conjugated forms. So from the outset the poetic translator into English is working at a serious disadvantage.

In all fairness, my view of English as rhyme-poor is not universal. No less a figure than Norman R. Shapiro, a masterly practitioner who produces award-winning metrical and rhymed translations of French poetry, expressed an opposing outlook in a letter to *Source* (Summer/Fall 2000):

> True, the Romance languages have a certain natural advantage, but it is more than compensated by English's vast lexicon, considerably larger than that of its rivals... English has a number of rhyme-potentials that other common Western languages enjoy to a lesser degree, if at all. One of them is the easy rhymability of plural nouns ... with verb forms... For example, *apples/dapples, sexes/hexes, facts/acts*... Italian and Portuguese are poor relations in this regard, and Spanish, poorer still... [T]he aspiring translator of poetry should not be put off from attempting formal renderings by the too-facile claim that English is rhyme-deprived. Granted, it's often a challenge. But that's where the feeling of accomplishment, and the fun of it, come in.

Even in rhyme-friendly Spanish the best writers may rankle at the tyranny of rhyme. The Spanish Golden Age poet Francisco Quevedo (1580–1645) voiced his sentiments thus:

> Pues porque en un soneto
> dije que una señora era absoluta,
> y siendo más honesta que Lucrecia,
> por dar fin al cuarteto la hice puta.

(Because in a sonnet / I said a lady was absolute, / and more honest than Lucretia, / to end the quatrain I made her a whore.)

Just how critical is rhyme to poetry? Time was, the unquestioned rule was 'translate prose as prose, verse as verse.' To the best of my knowledge, recently no one has seriously proposed rendering a prose work into verse, but over the centuries many have felt that only a translation in verse can do justice to a poetic work. It should be noted that 'verse' is not synonymous with rhyme; classical Greek and Roman poetry was unrhymed, just as 'verses' in the Bible did not rhyme in their original Hebrew and Greek.

Must one be a poet to do poetic translation? No, though I am convinced that the translator must possess a poetic sensitivity, even if he or she has never written a line of original poetry. A poetic sensitivity encompasses, but is not limited to, an appreciation for nuance, sonority, metaphor and simile, allusion; the ability to read between and above the lines; flexibility; and ultimately, humility. In fine (a crib from E.A. Robinson's 'Richard Cory'; notice the poet didn't say 'in short'), anyone who can't read an English-language poem with feeling and more than surface comprehension is an unlikely candidate for poetic translation.

Any translation should – make that *must* – be read aloud for sonority. Sound is paramount to poets, and more than one translator has been told by the SL poet, 'When it's impossible to preserve both meaning and sound, go with the sound.' Although not all poems (both translations and originals) that sound good *are* good, it's a pretty safe bet that a translation that sounds bad is, well, bad.

As with any other translation, if you can get the author's input, by all means do so. This is especially vital in poetry, where ambiguity is often a conscious objective. For example, in translating 'Brejo da Cruz,' a poem by the renowned Brazilian composer Chico Buarque, many of whose lyrics rise to the level of poetry, I came across a particularly tricky line. It referred to the many adaptations experienced by migrants to the cities from the eponymous small town in the interior; the original reads '*Uns vendem fumo, tem uns que viram Jesus.*' The first half is no problem: 'Some sell marijuana.' But what about the verb *viram*? In Portuguese, it is the third-person plural for both the present tense of *virar* 'to become' and for the past tense of *ver* 'to see'. The phrase can be read as either 'There are some who have seen Jesus' or 'There are some who become Jesus' (presumably a reference to long hair and sandals, or perhaps to martyrdom). When I queried the author about this ambiguity, he expressed surprise and pleasure; apparently the double meaning hadn't occurred to him on the conscious level. There is no source better than the author, but in poetry even he/she may not know exactly what a given allusion 'means.'

In any language, poetry is probably the most extreme instance of linguistic concision. Every syllable counts. This phenomenon is heightened even more if the SL is one that, like Spanish, customarily incorporates the subject pronoun in the verb form itself (*piensa*: he/she/it thinks). For most occurrences of verbs, then, an extra syllable in the English version would be required for the pronoun. Conversely, to effect a metrical translation it is frequently necessary to pad, adding feet to make the line come out right. This often means introducing semantic elements not present in the original. Translators must determine individually the extent to which they are comfortable with this practice; no hard-and-fast rules exist for what is essentially an aesthetic decision.

A case study of how demanding poetic translation can be – and an illustration of why we translators of 'mere' prose stand in awe of successful poetic translators, especially those who preserve meter, rhyme, *and* meaning – is John Du Val's account (in *Delos*, October 1995) of his attempt to translate a deceptively simple five-line poem by Trilussa. Written in Romanesco, the dialect spoken in Rome, and followed by a literal translation, it goes:

La Felicità	Happiness
C'è un'Ape che se posa	There is a bee that settles
su un bottone de rosa:	on a rose bud:
lo succhia e se na va ...	it sucks it and goes away...
Tutto sommato la felicità	All in all happiness
è una piccola cosa.	is a little thing

Du Val's first effort, which was duly published, yielded this compact version:

A bee settled
on a rose petal.
It tasted, and off it flew.
Happiness, too,
requires little.

One problem, the author states, was in the last line, which is 'seven light, delicate syllables to express the light, delicate quality of happiness. But the four English syllables, 'requires little,' read like there's bread in the mouth.' Du Val humorously relives the various drafts that seemed to lead further and further away from the goal: 'This shows / what a little thing happiness is'; 'Happiness when all is settled / is a little thing when it comes'; 'What a little thing happiness is!', 'Happiness is something little,' etc. He finally published a second version:

A bee settled
on a rose petal.
It sipped, and off it flew.
All in all, happiness, too,
is something little.

Even years later, however, he still catches himself reworking the poem, proving that Paul Valéry's dictum that 'a poem is never finished, only abandoned' also applies to translations.

Translating humorous verse

Opportunities to translate comic verse are rare but constitute an unusually provocative challenge. Doggerel may not be true literature, but if its effect is to transfer across languages, the translator must be cognizant of certain principles.

(1) *Humorous verse must rhyme*. Not only that, the rhyme must be unmistakable. For example, the rhyme can't be on a word with two equally

acceptable pronunciations (bow, either, row, route, envelope) because a portion of the readership will choose the alternative and fail to see the humor.

(2) *Brevity is the soul of wit.* Unlike Shakespeare, who was having his jest by putting these words into the mouth of rambling, loquacious old Polonius, comic verse has no room for verbosity or even extra syllables.

(3) *Save the humorous rhyme for last.* Have *'lederhosen'* come *after* 'frozen,' not before. Probably nowhere is thus more evident than that quintessentially English-language humorous verse form, the limerick.

(4) *Sound trumps meaning.* Years ago I read an ingenious comic 'poem,' recounted by a vampire, that began something like this: 'A dolorous and disconsolate wraith I en- / countered in a Carpathian / mountain pass...' Turns out the legends are wrong and that the biter rather than the bitee is transmogrified; the narrator had bitten Ogden Nash! Obviously, anyone translating this trifle out of English would have free rein to interject whatever it took to retain the comic tone – rhyming *Drácula* with *imacula- / do* in Spanish?

And then there's the matter of time-honored examples of English words that supposedly have no rhyme – e.g., *orange, silver, Wednesday, purple, month.* Well, as the aforementioned Ogden Nash proved (he did after all rhyme Kleenex with V-necks), given sufficient ingenuity, and assuming humor rather than deathless literature is the goal, *anything* can be rhymed. For example, the plea of a claustrophile: *Please fence me in / Understand I deplore range; / I'd wear a grin / Even inside an orange.* Or this: *Lusting after beaucoup silver, / Relatives came to hear the will ver- / batim.* Or, *hen's day, Penn's day, men's day* (you get the idea). *If a public yawn won't make you blush purple, / Rest assured that a good loud burp'll.* As for *month*, offered for your approval: *She tried and tried, a hundred times / To find a rhyme for month. / The hundredth time she failed again, / But not the hundred and oneth.*

This brief discussion has barely scratched the surface of what is arguably the most complex area of translation. For additional information, there are a numerous books on the topic. A good primer on the mechanics of verse is the introduction to Clement Wood's *The Complete Rhyming Dictionary* (revised by Ronald Bogus), a Dell paperback. For more advanced insights into poetical translation in practice, read *Translating Poetry: The Double Labyrinth*, edited by Daniel Weissbort (University of Iowa Press, 1989), in which a score of working translators talk about the translation process as applied to their own work.

Other areas of literary translation

The bulk of literary translation takes the form of translating fiction, the dominant mode, and poetry. But there are other possibilities, and some translators specialize in non-fiction, drama, and even children's literature.

Translating non-fiction

Some are under the erroneous impression that literary translation comprises only the genres of poetry, drama, and fiction. But the same ideals that drive translators of these genres can also inspire translators whose métier is non-fiction. And let there be no mistake: non-fiction is part of literature and translation of non-fiction can properly be considered literary translation.

Even leaving aside the fact that some writers of non-fiction create prose with all the painstaking skill of our best authors of fiction (Winston Churchill is a good example), the techniques employed in translating poetry or fiction stand one in good stead when rendering a biography, a history, or a memoir into English. Furthermore, the translator of non-fiction enjoys several advantages: use of footnotes is not a deterrent, allowing the translator to point out any problem words or phrases and explain cultural contexts; the tone of the work usually remains constant, maintaining a single voice throughout; factual content is normally more important than style (although the latter cannot be ignored); often, a translator's foreword is permissible, providing a wider latitude for explanation of the translational choices made; and especially long, multivolume works are frequently divided among two or more translators, which reduces the length of time one must devote to a single project. Finally, government-sponsored translation is virtually always non-fiction, and the prospect of repeat business is greater because governmental bureaus tend to rely on proven practitioners.

All that has been said about translating narrative fiction applies to translating non-fiction: the same issue of the author–translator–reader relationship, the same sensitivity to nuance, the same sense of dedication. There are no uniquely non-fictional translation skills. While not every translator of non-fiction can make the switch to translation of novels and short stories, it's a safe bet that almost every translator of fiction has at some time translated non-fiction. In its way, translation of non- fiction can be viewed as a subset of translation of fiction, minus some of the more vexatious elements.

Translating for the theater

Translating for the stage differs in significant ways from other genres of translation. The essence of theatrical translation, at least from the stand-point of the spectator, is its 'speakability.' Most other considerations – meaning, fidelity, precision – are secondary to this primordial character-istic. Even style, which is by no means unimportant in dramatic translation, sometimes must yield to the reality that actors have to be able to deliver the lines in a convincing and natural manner. The 'illusion of the first time' can be fatally undermined if the dialogue strikes the audience as somehow off-register or odd.

Eric Bentley in *Thinking about the Playwright* listed four different 'phe-nomena' all of which have at one time or another been called translations:

(1)   The rendering that is so meanly literal that Arthur Miller has used the expression Pidgin English to describe its vocabulary and style.
(2)   The rendering that is in correct and cogent English but otherwise sticks as close to the original as possible.
(3)   The adaptation. This can have (2) as its basis but then take such liber-ties as: making cuts and interpolations and changing the style and/or tone.
(4)   The variation. This verges on an original play merely 'based on' a foreign one.

Of these possible versions, as Victor Dixon has noted in his commentary on Bentley's typology, 'all but the first ... have a claim to be performed; but only the second can in honesty be called a translation. The third and fourth should advertise their nature without equivocation.' The following discus-sion will not deal with the fourth possibility (the 'variation'), which belongs more to the realm of creative writing than translation.

As Eric Bentley remarked in *The Life of the Drama*, a play exists in a dual sense: as a written text and as a performed script. Reading a play is in every way different from seeing that same play presented on stage. By and large, the translator's duty is to produce a version that honors the latter without shortchanging the former. In the same vein, in his article 'Text and Ideotext: Translation and Adaptation for the Stage' David Johnston aptly observes:

[R]ather than giving new form to an already known meaning, translation for the stage is concerned with re-constructing meaning both as text and as theatre through a process … which is no less dramaturgical than it is linguistic.

In translating drama, whose very *raison d'être* is performance, the translator has unseen collaborators: the actors and the director. Both can make explicit elements that on the printed page might forever remain cryptic. But in order for meaning to journey from paper to spoken word and gesture, the translator must provide the extratextual clues through explanatory notes. As in any other field of literary translation, culture has a leading role. Here again, David Johnston's views are worth citing:

> [T]he translator as dramaturge must provide, in the sense of making explicit, in the target language text (and, in an ideal world, subsequently through active participation in rehearsal) an array of information which is encoded in the culture-specific frame of reference or the paraverbal elements of the original, so that the final process of reconstitution can take place on stage in as complete a way as possible.

For instance, in a Brazilian play in which *candomblé* figured prominently, the translator should offer information about that African-Brazilian fetishistic religion and, if relevant, its belief in communication with the dead.

Light drama such as farces and throwaway comedies are often adapted rather than translated. Some fine examples of this can be found in Norman R. Shapiro's adaptations of the works of Georges Feydeau and other French farceurs. The titles themselves bespeak the degree to which Shapiro has adapted these frothy entertainments to the tastes of an Anglophone audience: *A Flea in Her Rear, Caught with His Trance Down, The Pregnant Pause,* or *Love's Labor Lost.* I remember seeing in Santo Domingo an adaptation of Jean Anouilh's one-act play 'L'Orchestre,' a more serious work, in which the director had introduced a bizarre but surprisingly effective change: all the members of the five-woman orchestra were played by men in drag! The ruse was so well done that only at the end, when they removed their wigs, did the mechanism become apparent. Adaptations frequently modernize the work and introduce local topical references to make it more appealing to a contemporary audience. The essential requirement is to retain the humor, suspense, satire, or any other preponderant effect of the play, however much it may entail textual modifications. For example, when I translate Patrícia Melo's black comedy *Two Women and a Cadaver,* I will have no compunctions about giving all three characters American-sounding names and changing several references that situate the action somewhere other than locally.

One feature of translating drama has both a positive and a negative side.

It is not uncommon for retranslations of existing classics to be commissioned for a new production, often by regional or university-affiliated theaters. This increases the demand for translations, to be sure, but it also means that at any one time there may be two or three competing English versions of *The Misanthrope* or *Blood Wedding*. Because more often than not translations of drama are not published except for use as scripts or occasionally in a theater-oriented magazine, they seldom engender the recognition that publication in book form or in a more widely circulated periodical would bring.

Because it is a highly specialized area, anyone intending to embark upon translating for the stage is well advised to read a number of successful translations of drama in addition to the musings of well-known drama translators.

Translating children's literature

I'm sometimes asked whether there are any special requirements for translating children's literature. Golly gee, you betcha. Like writing original material for children, translating the stuff is a field all its own. Some of the best translators of fiction and poetry for adults have come a cropper when attempting to find the voice of a work written for six- and nine-year-olds.

Most of the challenges of translating literature for adults – for example, fluency, accuracy, register, flexibility, a feeling for style, an appreciation of nuance, and transparency – are also present in translating children's literature. But in addition there are special needs in translating works aimed at children, particularly those under ten or so. Age-level must be taken into consideration: what is right for a ten-year-old will usually be beyond the grasp of a seven-year-old, while kids on the verge of adolescence feel they're ready to read so-called young-adult literature. Appropriate illustrations must be found, though sometimes those from the source language can be used. In the United States, considerations of political correctness are a major concern; nothing capable of offending any racial, religious, or ethnic group can be included, and gender bias is also an issue. One must come to terms with certain themes such as magic, which some Christian fundamentalists view as witchcraft (the Harry Potter books have come under criticism from some quarters for this very reason). Sexuality in any form is a no-no. Death and illness must be handled with extreme care. Family strife and divorce are touchy subjects.

I still remember ruefully, a full decade later, the disappointment surrounding my translation of a lovely, nostalgic little story by Marcos Rey,

'Doutor por Correspondência' (Architect by Correspondence). Commissioned by a major New York publisher for a collection designed for high-school courses in foreign literature, the tale recounts long-ago childhood memories when a cousin from the hinterlands comes to live with narrator's family in São Paulo. Ambitious but with undeveloped ethical sensitivities, he sets about on various moneymaking schemes: running a kind of Turkish bath in a shed in the backyard, getting a correspondence-school diploma in architecture, concocting various kinds of ersatz alcohol – whiskey, rum, gin, differing only in coloring agents, flavorings, and labels – in the family bathtub. It was this latter allusion that caused the belated rejection of the translation after the editors had accepted it. The publishers were afraid that school districts in certain areas of the country would object to the mention; it might give the impression that drinking was somehow condoned.

Yes, many of the points cited here are more marketing concerns than translational issues, but because publishers are acutely attuned to the bottom line, a translator must be aware of the pitfalls.

At the outset, one difficulty is finding material. The works of the Grimm brothers and Hans Christian Andersen are pretty much mined out. Also, while there are exceptions such as Lewis Carroll's marvelous tales, *Bambi*, and *Pinocchio*, children's literature often doesn't travel well. And although new children's works appear frequently in other cultures, English-language publishers take a lot of convincing about their viability in a highly competitive market dominated by homegrown originals.

In kiddie lit, both vocabulary and tone are crucial. Words that a fifth grader might know may be beyond the grasp of his counterpart in the second grade. You will have to consciously reduce your range of words (some publishers provide a list of 'suitable' words) to translate in this field. The first thing a publisher will ask is what age group the work is aimed at. Be prepared to answer within a two- or at most three-year range; 'pre-teens' isn't precise enough. Also, commercial houses are loath to deal with the dark side, whether of human nature or of impersonal forces. Any subject that might cause insecurity in the very young – e.g., divorce, debilitating illness, or death – is a no-no for the pre-eleven set.

If you translate children's literature in verse, rhyme is a *sine qua non*. Children, especially young children, are unequipped to appreciate more sophisticated metrical formats like blank verse or free verse. In addition, rhyme is a significant aid to memorization, and one of the purposes of literature for children is to encourage, and sometimes teach, them to read. Where the rhyme is humorous, it's imperative to find an equivalent in English, even at the cost of adapting rather than a close translation.

It is frequently necessary to exercise much greater freedom with text in children's literature than with adult literature. An analogy can be made with film, in which complex novels are often brought to the screen with major changes, including omissions, composite characters, and dramatic liberties. For one thing, children are less likely than adults to find attraction in the customs of other cultures. The *Arabian Nights* à la Disney aside, children are most comfortable with the familiar, and adaptations may have to be made if the goal is to achieve commercial success. Generally, in children's literature the less familiar the source culture the more magical it must be to succeed. (Like all other 'rules,' there are exceptions.)

One wonders whether the success of the Harry Potter series had any effect on the industry. I'm not an industry insider, but speaking as a translator I believe the Harry Potter phenomenon is a once-in-a-generation occurrence. While it's good that it has many young people reading again instead of vegetating in front of a television set or jabbing away at video games, I doubt that it will have much effect on translated children's literature in the English-speaking world. The Harry Potter series, after all, was written in English and takes place in a familiar cultural setting albeit one tinged with magical elements. If anything, its major impact to date has been to stimulate translation of children's literature from English to other languages.

Before attempting it, be forewarned that children's literature is one of the most competitive genres and among the toughest to break into. In this area, parents are brand-name consumers who gravitate toward authors they (and presumably their kids) have enjoyed in the past.

It must also be acknowledged that because of its restricted range, children's literature may not allow full expression of a translator's talents – a limitation that some find chafing.

On the plus side, if you find pleasure in reading to your toddlers, you might like translating similar material. Because the works are short, your initial investment in time would be fairly small. And there are several specialized publishing houses that welcome fresh offerings in children's literature.

If you wish to investigate the field, there is no shortage of published information. Though most manuals focus on writing rather than translating children's literature, the principles of both are largely the same. *Writer's Digest* has published a guide to the genre, and any good public library will have works on the topic. A useful Internet source is the Children's Writer's and Illustrator's Resource List, at:

http://www.pfdstudio.com/cwrl.html.

Puns and word play

There is perhaps no aspect of translation that is simultaneously more frustrating and potentially more rewarding than metalanguage – in effect, a language talking about itself. For example, the fullness of an English sentence like *'Ain't* ain't a word' is probably beyond capture in another language. (*'Ain't, n'est pas un mot'*?) In a tongue that lacks a non-standard first-, second-, and third-person form of *be* it simply loses the facetious flavor of the original. Similarly, in Spanish, *Le dije usted, no tú* would often call for something as circumlocutory as 'I addressed him in the formal, not the familiar, voice.' Hardly deathless prose. Of course, for those languages that distinguish between familiar and polite *you*-forms (which include most major European tongues) there may be a workaround. In English, we can indicate a sudden emotional distancing by several devices, among them a mother addressing her child by his or her full name: 'James William Henderson, did you break that vase?' In Portuguese, use of a direct-address *doutor* indicates not medical training but simply the inferior social position of the speaker in relation to the listener. In the same language, *seu*, a corruption of *senhor*, is an honorific best conveyed in English by adding a 'sir' to an utterance or prefixing a 'Mister' to the name.

The most frequently encountered use of metalanguage, and the one most likely to cause translators sleepless nights, is the pun. Nowhere do the joys and travails of translation coexist as visibly as in the close combat between a translator and a play on words. Not all word plays are puns; there are also alliterations, coinages, malapropisms, hypercorrections, and the whole range of verbal resources that a skilled writer marshals to convey character or define individuality. But puns are among the most time-honored (if that's the appropriate adjective) form of playful linguistic expression.

It should come as no surprise that translators are notorious punsters and that few things are as gratifying to the literary translator as discovering a perfect TL equivalent of a SL play on words. To transfer a joke from one language to another calls on the ability to 'think outside the box,' and while not every attempt to translate a witticism pans out, a successful effort can make the translator's day.

It is a fact of life that many if not most puns will be untranslatable. But, like other special uses of language (humor is one instance), the effect can often be reproduced by transferring the word play into a different setting in the same text. Maintaining the tone is the principal concern. In translating Patrícia Melo's *Inferno*, for example, I wrestled with a common informal phrase, *tudo azul*, that ordinarily would not have presented a major problem. Literally, 'everything blue,' its meaning is really 'everything peachy, rosy.' Searching for a TL equivalent based on color was fruitless, however, precluded by circumstances in the novel: an expected police raid on drug dealers in a Rio *favela* was predicated on their looking for a house with a blue door. The wily traffickers provided free blue paint for the inhabitants and urged them to change the color of their doors – thus 'everything blue,' which in context is 'everything cool.' But the pun is lost because in English the color blue is associated with sadness, as in singing the blues. Unfortunately, no way occurred to me that would save the double meaning.

In *A Samba for Sherlock*, the crucial word in the denouement was totally different in Portuguese and English. This forced a key modification in the TL: the serial killer taking flaps of skin instead of cutting off his victims' ears. Subsequent changes were then necessitated – for instance, a wag saying, '*Não há de ser por ganância. Nenhuma das vítimas usava brincos*' ('It can't be from greed. Neither of the victims wore earrings'), became 'It can't be because he's an art collector. Neither of the victims was tattooed.' Coincidentally enough, another translational solution in an earlier novel hinged on the same word, *orelha*. In *Bufo & Spallanzani*, the first-person protagonist, a writer, remarks that it's the material on the dust jacket (*orelha*, which in Portuguese means both 'ear' and 'flap of a book jacket') that sells his books in translation, each foreign edition being carefully slanted to appeal to certain national expectations:

> On the jacket flap the publisher will say something to enlighten and motivate the reader. In France ... they'll say the book is a metaphor for the violence of knowledge. In Germany, that it's a denunciation of the abuses perpetuated by *Homo sapiens* against nature... In the United States they'll define the book as a cruel reflection on the utopia of progress. The word 'hubris' will be used anathematically. We'll seduce the prospective reader by creating quite a flap.

The original read 'We'll grab the reader by the *orelhas*.' The author was pleased with 'creating quite a flap.' I recall this minor triumph with perhaps undue pride as compensation for the many times I have been unable to find a suitable replacement for a pun.

Stalking the treacherous typo (*Lapsus calami*)

It was maddening. For over a month I'd been looking for the translation of a single Portuguese word, *viago*. I had consulted native speakers, exhausted my collection of dictionaries, asked everyone with a knowledge of the language, all to no avail. If not a translator's nightmare, it was close enough.

Today I know how to cope with problems of this nature, but at that time I had translated only three novels. I felt that I had to find out what *viago* meant or be a failure as a translator. We'll come back to that.

Though occurring only once, *viago* was crucial to the passage where it appeared. And to complicate matters, it bore such a close phonetic resemblance to *viado* (one spelling of a slang term for homosexual) that a number of my interlocutors 'heard' that word when I queried them. A little background is in order.

I was working on a short story by Marcos Rey, whose *Memoirs of a Gigolo* I had published a couple of years earlier. 'Me and My Beetle' ('Eu e Meu Fusca') deals with a reform school graduate whose passion is his Volkswagen, which he has embellished with countless accessories and in which he cruises the streets of São Paulo in search of a good time, as well as other more sinister pleasures.

As the story opens, he is chatting with Januário, the mechanic who's checking his car: '*Hoje vou faturar uns duzentos. Não, nada de Santos. Quem gosta de areia é siri. Meu negócio é o asfalto. Esta cidadona tem* **viago**. *Ciau, Janu* (…)' With the exception of that nettlesome word *viago*, the meaning of the passage is clear: 'I'm gonna make a couple of hundred today. No, not at the beach in Santos. Sand is for crabs. Asphalt's my thing. This [big] city's got **viago**. Ciao, Janu.'

Fruitless searches through dictionaries bolstered the conviction that it must be slang, and very recent slang at that, or possibility a localism peculiar to São Paulo, since no native informants were familiar with it. The speaker is apparently referring to racing in Santos, but he prefers the city with its *viago*. Could it mean 'drag strip' or 'automobile race track'? Makes sense. I even conjectured that it was a neologism on the order of *ciclovia* 'bike trail'. *Via* = way, path; *go*, from the English 'go' (English for commercial establishments is considered chic in Brazil). I was quickly beginning to persuade myself.

Feeling smug about my cleverness, I sought confirmation with *paulistas* living in the US. The conversations usually went something like this:

'Do you know the word *viago*?'
'Of course, but don't you mean *viado*?'

Confronted with a printed version of the spelling, they confessed ignorance of the term. Back to square one.

It was time to suspend wrestling with *viago* and turn to the rest of 'Me and My Beetle.'

The narrator lives in a low-rent boarding-house run by the motherly Dona Itália, who dotes on him. Among the other residents are Clô, an effeminate hairdresser; 'Cary Grant' and 'Bette Davis,' a middle-aged married couple; and the Wolfman, a confirmed bachelor. (The protagonist, who like many of Rey's characters remains nameless throughout, has the habit of conferring private nicknames on everyone he deals with.)

At one point the dinnertime conversation turns to a series of gunshot murders in the city:

> Desço para o jardim de inverno. O Lobisomem e o Cary Grant ainda falam do atirador. A eles, junta-se agora o Clô, o cabeleireiro.
> – Mas ninguém viu a cara dele? – indaga a bicha.
> – Quem viu morreu – respondeu Cary.
> – Mesmo quem morreu não viu – corrigiu o encalhado. Ele atira a distância.
> – Mas por que mata? – arrepia-se o **C18**.
> – Para se divertir.

I go downstairs to the solarium. The Wolfman and Cary Grant are still talking about the sniper. Clô, the hairdresser, joins them.
'But hasn't anyone seen his face?' the fag asks.
'Whoever saw him is dead,' Cary replied.
'Even the dead ones didn't see him,' the bachelor corrected. 'He shoots from a distance.'
'But why does he kill?' – – – asks, his flesh crawling.
'For kicks.'

What does 'C18' signify? Contextually ('his flesh crawling') it seems to refer to the gay hairdresser Clô. Is this some kind of number-code used by Brazilians like '24' (*vinte-e-quatro*), denoting a male homosexual? (For the curious, the number 24 corresponds to the stag – *veado* – in Brazil's illegal *jogo do bicho*, a lottery based on animals.) I drew a blank in standard dictionaries and their slang equivalents. Native informants were equally baffled.

I finally concluded that C18 must be the number of the room in which Clô lived, Room C18, despite misgivings that Dona Itália's boardinghouse didn't seem large enough to necessitate numbering the rooms (and could there be as many as 18 rooms, given the small number of people at dinner?); I reluctantly opted for 'the boarder in C18.'

Wrong again.

Dissatisfied with my tentative rendering of both *viago* and C18, I did what I should have done earlier and wrote the author. A reluctance to bother the author with trivial questions had forestalled my resorting to the source. Nevertheless, before the manuscript went to the publisher, I wanted to eliminate any howlers.

The answer came by return mail. But first let's look at another example.

In this case the author was unavailable for consultation, having departed the world in 1922. I was translating a classic piece of short fiction by Lima Barreto, a droll and satirical short story called 'O Homem que Sabia Javanês' (The Man Who Knew Javanese), from the anthology *Obras Primas do Conto Brasileiro* (Almiro Barbosa and Edgard Cavalheiro, eds). Some of the antiquated vocabulary presented problems, but the real difficulty in such cases lies not in obvious typos or even patent errors of fact or of terminology, which can easily be corrected. (And no, this is not 'improving on the original.' The author never intended for such a slip-up to appear in print. Too late to correct in the original, at least it can be prevented from perpetuating itself in a foreign edition.) Rather, it is those subtle errors that masquerade as valid words that offer the real trouble. For example, the phrase 'este calungas' was clearly a misprint for *estes calungas* (these figures); no problem there.

For the non-native speaker, which describes my standing in Portuguese, there is always the possibility that a given term may simply be of sufficient rarity as to have never come to one's attention. Many English speakers, for instance, would not recognize the word *dour* when pronounced (correctly) to rhyme with 'moor' instead of 'sour.' By the same token, a perfectly valid term like *nonce* may not be in the recognition vocabulary of many educated Anglophones. An example of my ignorance occurred when the protagonist of the story, about to begin a vertiginous professional and social ascent based on his supposed knowledge of Javanese, is asked by a low-level functionary in the Foreign Office if he knows **canaque**.

Contextually *canaque* is a language, but which one? No Portuguese-language dictionary lists it. Was Lima Barreto inventing it as a jape? Or was this a case of linguistic change of the last 80 years or so? There is a word, *canaca*, that seems to fit: 'a native of the South Sea islands, Polynesia, Micronesia, and Melanesia.' An unabridged English dictionary yielded *kanaka*, a Hawaiian word with the same meaning. Even if wrong, it seemed close enough to do no real violence to the author's intent, for *kanaka* is as esoteric in English as its counterpart in Portuguese.

The story still wasn't through with its terminology mischief. It was reprinted in *Antologia Brasileira de Humorismo*, edited by Paulo Mendes Campos (1965), but finding a second version of the work, far from resolving doubts, raised even more. These are some of the differences between the two editions: *aprendera/aprendi* (had learned, learned), *bibliografia de história literária/bibliografia e história literária* (bibliography of literary history/bibliography and literary history), *posteridade/prosperidade* (posterity/prosperity), *papel amarelo/papel amarelado* (yellow paper/yellowed paper), *diligente/inteligente* (diligent/intelligent), *extático/estático* (ecstatic/static), *aprenderem/entenderem* (to learn/to understand), *convidava-me/convida-me* (invited me/invites me).

It reminded me of the hoary observation that a man who has a clock always knows what time it is; a man with two clocks never knows what time it is. *L. calami* can be a devilishly tricky beast. While some variations are insignificant because they become invisible in translation, others are substantive and seriously change the meaning: *posterity* vs. *prosperity*, *ecstatic* vs. *static*, *learn* vs. *understand*. And the subtle distinction between yellow (*amarelo*) paper and yellowed (*amarelado*) paper is worth preserving. Literary translation lives by such fine gradations of meaning.

When dealing with a classic, oft-reprinted work, the translator should always entertain the possibility of corruption in the text. In the real world, of course, we are sometimes given a photocopy of a work from, say, Algeria and must make do with no basis of comparison and little opportunity for checking against the original. Still, often there are resources available for confirmation, like interlibrary loans.

Searching for the *Urtext* is frustrating at times, for even first editions contain errors, often (especially where the author is deceased) perpetuated in later printings. Viruslike, the typo once introduced tends to displace the original word and reproduce itself in subsequent editions, which frequently are made from the same plates.

Which brings us back to Marcos Rey and 'Me and My Beetle.' As his letter confirmed, both *viago* and C18 were *erros de impressão*, simple typos! *Esta cidadona tem viago* should read '*tem visgo.*' (*Visgo* denotes a sticky substance, often used figuratively.) The meaning: 'There's something in this city that grabs holds of you.' As for the cryptic C18, the author replied laconically, 'Printing error; should be Clô.' That sudden sharp sound was my palm slapping against my brow.

Mystery solved, I could once again concentrate on translating the tale of how the narrator and his true love Marianna Catkiller demonstrate that the couple that slays together stays together. But that's another topic...

The dilemma of dialect

A frequently encountered problem in literary translation is how to convey dialect. As translators we are familiar with the variants found within the range of native speakers of the SL with which we deal. They are as real and as conspicuous to us as an Irish or a Yorkshire dialect would be to an Englishman or a New England or Southern dialect to an American. Can they be translated?

First, a definition. In popular usage, 'dialect' often denotes a supposedly substandard or 'inferior' speech pattern varying in pronunciation, vocabulary, grammar, or syntax from the societally accepted norm. But standard English – or standard Latvian, for that matter – is merely the dialect spoken by a privileged segment of society that includes its political leaders, its opinion-makers, and its literati. Max Weinreich's famous definition of a language comes to mind: 'A language is a dialect with an army and a navy.'

That we seldom think of 'BBC English' as a dialect is reflected in the lack of difficulty in choosing a suitable register for translating it into another language. 'Good' and 'correct' language is always easier to translate than is the speech of the uneducated or speech that displays strongly characteristic regional markers.

Dialect is a challenge unique to *literary* translation; commercial and technical translations invariably demand standard English. Deeply steeped in the SL culture, the translator understandably wants to convey every inflection, every nuance that distinguishes the dialect group. This is a goal that speaks well of the translator's seriousness and dedication, but it is also an impossible one.

Deep inside, the conscientious translator believes, *wants to believe* that there exists some apposite way of rendering the speech of the Polish *shtetl* into equivalent English. What if I give them a Yiddish accent? But people don't have a foreign accent in their native language... Maybe I can capture Guatemalan peasant dialect by borrowing a bit from Appalachia. But there's no admixture of Indian vocabulary and syntax in even the most uneducated West Virginian...

I once saw on television Marcel Camus's classic *Black Orpheus*, a film set in Rio de Janeiro and one with which I was familiar. Anticipating the musical cadences of *carioca* Portuguese, I was stupefied to find that instead of carrying subtitles the film had been dubbed and – horror of horrors! –

dubbed in Caribbean English! I could only take 15 minutes of it before lunging for the remote to seek relief in an infomercial.

No dialect travels well in translation. However reluctantly, the translator must recognize that dialect, at least at the level of one-to-one transference, is untranslatable.

Dialect is inextricably rooted in time and space. Whether based on vocabulary or on accent, the listener unconsciously associates such speech patterns with a region or a chronological period. 'I got a hankering to do that' or 'We don't cotton to strangers here' are not constructions heard in contemporary urban settings. *Thang*, dialect for 'thing,' fairly screams Texas or parts of Tennessee, as *pak* (park) does Boston.

It *is* possible to hint at unorthodox ways of speaking, if done sparingly. In *The Golden Harvest* an immigrant peddler from the Middle East mangles Portuguese in a manner that was fairly easy to reproduce:

> 'Is highest quality, customer...' the Syrian said in his clumsy speech, pointing to the glass of the rings and displaying cheap, cheery necklaces... The Syrian raised his hands in strange and impressive oaths. 'I swear from God, customer. Customer never see a more pretty present...' He pronounced it 'bresent,' his tongue suffering from forming what for him were difficult words.

Where extended passages in dialect are the case, the best we can hope for is a kind of generalized adaptation to spoken discourse – e.g., a plausible reproduction of non-specific rural, as opposed to Cajun or Ozark, speech. Any rendering of SL dialect that consciously or unconsciously evokes an existing TL dialect is probably self-defeating. Whether or not it 'reads well,' it still falls short of the original by introducing an element markedly different from that in the SL.

More calamitous still is the *invented* dialect. There are those, for example, who still have not forgiven Norman Mailer his three-letter euphemism 'fug' in *The Naked and the Dead*, which seemed self-conscious even in the uptight 1950s. An invented dialect, except perhaps in the hands of some James Joyce of translators, is almost certain to be both ephemeral and off-putting to all but the most forgiving and open-minded of readers.

Summing up, dialect is always tied, geographically and culturally, to a milieu that does not exist in the target-language setting. Substitution of an 'equivalent' dialect is foredoomed to failure. The best advice about trying to translate dialect: don't.

Special problems in literary translation

Because every translation is unique, a translator may go a lifetime without running into a specific problem that a colleague encounters fairly frequently. This section deals with some of the less common challenges that a translator should nevertheless be prepared to grapple with if the occasion demands.

English before there was English

A problem unique to literary translation arises when the SL original dates from, or is set in, a period before the TL emerged as a discrete linguistic entity. The dialogue in a play by Sophocles, for example, or the content of a poem by Catullus, might be conveyed using a wide range of English vocabulary, within limits. But just what are those limits?

This problem is not one that every literary translator will face. Still, it is more common than might be supposed. Gregory Rabassa confronted this challenge in his excellent translation of the Pegasus Prize-winning novel *A God Strolling in the Cool of the Evening*, by the Portuguese writer Mário de Carvalho. The 4th century AD is the setting for this beautifully told story of a Roman governor struggling to maintain peace in an atmosphere of decadence and decline, with barbarians drawing near and Christians undermining the established order. Naturally enough, his language, the one in which the novel is purportedly written, is Classical Latin.

In dealing with text actually or supposedly antedating English *qua* English, one approach might be what I call the accommodation model and others might see as more of an example of Robert Frost's oft-quoted swipe at free verse: 'playing tennis without a net.' The accommodation school of thought would argue that at any point earlier than roughly 1000 or 1100 years ago English had not yet acquired a separate linguistic identity and was clearly not a written language with a codified grammatical structure. By the time Shakespeare did for English what Dante had done centuries earlier for Italian, other languages – e.g., Greek, Latin, Arabic, Chinese – were either flourishing or had been relegated to liturgical or scholarly applications. Therefore, the argument goes, in translating a work set in, say AD 357, one is justified in using any English word, modern or archaic, that is aesthetically and semantically apropos. After all, since *no* English words existed at that time, why limit oneself to those that entered the language before some arbitrarily chosen date such as 1900?

The issue is of course not solely one that affects translators. In *I, Claudius*, recently chosen as one of the 100 best English-language novels of the 20th century, Robert Graves exercised throughout meticulous care in choosing words to create natural yet atmospheric dialogue. In one scene, Livia, the scheming and dangerous wife of Emperor Augustus, invites a fellow poisoner to dinner. After an exchange of professional chitchat, the other woman suddenly experiences stomach pains and looks in horror at her royal commensal. 'Don't be silly', Livia tells her. If she wanted her dead she could order her throat cut in an instant. 'It's just wind,' she says reassuringly.

Today we would say *gas*. But Graves, with his poet's sensitivity to the subtleties of language, knew that *gas* was invented out of thin air, so to speak, by the Flemish chemist J.B. van Helmont in the 17th century, based on the Greek *chaos*. The Romans had no such concept. While he might occasionally use a modern-sounding term for clarity or conciseness, Graves sifted through the enormous lexicon of 20th-century English to come up with *le mot juste* – though the French cliché is of course nowhere to be found in his marvelous tale of the first four Caesars.

When asked by HarperCollins to translate *The Fifth Mountain* by Paulo Coelho, I was mindful of such linguistic boundaries.

Any translation destined for publication carries with it the translator's responsibility to both author and reader, but in this case the weight of accountability was greater than usual. I was told that the English translation would be the model by which translations into less widespread languages would be judged by their publishers. (It was too much to expect that, say, Lithuanian or Slovenian literary translators would know Portuguese.) It would be the basis for an indirect translation – i.e., one from English to a second TL, without reference to the original language. And in fact I later received e-mail from my Japanese counterpart, who was using the English version to bring *The Fifth Mountain* into his own language, with questions based on my translation.

Before beginning the translation I laid down a few ground rules. Some I was able to adhere to firmly; others were modified or discarded under the bludgeoning of reality. To understand why they were important, it's necessary to know something about *The Fifth Mountain*.

The novel is a departure for the internationally best-selling Coelho, his first with a biblical theme. Its aim is to invoke through language the grandeur and wonder of a turbulent time. In the 9th century BC, the beautiful Phoenician princess Jezebel persuades her husband, King Ahab of Israel, to instate the worship of Baal. Prophets decry the practice, chief among them Elijah. He is 23 and is considered a prophet because all his life he has heard voices from angels. He also enjoys the protection of a guardian angel to whom he speaks in times of trouble. When he confronts Ahab to demand restoration of worship of the One God, the queen convinces her husband to order all prophets of the God of Israel to renounce their beliefs or be put to death. Elijah flees to the Phoenician city of Akbar, where he takes lodging in the humble dwelling of a young widow. The citizens view the newcomer with suspicion, but the widow defends him. When her young son dies suddenly, Elijah is commanded by the High Priest to climb the Fifth Mountain, where the gods of Akbar will slay him; if they choose not to sully their hands, he will be executed in the square upon his return. On the mountain, an angel bids him to descend and raise the boy from the dead. The miracle establishes Elijah as a prophet but wins him the implacable enmity of the High Priest. Gradually, he and the widow fall in love, bringing Elijah a joy he has never known. But the specter of war will end his newfound happiness, jeopardizing the people he has come to love and threatening his very existence. From tragedy will come the lesson of the uses of the unavoidable, and from the ashes Elijah will forge a new Akbar and a new life.

Neither hagiography nor religious tract, *The Fifth Mountain* portrays in human terms an imperfect, often cantankerous individual willing to die if necessary for a God he sometimes doubts, sometimes disobeys but never stops loving.

Here are some of the ground rules I set for myself:

- Exclude as much as possible foreign words in any language but Hebrew. However useful or apropos (oops!) *et cetera, hoi polloi,* or *rendezvous* might have been, they were out, not to say *verboten.* The prohibition extended even to anglicized words of obvious foreign origin like *imbroglio.* My objective was to avoid dislodging the reader from the natural-appearing atmosphere created by an otherwise seamless English that was a surrogate for the (supposed) Semitic languages spoken in the novel. Where an awkward, lengthy circumlocution was the only alternative, and assuming the word was sufficiently assimilated into English (like *coup*), I made an exception.

- Obviously, no anachronisms. In an earlier translation I had occasion to remind a different author – alas, too late to change the text – that a study cited in the novel had not yet appeared at the time the story was set. Fortunately, it was a postmodern work, so no irreparable harm was done.

- Words or phrases that, though perfectly good English, sounded too modern were also out. *Future generations, in the final analysis,* even *parents* was excised. (My tie-breaker was whether a word appears in the King James version, which refers to one's progenitors as 'father and mother.') Some phrases, such as *peaceful solution,* while having a definitely modern ring, offered no preferable alternative. *Pacific solution, non-belligerent sol* – Let's stop there.
- Slang is too linked to time and place to work here. Further, its lower register is at odds with the desired stateliness of the text.
- Use *thy, thou,* and *thee* sparingly, only when a character is addressing the Lord (as the Deity is usually called in the text) or when an angel is speaking to Elijah. The same with *-est* and *-eth* verb endings. Even so, one reviewer would subsequently refer to the translation's 'pseudo-King James' speech.

The intent governing these shibboleths was to maintain a colloquial but not overly colloquial tone that would undergird the depiction of Elijah as man rather than holy man. In my translation people say 'You don't' and 'I wouldn't'; that is, they use contractions. They do not, however, commit solecisms. In keeping with the somewhat elevated content, even the humble and unlettered speak in correct, if simple, sentences.

Should the language sound vaguely Shakespearean? Biblical? Victorian? Modern – and if so, how modern? A balance had to be struck between an English that was powerful yet concise and one that did not unduly distance the reader. I chose a register that without being slavishly imitative nevertheless resonated (perhaps subconsciously) on the King James version, the most familiar Bible translation and for most English speakers the one that 'sounds right.'

This short passage illustrates some of these points:

> The boy <u>rose</u> slowly and began to walk <u>toward</u> the <u>outer room</u>. After a few steps, he <u>dropped</u> to the floor, as if felled by a bolt of lightning. Elijah and the widow ran to him; the boy was dead.
> For an instant, neither spoke. Suddenly, the woman began to scream, with all her <u>strength</u>.
> 'Cursed be the gods, cursed be they who have taken away my son! Cursed be the man who brought such misfortune to my home! My only child!' she screamed. 'Because I have respected the will of heaven, because I was generous with a foreigner, my son is dead!'
> That evening, the <u>council of the city</u> of Akbar was convened, under the <u>direction</u> of the high priest and the governor. Elijah was brought to judgment.

rose: higher register than 'got up' or 'stood up.'

toward: marginally higher register than 'towards.'

outer room: 'parlor' and 'anteroom' sound too modern, and 'drawing room' would be wrong here.

dropped: can't say 'fell' because that would preclude the use of 'felled.'

strength: 'with all her might' is a cliché.

cursed: pronounced 'cursèd'; good biblical word.

council of the city: 'city council' is too modern-sounding.

direction: 'leadership' is too contemporary.

Similarly, a phrase like *Vá embora* could be rendered in a variety of ways: 'get thee hence,' 'go away,' 'leave this place,' 'off with you'; I opted for 'away with you.'

As mentioned, at the time of the novel's setting, English did not exist; nevertheless, the problem of anachronism can still arise. In the original the phrase *silhueta escura das montanhas* 'dark silhouette of the mountains' is anachronistic. (The eponymous M. Silhouette lived in 18th-century France.) I went with 'dark outline of the mountains.' It brought to mind my reaction when, reading an English translation of a novel set in 16th-century Brazil, I came across the word *shrapnel*, which was named after its inventor Henry Shrapnel (1761–1842), an English army officer. Motivated by curiosity rather than any desire to one-up a fellow translator, I checked the Portuguese original, which turned out to 'metal shards.' Because the word occurred in dialogue rather than the authorial voice, there was no escaping the anachronism, which nonetheless probably went unnoticed by everyone but me and Prof. Horrendo.

English with a restricted vocabulary: a case study

A Samba for Sherlock (1997) is a pastiche in which Sherlock Holmes and Dr Watson journey to 1886 Rio de Janeiro to solve the mystery of a stolen Stradivarius at the behest of Emperor Dom Pedro II. There, they soon confront a series of horrific murders, leading Sherlock to coin the term 'serial killer.' A departure from any previous Holmes adaptation, in *Samba* the redoubtable detective succumbs to the lures of the tropics, acclimatizing himself to such novelties as 'Indian cigarettes' (marijuana) and abandoning his cocaine habit; he also falls in love, with a beautiful mulatto actress. Intended as a popular entertainment, the novel is also a loving re-creation of a bygone period, the final years of the Second Empire. As an *hommage* both to a vanished era and to the world's greatest detective, the novel commingled historical figures with fictional personages such as Holmes, Watson, and certain of the characters representing the decadent aristocracy of the

Empire's waning years. Jô Soares established strict rules linguistically: he excluded any word or expression not in use in 1886.

The reader of the English-language edition may have difficulty distinguishing actual historical figures from those that sprang from the novelist's rich imagination. Dom Pedro II and Sarah Bernhardt (then on her first triumphant tour of South America) are obviously taken from life, as are men of letters like Olavo Bilac, Aluísio Azevedo, and Machado de Assis. Some important characters like the baroness of Avaré, the bookseller Miguel Solera de Lara, and the police inspector Mello Pimenta are fictitious. Even if the SL reader comes to accept one of Soares's imaginary characters as real, the confusion in no way diminishes the enjoyment of a provocative and highly original work that seamlesly merges fact and fiction.

In some cases the vocabulary in the translation may strike readers as anachronistic. (Did the usage 'the beer is on us' exist in 1886?) The authority in all such instances was the *Oxford English Dictionary*, although admittedly the notations 'mid-19th century' and 'late 19th century' leave some room for doubt. Otherwise, the vocabulary and diction was chosen to hew to a middle ground between overly stilted and formal language, more characteristic of Jane Austen than authors of the late 19th century, and an overly colloquial modernized English that would fail to convey the ethos of the era.

Because Brazilian Portuguese, unlike English, underwent several spelling reforms in the 20th century, the author's task of creating a 19th-century atmosphere was somewhat easier than the translator's. American English, with some minor modifications (e.g., we now write 'tomorrow' rather than 'to-morrow') codified its spelling with the appearance of Noah Webster's first dictionary. The result is that much of the vocabulary and dialogue in the translation appears more contemporary than in the original, an inevitable artifact of the differing rates of linguistic and orthographic evolution

The limiting of vocabulary to that existing in 1886 obliged me to a painstaking search for the provenance of word and phrases and a heightened sensitivity to what I dubbed the CC (chronologically correct).

On the very first page are clues to the killer's identity, through words that will later point to his profession. The problem is that they don't have the same double meanings in English. For example, *capa* is only 'cape,' the article of clothing; *volume* won't do for 'shape.' Workaround: restructuring to incorporate clue words (e.g., 'wearing a cape that *covers* him to his feet').

Goela escancarada: 'gaping gullet' would be nice except for the unwanted alliteration; by itself, either word fit nicely. As for 'yawning gullet,' the less said the better. I had to settle for 'open gullet.'

Recamier: unfortunate, the use of 'récamier' (uncapitalized, named after Madame Récamier) did not enter the English language in the sense of an item of furniture until the 1920s, so I opted for *'chaise longue.'*

[*Ele*] *logo viu que tinha uma boa nota para sua seção*: 'He [a newspaper writer] saw right away that he had' – what? *Boa nota* in the context actually means a journalistic scoop, but that usage didn't come in existence until shortly after the novel's time frame. (The Brazilian equivalent, *furo*, is also of more recent vintage than 1886.) So I went with 'a good item' for his – his what? Surprisingly, 'column,' in the sense of a recurring space devoted to the same writer, was already in use by then, although 'columnist' would not gain currency until the early 20th century.

Who would guess that 'vest,' in its current sense, was an early 20th-century usage? So I opted for 'waistcoat,' whose pedigree goes back several centuries.

Avental médico: should be easy enough: 'medical gown.' Wrong. According to *The New Shorter Oxford English Dictionary*, that term only entered the language early in the 20th century. Stick with 'apron.'

Passar carona means to dupe someone or fail to pay a debt. 'Welsh' (or 'welch') barely squeezed by chronologically.

Can't use 'hangover' for *ressaca*; it only came into use around 1900. Found 'wineache' in one slang dictionary but no dictionary confirmed it. Had to make do with a circumlocution.

A chacota daquele bando boêmio: is *chacota* 'banter' or 'satirical verse'? And what about *bando boêmio* – band of bohemians? Unfortunately, that would give us 'the banter of that band of bohemians,' an unwanted triple alliteration. Maybe 'pack of ...' On second thought, by going with 'persiflage,' I was able retain the alliteration of *bando boêmio*.

Podia-se ouvir uma mosca voar: could hear a *fly flying*? Hardly. Settled for 'a fly buzzing.'

Será que o sujeito é maricas? A nice old-fashioned word for a male homosexual. How about 'nancy-boy'? Too modern; dates from early 20th century. So do 'nance,' 'pansy,' 'flit,' 'pink,' 'nelly,' and most other such terms. I've got it – 'poof' (c. 1850).

... aborrecido pelo fato da notícia já correr à boca pequena. Another opportunity to set the feel for the period: '... irritated that the news was already being bandied.' Note that 'bandied about' is a more modern usage; also, 'being bandied about' has too many *b*'s.

It is Soares's conceit that, the year before he met Dr Watson, Sherlock Holmes spent six months in Macao studying with a Portuguese scientist specializing in poisons. There Holmes learned to speak flawless Portuguese, naturally with a marked *lisboeta* (continental) accent. Throughout the novel Holmes's vocabulary and diction are contrasted humorously with the (to Brazilian readers) 'normal' mode of expression. As is so often the case with metalinguistic questions, this distinction proved impossible to reproduce for the TL reader. Having Holmes speak British English would be inadequate because he *was* British. And if he spoke American English he would both appear unnatural and represent a betrayal of the Holmes that readers worldwide have come to know. I finally had to go with a semi-neutral, British-tinged English.

Nitrato de celulose? Easy enough, 'cellulose nitrate,' right? No, not if we're adhering to vocabulary in use in 1886. That phrase dates from 1890–95. Luckily, an early phrase, 'nitrocellulose,' just makes it under the wire (1880–85).

Redingote vermelho: 'red redingote' is cacophonous; let's go with 'scarlet.'

TL failure: '[Watson], *que tinha o sono leve dos médicos, dormia profundamente.*' The problem lies in *sono/dormia*, both of which are 'sleep' in English. To avoid a puerile turn of phrase ('who was a light sleeper ... was deeply asleep') I had to recast: 'He saw his friend, who, like all doctors, was a light sleeper, resting calmly.'

What word to use for the antiquated '*sala de banhos*'? Privy? Water closet? W.C.? Latrine? Bathroom?

Cavaquinho, a musical instrument akin to the ukulele. But the latter, although introduced to Hawaii c. 1879 and an offshoot of the Portuguese instrument, has its first recorded English use only in 1896. Can I use 'bandore'?

One would think that a term like 'gigolo' was international and had come into use in various Western languages more or less simultaneously. Not so; although it was used in Portuguese in the period of the novel, the earliest citation listed in the OED is 1922! So I went with 'kept man.'

Para afinar os últimos detalhes – what could be easier? Oops. 'To refine the final details' is cacophonous. 'Last details' is not idiomatic. 'Sharpen the final details'? It's this sort of thing that can take hours of a literary translator's time, even when the meaning is absolutely clear. (I ended up with 'polish.')

... *se abanaram com seus leques pintados*. '*Fanned* themselves with their painted *fans*' sounds infantile, on the order of 'the rain is raining.' Since there is no common synonym in English for either the noun or the verb, I must resort to a subterfuge. In a novel full of Gallicisms (reflecting the dominant cultural influence of the age), one more French term – especially one whose meaning is clear from the context – isn't going to hurt. 'Fanned themselves with their painted *éventails*.'

Another example of TL limitations: *trajes mais leves e um terno claro* both require 'lighter/light' in English, a stylistic infelicity. What about 'less-heavy clothes/clothing'?

'The guy is off his nut!' Sounds very modern, but according to the OED, both 'guy' and 'off his nut' were in use by 1886.

Extremamente bem-dotado – no problem in modern parlance: 'extremely well endowed' (sexually). But the OED doesn't list that specific meaning of the phrase until the mid-20th century. Have to use the less picturesque and more general 'extremely fortunate.'

Estava fundada a Roda dos Expostos: 'The Wheel/Turnstile of the Found-lings was – founded?' Make that 'created.' Or go with 'foundlings/estab-lished.'

What's a 19th-century term for *'zona do meretrício'*? The obvious 'red light district' is early 20th-century. I had to look in three thesauruses to find one with 'red light district' as a term. The Merriam-Webster *Collegiate Thesaurus* yielded a usable synonym: 'street of fallen women,' which has the desired Victorian feel.

What's CC for *alienado*? 'Mentally ill,' 'psychologically disturbed,' 'deviate,' 'unbalanced' – all are too modern.

Era de se lamber os dedos – a perfect translation would be 'It was finger-licking good'! But that's not CC. I chose 'a real thumbs-up.'

How did they say 'finish line' (racing) in 1886? They didn't, just 'finish.'

Referring to a well-known eating establishment with a Greek architec-tural motif, the author states:

> *Os estudantes boêmios deram-lhe a alcunha altamente pornográfica que persiste nestes dias: Café 'Cu da Mãe.' Na presença das senhoras, a ele se referiam como Café 'C.D.M.' ou Café 'Casa da Moeda.'*

Here's another instance where adaptation must supplant translation. Since *Casa da Moeda* means 'the Mint,' this is another instance when an adaptation must replace the translation: 'The bohemian students gave it the highly pornographic nickname that persists to this day: the "Mother's Ass" Café. In the presence of ladies, they referred to it as the "M.A." Café or "Modern Athens."'

Working with subtext

Especially but not exclusively in poetic translation, the translator must be constantly aware of subtext. This is defined as the implicit or underlying meaning of a literary text (the term, only about 60 years old, is a calque from the Russian *podtékst*). To cite one familiar example, the tale of Little Red Riding Hood has as its subtext a caution to pre-adolescent girls about sexual predators. A similar subtext has been adduced in other fairy tales. Why does the fair maiden's kiss transform the frog into a handsome prince? Because the subtext is one of sexual awakening; what, after all, looks sillier than a frog (i.e., sexuality to children still in the latent phase of development)? Yet suddenly at puberty it becomes – well, we all know what it becomes.

A more popular culture example of (alleged) subtext is the flap over the syndicated television series *Xena, Warrior Princess*, which engendered a gaggle of 'Xenites' furiously exchanging Internet chat room missives on whether the show had a lesbian subtext.

But I digress. I am not implying that subtext must be sexual; it may be political or take on any of a number of shapes. Examples: *High Noon*, one of the premier American films of the 1950s, had as subtext the McCarthy-inspired communist hysteria of the time; *Invasion of the Body Snatchers* had a similar paranoid subtext; the subtext of Arthur Miller's drama *The Crucible* was the figurative witch-hunting that the play dealt with literally.

Subtext differs from allegory in that the latter often makes use of openly symbolic characters (*Pilgrim's Progress*, for one) while a work with a subtext is normally realistic on the surface. This makes subtext more difficult to spot than allegory, and the translator should always be alert to the possible existence of a subtext.

In a very real sense, subtext in a written work can be compared to a layered performance by an actor. A truly fine actor can display simultaneously conflicting emotional states on his or her face without uttering a word. For a classic example of the opposite, a surface performance, rent the video of *The Barefoot Contessa*, made before the beautiful Ava Gardner learned to act.

Subtext can be subtle enough to escape conscious detection or obvious enough to demand the translator's active participation in the act of re-creation. Not all writing has a subtext, and non-fiction is more likely than fiction to lack it. But where a discernible subtext is present, the translator's obligation is to choose words that best reproduce it. Some of the challenges can be seen in the following case study in subtext, which originally appeared in *ATA Source*. Authored by Cristina Lambert, a Spanish-to-English translator, it analyzes a poem with a highly charged erotic subtext, 'Eva o el pecado original,' by the Cuban poet Odette Alonso

Yodú and translated into English by Mirtha Quintanales. It is also an insightful look at the dynamics of poetic translation.

Eva o el pecado original	**Eve or Original Sin**
Nada fue como dicen. MOIST? DAMP? WET? SL PLUS	Nothing was as they say. CORRECT FOR EROTIC SUBTEXT
Yo descubrí mi cuerpo mojado en la maleza	I discovered my body wet among the reeds.
y lo empecé a palpar.	and began to touch it. PREFERABLE TO 'SWELLED'
Era mi cuerpo solo el que se hinchaba	It was my body by itself that suffused
inflamada mi vela. SL PROBLEM WORDS	my candle inflamed.
No supe qué corría por mi vientre SL PROBLEM WORD	I never learned what ran thru my belly
trepaba hasta mi pecho —CHEST? BREAST? BOSOM?	rose to my breast TL PROBLEM WORD
enceguecía. PRIVILEGE SUBTEXT IF POSSIBLE	blinded. EXCELLENT SUBTEXT ADAPTATION
Tuve miedo y grité 'ROLL' OK HERE...	I felt fear and screamed REPLACES MOJADO/MALEZA ALLITERATION
tuve miedo y rodé por la maleza.	I felt fear and rolled among the reeds.
Era fuego era sangre era lava de volcán	It was fire it was blood it was lava from a volcano
era espejismo. SL PLUS NOT 'DRIZZLE'	it was a mirage. NOTE REINFORCEMENT IN SL REPETITION
No supe qué pasaba y tuve miedo ... BUT NOT HERE	I never knew what was happening and felt afraid − NOTE CHANGE
pero dejé rodar mi cuerpo y la llovizna	but I let my body tumble and the fine rain
y algo estalló vibrante quién sabe en qué recodo.	and something exploded vibrating in some unknown place.
Después dormí tranquila ANATOMICAL RESONANCE	Later I slept peacefully
un tiempo inexplicablemente largo.	a time too long to be explained.
Después quizá llegara Adán pero ya no lo vi	Perhaps Adam appeared later but I didn't see him
otra vez la llovizna humedeció mi cuerpo COGNATE 'FELT' WOULD BE WRONG UNPOETIC	once again the rain moistened my body
y me sentí gritar.	and I heard myself scream. NO NEED TO ELABORATE

Maleza means weeds, brush, scrub, undergrowth, but none of these is right poetically. 'Reeds,' though slightly different in denotation, has the desired connotation and in addition resonates on the biblical (Moses found in the reeds). *Maleza* has an extra lacking in the TL: it resonates nicely on *mal, malo, maldad*, and therefore on evil, reinforcing the idea of original sin.

    Era mi cuerpo solo: the word *solo* of course means 'alone' (not to be confused with *sólo*, an abbreviated form of *solamente* 'only'). But here it is of extreme importance to find the proper connotative translation for it. 'By itself' is good because it underlines the status of Eve alone in the garden, before Adam. (The poet has every right to retell the Genesis creation story as she chooses, giving Eve seniority over Adam.)

Vientre is a difficult word to translate into English. 'Belly,' the translator's choice, normally would have the wrong register, except perhaps in phrases like 'the belly of the beast' or 'the soft underbelly of Europe.' 'Stomach' is too prosaic and 'abdomen' too clinical. 'Womb' is a possibility, but in the context 'ran through my womb' doesn't sound quite right. The translator perhaps considered and rejected 'loins,' which has a poetic quality and would strengthen the image of Eve, from whose loins all humans sprang, the mother of us all.

Trepaba hasta mi pecho: the term *trepaba* resonates in Spanish on vines and creeping things like serpents, and 'crept' must have occurred to the translator, but she wisely selected 'rose,' which has a lovely association with garden. Also, *pecho*, which is not connotatively equivalent to *seno*, led the translator to 'breast' rather than 'chest.' From a lifetime of exposure to art, most of us have a mental image of a nude Eve whose breasts symbolize nurture.

Tuve miedo is in the preterit tense in Spanish, a completed action in the past, as opposed to *tenía miedo*, imperfect or continuing action in the past. Presumably this fact inclined the translator to choose 'I felt fear,' ignoring the slight alliteration it introduces, over 'I was afraid.'

Era lava de volcán: a clear-cut instance of SL superiority over TL. One of only three lines in the translation ending on a trochee. In each case, the choice seems unavoidable ('peacefully' and 'body' are the others). In general, with some exceptions for effect, in English prosody a trochee is perceived as less poetic than an iamb. Here, no recasting would work: 'lava' (for example, 'a volcano's lava') is itself trochaic, and it would be intrusive to rearrange the order of the elements, which build in intensity to climax in the eruption symbolizing Eve's erotic catharsis. In Spanish the line ends with a power imparted by the stress on the final syllable, something that cannot be captured in English translation.

Dejé rodar mi cuerpo: the key word is *rodar*, which literally is 'roll,' with additional meanings like 'roam,' but there are problems of connotation with the word in English. The juxtaposition of 'body roll' carries an unfortunate, perhaps subconscious, resonance on the roll of excess flesh around one's middle, and maybe even on 'jelly roll.' Better to avoid these difficulties by finding another word, and the translator did. From among several alternatives such as 'fall,' 'drop,' even 'move about,' she chose 'tumble.'

Llovizna: the usual translation is 'drizzle,' an adequate word semantically but completely wrong for this poem. The translator rendered it as 'fine rain,' a marvelous adaptation. The word's second appearance, now that the quality of the rain (fine, not a downpour) has been established, is simply 'rain.'

Recodo means 'bend of a road,' 'twist (or turn) of a river,' 'nook,' 'recess.' In Spanish it resonates on *codo* 'elbow' and thus enhances the poem's anatomical subtext. But since the word is not specifically a reference to body parts, the translator's generalized 'place' is preferable to 'corner,' 'bend,' and certainly to 'nook.'

Another passage difficult to deal with is *un tiempo inexplicablemente largo*, which reads well in Spanish but presents problems in English. The literal 'an inexplicably long time' is too prosaic. The translator's choice, 'A time too long to be explained,' is probably the best of several less-than-ideal solutions, among them 'a time too long to explain,' and 'a time beyond explanation.'

Después quizá llegara Adán: the principal word is *llegara*, the imperfect subjunctive for 'arrived,' which here sounds odd in English. 'Showed up' is obviously the wrong register, and 'came' is out of the question. 'Appeared' is definitely the correct selection.

Me sentí gritar: the translator avoids a trap here. *Sentir* means 'to feel,' but 'I felt myself scream' is not good English. An additional meaning is 'to hear,' thus 'I heard myself scream.' Also: 'scream' is the best of various meanings of *gritar*, far better than 'shout,' 'yell,' or (laughable in this setting) 'holler.'

Taken as a whole, what Ms. Quintanales has produced is a carefully considered, excellent translation of a fine poem.

My own comments: sensitivity to the subtext allowed the translator to find words that subtly add to the overall erotic effect: 'wet,' 'touch,' 'suffused.' Subtext is found in both prose and poetry, and being attuned to it increases the likelihood of bringing the SL text into English in all its richness and overtones.

Indirect translation

Indirect translation is translation into Language C based on a translation into Language B of a source text in Language A. Tolstoy's *War and Peace* was sometimes translated into various European languages via French rather than directly from Russian; the result was an indirect translation. What are the pros and cons of indirect vs. direct translation?

the plus side, it's safe to say that certain classic works of world litera-
ould not have found their way into languages of limited diffusion

had it not been for indirect translation; at the very least their appearance would have been delayed. With close to 350 million native speakers of the language of Shakespeare, discovery of a long-lost Tibetan text may in relatively short order lead to an English translation, but what are the chances of finding an Afrikaans or Basque speaker schooled in Tibetan? Recourse to a French or English translation may be the only solution.

Pitted against this advantage are several negatives. First and most important, any error or misinterpretation in the first-generation translation (T1) will inevitably be reproduced in T2 (the second generation) with no chance of correction through comparison with the SL. Thus T2 is automatically further removed from denotative fidelity than T1, even if T2 introduces no further errors into the translation. But because such second-stage errors *are* likely to occur, a degrading of meaning sets in, and something akin to the Xerox effect takes place: a copy of a copy of a copy loses sharpness and detail with each successive passage through the process.

In my view, indirect translations are to be avoided if possible, and an ethical translator is duty-bound to inform readers, perhaps in a translator's introduction, that the text at hand is not a first-generation translation. This is not to deny that certain excellent and even indispensable translations have been indirect. At the beginning of the Renaissance, the 'lost' works of Greek antiquity (lost to Europe but kept alive in Arab cultures, more advanced than their counterparts in Christendom) re-emerged through indirect translations into Western European tongues, thus reclaiming Plato and Aristotle for new generations. The 'Spanish' classic *Calila e Digna* was a fourth- or fifth-generation translation from Arabic via Old Persian and Sanskrit. But in today's world there is little justification for indirect translation, certainly not when two major languages are involved.

Predicated on what I consider the sound translational principles listed above, I have never done an indirect translation and have no plans to do one.

Pitfalls and how to avoid them

Both experienced and neophyte translators can fall prey to certain errors that at first glance may not appear to be mistakes at all. In some cases they can masquerade as 'faithfulness'; in others, they may take the form of excessive fastidiousness. This section looks at some of the more common lapses that the translating class is heir to.

Errors of frequency

Look at this paragraph in French (emphasis added):

> *Le Paris que j'évoque ici est celui de quelqu'un venu s'y exiler pour écrire et qui a porté sur cette ville un regard d'écrivain. Ce n'est pas le Paris que le Parisien voit dans son quotidien – celui de l'espace qu'il traverse noyé dans ses soucis. Ce n'est pas non plus celui que visite le touriste soumis aux impératifs de son guide. C'est la ville de celui qui marche sans autre but que se laisser surprendre et écrire, autrement dit de qui se laisse porter par ses pas et saisir par la surprise que lui procure son errance, pour ensuite s'adonner à l'écriture.*

This passage, from Betty Milan's introduction to the reader in her non-fiction work *Paris Never Ends*, is in perfectly good French, but care must be taken if it is to be translated into comparably literate English. The thorny element here is *celui* – not grammatically, for its meaning is clear, but in terms of a translational pitfall: errors of frequency. Let's begin with the first sentence: '*The Paris that I evoke here is that of one who chose it as a place of exile to write and who brings to that city a writer's eye.*' In the above paragraph, *celui* may variously be translated as *that which, that of, him who*. In normal English, all of these constructions are rather high-register but individually would not call undue attention to themselves. When all four occur in the space of a few lines, the result is an artificial, un-English sound to the text.

Errors of frequency, one variety of SL interference in the TL, occur when a grammatical feature of the SL is allowed to influence the structure of the TL. French and other Romance languages use demonstrative pronouns like *celui* much more often than does English, and any attempt to replicate the syntax of the TL will yield a stilted, 'bookish' translation. In similar fashion, the ubiquitous *para* + verb construction (*in order to*) in Spanish and Portuguese sounds right in those languages but quickly becomes obtrusive – at least in fiction – if it pops up too often. 'Too often' is a subjective term but in practice probably means no more than once every ten lines or so. It is a challenge to the translator's ingenuity to come up with ways of expressing the idea without either conspicuous repetition or tortuous circumlocution.

A related issue is less clear-cut. In English prosody, the tradition is not to repeat a word in the same sentence or, if possible, even the same (short) paragraph. But in many languages even the best writers utilize the same word with a frequency that in the United States would have Elementary Composition instructors sharpening their blue pencils. A translator faces the problem of whether to reproduce this, honoring the author's style, or to shape a more readable English. (See 'The author–translator–reader triangle.') Ultimately, it's a case-by-case decision.

A common mistake of beginning translators is the fear of 'betraying' the author by leaving out some shade of meaning from the original – e.g., translating a repeating term like Portuguese *sobrado* as 'two-storey house' in its second, third, *n*th appearance. We don't do this in English – after the first mention of the dwelling an author would normally refer to it simply as 'the house,' 'the large old house' or similar – and to force the TL into the SL mold is to do violence to both. A betrayal does occur, but it is the betrayal of the TL audience.

'Landmine' words: hidden traps in translating common vocabulary

Pound for pound, dialogue in fiction presents more translational challenges than description. Where the authorial voice dominates, as in most third-person narration, the level of discourse is usually 'standard' – that is, conforming to conventional norms of syntax and vocabulary – and while snatches of dialogue may vary enormously they usually do not set the tone for the work as a whole. In first-person narrative, however, in effect every line is dialogue. In any case, whether isolated snatches or the whole of the text, dialogue must be carefully parsed for what I call landmine words, those that in their apparent innocuousness hold concealed dangers for the translator.

No one would expect simple unlettered peasants or other uneducated folk to use words like *vagaries, adroitly,* or *sesquipedalian* (which someone once defined as the tendency to use words like sesquipedalian). In works of fiction, the focus of this guide, the danger in translating spoken language lurks rather in the small words that many of us use – and sometimes misuse – on a regular basis.

Probably no three-letter word separates the well-educated from the incompletely-educated as readily and as frequently as *lie*. (And that's the truth.) When the word means to prevaricate, there's no problem (the politician lies today, lied yesterday, has lied throughout his career), but when it means 'to recline,' watch out! (I assume that no literary translator would make the opposite mistake – e.g., 'The knife was laying on the table,' or, horror of hypercorrective horrors, 'He told me to lie down my weapon.') Even – or perhaps especially – native speakers of English have difficulty with this word. I recall seeing a few years ago a newspaper article with the headline CAR KILLS MAN LAYING IN STREET, to which I could only cluck my tongue and think: 'The wages of sin is death.'

The *lie/lay* perplex is complicated by the fact that *lay* is the (correct) past tense of *lie*. As for the other tenses of *lie* (recline), it's unlikely that half of all American college graduates can name its past participle – *lain*, as in 'The ruins of Babylon had lain untouched for millennia.' But not even an unrepentant member of the discourse police like me would normally say he'd 'lain' on the sofa for hours. Using a variant of Safire's Law ('When *whom* is correct, recast the sentence'), I would incline toward something on the order of 'I've been lying on the sofa for hours.'

Confusion between *lie* and *lay* has an additional facet: the sexual term *lay*, which of course opens endless possibilities for deliberate and/or unintended word-plays, as in the example above. Typically, however, such questions seldom arise in translation; the major problem occurs with the past tense and the present perfect of *lie*.

In other words, *lie* is what I call a *marker*, for the choice will mark the translated text with a specific register and tone. In English, these markers occur most often in dialogue, which exhibits greater variation than the descriptive, or authorial, voice. In general, and allowing for idiolectal variation, careful writers work in the prestige dialect ('the Queen's English,' Standard American, etc.). But when their literary creations speak for themselves, the range is wider, often constituting a problem for translators. A marker separates its users into two categories, and it means the translator must constantly avoid the misstep of putting it into the mouth of someone unlikely to employ the word correctly if he or she were speaking English. Accurate use of *lay* (which hereinafter will denote only the past tense of *lie*) is one hallmark of an educated person, one who has an interest in oral expression and is what laymen often call 'well spoken.'

Given the absence of exact equivalents of English-language markers in the SL text, the translator must decide which if any to introduce into the TL version. Only a thorough knowledge of both languages can determine the extent to which a given SL variant has an English counterpart. Some other common markers in English:

- the double conditional: 'If I would have known, I would have come earlier.'
- the double negative: 'He doesn't do nothing right.'
- adverb/adjective confusion: 'Monty reads good but he doesn't understand everything he reads.'
- failure of subject/verb agreement: 'She don't work here anymore.'

When translating Patrícia's Melo's novel *O Matador* (published in 1997 by Bloomsbury Press in England and Ecco Press in the US as *The Killer*), I confronted an illustrative example. It is a first-person narrative by a young man whose formal education presumably stopped short of finishing high school, yet who speaks a grammatical and mostly correct Portuguese, dotted here and there with slang. When he says '*Deitei no sofá*,' could I accurately translate it as 'I lay down on the sofa'? This was a decision I had to make early in the project and adhere to throughout.

Lie/lay may well be a case of what Steven Pinker, author of *The Language Instinct*, is referring to in arguing that when a grammatical construction becomes too difficult for children to assimilate, it eventually drops out of the language. Even if I can foresee a future in which *lay* replaces the intransitive *lie*; until that happens, translators should in the interests of educated levels of discourse continue to make the distinction. Alexander Pope's admonition about words still rings true: 'Be not the first by whom the new are tried / Nor yet the last to lay the old aside.' (Following the latter half of his advice, I consistently write *goodbye* without a hyphen.)

Surprisingly, certain 'uncultured' words in English are not necessarily characteristic of the educationally challenged. *Ain't* is likely to occur – humorously, to be sure – even in the speech of PhD's, as in 'He lost five thousand in Las Vegas, and that ain't hay.' I wish to emphasize that this discussion is not intended to be prescriptive about the use in English of such constructions as double negatives, 'he don't,' *lay* for *lie*, and the like. Its intent is point out the implications attendant to the choice of either alternative insofar as the reader's perception is concerned. For excellent non-prescriptive discussions of English usage, see R.L. Trask, *Language: The Basics* (Routledge, 1995), Lars-Gunnar Andersson and Peter Trudgill, *Bad Language* (Penguin, 1990), and Steven Pinker's *The Language Instinct* (1994), Chapter 12, 'The Language Mavens.'

Experienced translators know it is far more difficult to translate the speech of peasants and illiterates than of doctors and college professors. Allowing for regional variation and accent, the highly educated, the intelligent, the articulate tend to speak a fairly homogenized version of the Queen's English, while there is a rich spectrum of non-standard usage that delights linguists as much as it horrifies purists.

Burst is another landmine word. *The pipe burst. The woman's words burst his bubble. A burst of gunfire/energy. He burst onto the scene.* With the exception of the last two (which are borderline set phrases), many Americans use *bust* in such lexical slots. Also, the use of *bust* is obligatory in such senses as 'The police plan to bust the crack ring' and 'Al's party was a big bust; almost no one came.'

For many translators, the biggest bugbear is one of our shortest words: *who* – or, rather, *whom*. It is not uncommon for languages to distinguish between subject- and object pronouns through case markers (German is an example), but I am unaware of any in which their subjective distance is as great as the English *who/whom* split. In our language, use of *whom* instantly labels one as educated, pedantic, a show-off, or all of the above. In Portuguese, a phrase like *para quem?* (for whom?) is invariable and would be used in identical form by the most unschooled and by members of the Brazilian Academy of Letters. The translator has to be constantly vigilant with *whom*, for perceptually its use by a character assigns that speaker to a rarefied social category, or at the very least connotes a privileged education. In England it might be a rough equivalent to hearing someone speak with so-called Received Pronunciation, the product of that country's public (American, private) school educational system. The translator must decide whether this is the desired impression to convey.

The two-letter word *as* would seem as simple a word as can be found in English, yet its use or avoidance can mark a speaker as unmistakably as a Yorkshire accent or a Bostonian broad *a* in *bath*. A phrase like 'As I was having breakfast ...' will probably be found at all levels of discourse and all degrees of formal education. But even something on the order of 'As they say, nobody's perfect' already begins to separate native speakers, many of whom would automatically produce 'Like they say ...' The usage is complicated by such set phrases as 'He did it *so as* to confuse people,' which is invariable and independent of discourse level, although many educated speakers might substitute the rather highfalutin *in order to*. And speaking of *highfalutin*, it's an excellent example of the tendency toward hypercorrection on the part of some: *highfaluting* is sometimes heard, perhaps from the same people who verbally add a *'g'* to the end of *kitchen* and *chicken*.

There are numerous doublets that constitute forks in the road for the translator. Some are fairly innocuous – *sneaked/snuck, sunk/sank, leaped/leapt* – while others, like *shined/shone*, are more fraught with implication for the subtle, quasi-subconscious impression they convey. Part of being a translator is developing and maintaining a sensitivity to such gradations of usage.

Change of address: problems of the English vocative

English enjoys, if that is the word, a culture-linked feature that causes problems when translating certain languages – Spanish and Portuguese are two of them – that would not occur in translating that same language into various other tongues. I refer to the vocative.

Sometimes called 'direct address,' the vocative is the form by which we call another person face-to-face. In the phrase 'John, please hand me that pencil,' the word John is a vocative. Some languages (Scottish, for example) actually have different noun forms for the vocative case; the name Hamish is the vocative of the Scottish version of James.

English not only lacks a separate vocative case – and I promise this is as far as the grammatical discussion will go – but, as will be shown, even demonstrates a reluctance to use direct address in certain circumstances, and this can raise problems for the translator into English.

In some cultures, especially those where Romance languages are spoken, it is common to address people by their profession. While English does this in the case of doctors, judges, lawyers ('counselor,' but not 'attorney'), professors, political officeholders, and military ranks, in France it would extend to policemen (*Monsieur l'agent*) and other occupations. In Latin American cultures, among others, pharmacists, engineers, teachers, and architects would be included.

There is also the ubiquitous Spanish 'doctor(a)' – doutor(a) in Portuguese. This honorific is applied to practically any college graduate or professional by persons of lower social status. I customarily substitute a simple 'sir' or 'ma'am' for it in translation without great qualms.

But the real problem arises when the SL, as do Spanish and Portuguese, is spoken in a culture in which it is normal and non-aggressive to address a person by his or her ethnicity or race. '*Árabe*,' '*judeu*,' or '*negro*' are acceptable in Brazil and are not considered offensive in such situations. (There are of course other terms for these same groups that Brazilians consider insulting, or at least disrespectful. For example, to call a person of Middle Eastern heritage '*turco*' 'Turk' is less than flattering, and there is no shortage of hateful words for Afro-Brazilians in the national vocabulary.)

In contrast, in Anglo-Saxon nations to say 'Hey, Jew,' or in some circumstances even 'Hey, you,' is offensive and indicative of prejudice. The same is true of such body-oriented terms as 'Fat man,' 'Skinny,' or 'Shorty,' though such usage is occasionally heard, presumably to the displeasure of its object. But in Spanish America, assuming the person is a friend, to address him as *Gordo, Flaco,* or *Bajito* can even convey affection.

How, then, to handle such SL phenomena when translating into English? Through experience and experimentation, I have concluded that with rare exceptions the only acceptable way – and this stems from the desire for translation correctness, not political correctness – is what is known as a *zero translation*. That is, omit the vocative altogether. Its absence will not be noticed, and its presence would be jarring at best and totally misleading at worst.

In Latin America at least, political correctness has not yet reached the point of visibly influencing writers' freedom to shape their prose as they see fit. One example is the ubiquitous 'he or she' or 'he/she' construction found in English nowadays. (Yes, the author of this guide is among the perpetrators of this inelegant and aesthetically wanting phrase.) In translating many European languages (the Romance languages among them), a single possessive adjective serves for 'his' and 'her,' and often for 'your' and 'their' as well. A Spanish-language author who writes *'Cada alumno tiene su valor'* ('Each student has his value/worth') was unconcerned about the fact that *alumno* is a masculine noun or that *su* encompasses both sexes. To translate the sentence as '… has his or her value' is not only a departure from the author's intent but also does violence to the culture of which the writer is a product. While the original statement may not have been consciously sexist, translating 'his or her' in this instance strongly implies that avoidance of even the appearance of sexism was a consideration by the author, which is most likely a distortion of reality.

In the past, there have been regrettable cases of translators rendering the term *'negro'* from Spanish or Portuguese as the hateful n-word. Such practice is unjustifiable on several grounds, but none more so than that of accuracy. The translator has no right to introduce his or her own notions into the text, above all when such accretion distorts the views of the author or warps the TL reader's perspective of the SL culture.

Every culture has pejorative terms for certain disdained members of its own and other societies, even where, as in Andean nations, a given racial group may constitute a numerical majority. In parts of South America, for example, *cholo* and *roto* are used in an offensive context to denote Indians. Even the term *indio* is often avoided in some Spanish American cultures, replaced by the more neutral *indígena*. To avoid accidental mistranslation of crucial racial and ethnic terms, any translator dealing with Latin American contexts should be familiar with Thomas M. Stephens's extremely useful *Dictionary of Latin American Racial and Ethnic Terminology* (University of Florida Press).

Few choices of words can have greater impact than those impacting race and ethnicity. The literary translator must be constantly vigilant to select the term that conveys not only denotation but connotation as well.

The all-important title

Would *War and Peace* have been as successful with a different title? Obviously, an imponderable. In their original language, works come complete with title, but in translation titles are sometimes altered beyond recognition. A few titles are outright mistranslations but have become so consecrated that any change would cause confusion – for example, Camus's *The Stranger* should actually be *The Foreigner*. The popularity of existentialism in intellectual circles at the time of publication may have had an influence, 'stranger' being perceived as more alienated than 'foreigner.' A more egregious example of poor translation of a title is the name given François Truffaut's *Les Quatre Cents Coups*, which made it to American shores as *The 400 Blows*, which is meaningless in English and was never elucidated in the film. In French, *faire les quatre cents coups* means 'to sow one's wild oats' or 'to run wild', which coincides perfectly with the content of the work.

Sometimes the most seemingly insignificant word can affect the rightness of a title. Helen Lane relates that when she translated Mario Vargas Llosas's political memoirs *El pez en el agua*, 'I entitled it *A Fish in Water*, without the article, and it was changed to *A Fish in the Water*, thereby losing the parallelism with the English idiom "a fish out of water."'

The ability to influence the choice of a work's title places a heavy responsibility on the literary translator. Approaches differ, but I am of the school that believes a title should be changed only when it cannot be left unchanged. A title change may occur because of cultural, linguistic, historical, or even geographical disparities between SL and TL. In all cases, the purpose should be to afford the TL reader easier access into the work by diminishing the potentially offputting 'otherness' of such writings – without, needless to say, adulterating or 'improving' the original.

Let's acknowledge the facts: major, and even most minor, literary works do not languish unpublished because of a poorly chosen title. Think of *Arrowsmith* (about an archer?), *Rebel* [noun or verb?] *without a Cause*, and *The Ugly American* (he was the good guy, not the villain). Possibly the worst title of all time was *Too Late the Phalarope*. What the blazes is a phalarope, and what was he/she/it late for? Still, a clever, appealing title adds to the attraction and saleability of a work, and nowhere is this more true than in translations of fiction. If anything, a serviceable title has even geater importance for translations than for English-language originals; given

Anglo-Saxon reluctance to read foreign works, translations need all the help they can get.

A mistake that translators sometimes make is settling on a title too early in the process. Where the title is straightforward (*Il nome della rosa* translates itself), the decision is often automatic. But other titles prove more elusive, especially where they relate to cultural referents or literary allusions, and the translator is best advised to save the selection of title for last or until inspiration strikes, whichever comes first.

As an illustration of the need for flexibility and imagination in selecting a title, here, courtesy of Adrian Room's *Dictionary of Translated Names and Titles*, are how some well-known novel and film titles fared when translated into French, German, Italian, and Spanish.

Title in English	French	German	Italian	Spanish
As I Lay Dying	As (While) I Lie Dying	As I Lay Dying	As (While) I Lie Dying	As (While) I Lie Dying
Bad Day at Black Rock	A Man Came Through	Town in Anguish	Damned Day	Conspiracy of Silence
Catcher in the Rye	The Heart-Snatcher	Young Holden	The Catcher in the Rye	The Hidden Hunter
Inherit the Wind	The Monkey Trial	He Who Sows the Wind	...And Man Created Satan	Inherit the Wind [in English]
Taxi Driver	Taxi Driver [in English]	Taxi-Driver [in English]	Taxi Driver [in English]	Taxi Driver [in English]
The Pathfinder	The Trapper	The Pathfinder	The Guide	The Pilot
The Tell-Tale Heart	The Revealing Heart	The Traitorous Heart	The Revealing Heart	The Denouncing Heart
Vertigo	Cold Sweat	From the Realm of the Dead	The Woman Who Lived Twice	From Among the Dead

Some clear patterns emerge that can be of use to those faced with choosing a less-than-obvious title in translation. As seen in *The Pathfinder* and 'The Tell-Tale Heart,' when the SL makes use of a feature not shared by the TL (in this case the ease of creating compounds in English) a workaround must be sought. Note that in German, which shares 'compoundability' with its cousin language, the problem did not arise. With *As I Lay Dying*, the choice in the Romance languages was to bring the verb into the present tense, perhaps because of the existence of the so-called 'historical present,' a literary device that allows past events to be recounted in the present tense and imparts an immediacy to the narrative. *Catcher in the Rye* provoked a series of adaptive titles, despite J.D. Salinger's insistence that the title be translated literally in any language; thematically, among the various versions the French perhaps comes closest and the Spanish is furthest from the mark, while German simply gives up. *Bad Day at Black Rock* is an example of how place names in titles can be vexing. (*West Side Story* was unchanged in all four languages, but interestingly enough became the maudlin '*Love, Sublime Love*' in Portuguese.) *Inherit the Wind* should have posed no translational conundrum, as it comes directly from Proverbs 11:29: 'He that troubleth his own house shall inherit the wind.' But apparently the TL cultures are either less prone to biblical citation or felt that other choices would be better box office. Hitchcock's *Vertigo* is worth consideration for the wide range of adaptations it spawned. Even though the medical term exists in other languages (in French, *vertige*), its limited currency called for thematic solutions. Finally, the film *Taxi Driver* was sufficiently succinct and descriptive to survive intact in all four languages, illustrating the concept that there are times when the original title can be safely maintained; *Les Misérables* and Zola's *Germinal* are cases in point.

Choice of title is critical because, while a textual inaccuracy may be over-looked, an error in the title will be there every time the book is referred to, and each mention will reinforce the mistaken impression it conveys. Further, since readers usually assume the title is indicative of the theme of the work, a bad title can color or even falsify their perception of its meaning. There is less margin for error in the title than in the body of the work because it is what the public sees first; indeed, in many instances it is the sole contact with the potential reader. Like a huge wart at the end of one's nose, an infelicitous title is hard to ignore; unlike the wart, which can be surgically excised, the title is here to stay – at least until a new translation comes along.

This fact underscores the need to do right by a translation the first time. Because even acknowledged masterpieces are seldom translated more than once every couple of decades, an inadequate translation deprives an entire reading generation of a version in a contemporary voice. In 1984, followers of Brazilian literature were distressed to see the long-awaited translation of Mário de Andrade's classic *Macunaíma*, which was poorly done and which forestalled any better rendering for the rest of the 20th century. Similarly, despite the shortcomings of the first English version (1963), after almost 40 years a retranslation of Guimarães Rosa's *Grande Sertão: Veredas* [Great Backland: Paths] has yet to appear.

Although in some cases the publisher makes the final decision on a title (as with *A Samba for Sherlock*), more often it is the translator's prerogative, within reason. The choice of title demands an apprehension of the work's thematic sinews and textual subtleties. If anything, the responsibility for translators is greater than for authors, who normally have only themselves to blame if the SL title is less than perfect.

But unlike the author, the translator has the existing title as a guide, with the option to retain, modify, or (the last resort) discard it in accord with the exigencies of taste and the marketplace. Just as a brilliant work can be enhanced by an astute title, an ill-chosen title can act as an anchor on the finest masterpiece, and absent overriding considerations the translator owes it to the author to preserve the sense of the original. Under any other title *The Name of the Rose* would not smell as sweet.

What do we look for in a title? Catchiness (*Cat on a Hot Tin Roof* sparks our interest more than '*Maggie the Cat*'). Thematic relevance (*Long Day's Journey into Night* fits a Eugene O'Neill work better than one by Neil Simon). Curiosity (just what is a Maltese falcon, what kinds of heights are 'wuthering'?). Sometimes, a literary allusion that resonates for a large portion of the potential readership (*For Whom the Bell Tolls, A Fine and Private Place, Brave New World* – this last an example of a title that, borrowed from Shakespeare by Aldous Huxley, has become more familiar than the quotation that inspired it). Usually, but not always, conciseness, on the theory that short titles are more easily remembered than long ones. (This rule can sometimes be broken with telling effect. A deliberately long, rambling title may be the right choice, as when evoking the almost encyclopedic titles of past eras. In Andrew Hurley's retranslation of a Reinaldo Arenas work, *The Ill-fated Peregrinations of Fray Servando* replaced the earlier *Hallucinations*. A lengthy title may also be desirable for conveying a sense of incoherence, irreality, or insanity: *Oh Dad, Poor, Dad, Momma's Hung You in the Closet and I'm Feeling So Sad*, or *Dr Strangelove, or How I Learned to Stop Worrying and Love the Bomb*, or the ultimate example of *The Persecution and Assassination of Jean-Paul Marat as Performed by the Inmates of the Asylum of Charenton under the Direction of the Marquis de Sade*, more commonly known simply as '*Marat/Sade*.') Finally, all things being equal, a dynamic, action-implying title is preferable to a more static one, as will be shown below in 'Title quest: a case study.'

Like some wines, certain titles do not travel well. For instance, titles with local place names unknown abroad (*84 Charing Cross Road, West Side Story*), snatches of proverbs of limited diffusion ('one foot in the stirrup' from the Turkish proverb 'Tell the truth with one foot in the stirrup'), plays on words, or any cultural referent familiar to the SL reader but meaningless or confusing to the TL audience. Several examples are cited below.

This discussion is limited to titles of complete works such as novels and plays, omitting consideration of collections, anthologies, and books of poetry. All of these offer fewer obstacles because one has the option of choosing the most striking or least difficult title and using it as the name of the book, followed by 'and Other Stories.'

Michael Scott Doyle offers a useful catalog of classes of translated titles: literal (examples would include the names of a character, such as *Madame Bovary*, or a foreign word or phrase used as title, like *Così fan tutte*), near literal (e.g., changing Carlos Fuentes's *Las buenas conciencias*, which is plural, to *The Good Conscience*), and what might be termed adaptive or allusive (e.g., Ana María Matute's *Primera memoria* [First Memory], published as *School of the Sun* in the US and *Awakening* in England).

There are titles already consecrated through previous, well-known translations that generate resistance to any alteration, even where the new title is clearly superior. In 1992, when D.J. Enright revised the venerable C.K. Scott Moncrieff and Terence Kilmartin translation of Proust's masterpiece and entitled it (correctly) *In Search of Lost Time*, he was not without his critics. But as Jerry Farber remarked in an article about Proust translations:

> [T]he title, I'm glad to say, is finally right. *A la recherche du temps perdu* does not mean 'Remembrance of Things Past'; what it means is what the 1992 Modern Library version is called: *In Search of Lost Time*. Scott Moncrieff borrowed his title from one of Shakespeare's sonnets; it's a pretty phrase, but inappropriate. Proust's title is more active; it implies a quest. What, unfortunately, remains untranslatable in the title is a secondary meaning present in '*temps perdu*,' which can mean not only 'lost time,' but also 'wasted time.'

In the case of Ibsen's *A Doll's House*, Irene Berman, who with Gerry Bamman has translated Ibsen for several stage productions, argues that *A Doll House* is more faithful to the playwright's intent but also acknowledges that it would be difficult to effect a change at this late date.

Another category where changes should be approached with caution is when the title is the name of a main character: *Doña Bárbara, Anna Karenina, Dom Casmurro*. Changing Ricardo Güiraldes's classic Argentine novel *Don Segundo Sombra* to *Shadow on the Pampas* weakened the impact by making explicit what had been implicit in the original – that the title character, a gaucho, was figuratively a shade (ghost) of a bygone era.

Place names that are essential to the theme and readily comprehensible to a TL audience also should not be changed on a whim. Rightly, Babel's *Odessa Tales*, Mann's *Death in Venice*, or Kafka's *Amerika* pretty much defy modification.

In all this discussion, keep in mind that, however inspired or apropos the translator's suggestions, the final choice of title rests with the publisher, who may wish a more salable or 'pizzazzy' title. Such was clearly the case of *A Samba for Sherlock*, whose title in Portuguese, *O Xangô de Baker Street* (*The Xangô of Baker Street*), obviously called for change. The publisher rejected the author's suggestion: *Elementary, My Dear Sarah*. A reference to Sarah Bernhardt, who figures prominently in the plot, it was also the title of the French edition. Of course this practice can be carried to extremes. Witness this excerpt from my 1996 interview, in *Translation Review*, with Helen Lane, one of the most renowned translators from Spanish, who complained:

> I'm really very upset when publishers change titles to vulgar titles to sell. The preeminent example is that of a tragic book by Elena Poniatowska, whose subject was the killing of unarmed demonstrators, largely students … in [Mexico's] Tlaltelolco Plaza in 1968 by police and soldiers. It had the wonderfully resonant title of *La noche de Tlaltelolco* [*The Night of Tlaltelolco*], referring of course to Cortés and the *Noche Triste*. It was changed to *Massacre in Mexico*!

Title changes can be of several types: *optional*, where the goal is a better title, one more saleable or more accessible to the TL audience; *capricious*, done for no evident reason except display of one's ingenuity; *disastrous*, as when the SL title is misleading or less attractive than would be a literal rendering of the original; and *obligatory*.

Let's examine what happened to titles by Jorge Amado, the most translated of all Brazilian writers, on their way to English.

- *Terras do Sem Fim* (The Endless Lands) emerged in Samuel Putnam's version as *The Violent Land*, which is pithy and thematically valid.
- *Dona Flor and Her two Husbands*; *Tieta* (*Tieta do Agreste*, a geographical reference); *Gabriela, Clove and Cinnamon*; *Shepherds of the Night*; *Tereza Batista: Home from the Wars*; *Jubiabá*; and *Captains of the Sands* correctly received more or less literal translations.
- *Tent of Miracles* (*Tenda dos Milagres*) faced a problem: *tenda*, while it can mean 'tent,' was in this context 'market stall' or 'small shop.' Neither of these would read as well as the technically less accurate 'tent,' so it is hard to fault the translator, Barbara Shelby.
- *Os Velhos Marinheiros ou o Capitão de Longo Curso* (The Old Mariners or the Seafaring Captain) appeared in English as *Home Is the Sailor* in Harriet de Onís's translation. For obvious reasons, 'The Ancient Mariners' was ruled out, and variants of 'The Old Seamen' perhaps smacked too much of Hemingway's *The Old Man and the Sea*.

- *A Morte e a Morte de Quincas Berro d'Água* (The Death and the Death of Quincas Berro d'Água) underwent a transmogrification in the proper name: Barbara Shelby chose for her translation *The Two Deaths of Quincas Wateryell*, thereby countering a trend in the previous few decades away from the renaming of characters. In this case it seems justifiable, given the nature of Quincas's nickname, a bellow issued when the inveterate drunkard accidentally drank water thinking it was rum.
- *Mar Morto* was published in America as *Sea of Death*, not quite 'The Dead Sea' but close.
- *Farda Fardão Camisola de Dormir* (Uniform, Ceremonial Gown, Nightshirt) became *Pen, Sword, Camisole* in Helen Lane's translation, an acceptable change given the difficulty of conveying to an English-speaking audience the cultural context in the original title.
- *Tocaia Grande*, a place name that means 'big ambush,' was renamed *Showdown* in Gregory Rabassa's translation.

Title quest: a case study

Which brings us to *São Jorge dos Ilhéus*, published by Avon in 1992 and the sequel to *Terras do Sem Fim*. In translating it I gained first-hand experience with the difficult problem of title selection. This was an example of obligatory change because the SL title communicates nothing to the TL reader. São Jorge dos Ilhéus, the eponymous city in the Brazilian state of Bahia, is in many ways the true protagonist of the novel despite its dozens of characters and various settings in the cacao-growing region of the state. Obviously, 'St. George of Ilhéus' would not attract any but the most brazilophile of readers, so a change was mandatory.

The novel, set some 30 years after the earlier work, depicts the struggle for control of the cacao trade. Unlike *The Violent Land*, which centered on the bloody battles of men who obeyed only the law of force, the sequel takes place in an ostensibly more civilized period. It focuses on the shady legal deals and political maneuverings by the exporters to wrest control of the lucrative cacao plantations from the 'colonels' who own them. A recurring motif is Amado's lyrical description of the cacao trees bearing their fruit, which shimmers with the color of gold in the tropical heat. Furthermore, to those vying for them, the cacao lands had the value of gold itself. Clearly, it was on this thematic terrain that I had to seek inspiration for the English title.

I first verified what translators into other languages had done with *São*

Jorge dos Ilhéus. In German it's *The Golden Land*; in Italian, *Fruits of Gold*. But these titles, while adequate, fail to do full justice to Amado's powerful, lusty tale of men and women in the era of the cacao boom of the 1930s. Throbbing with vitality and abounding with sympathy for the under-dogs, especially the plantation workers struggling under neofeudal conditions little better than slavery, it called for a title that reflected this raw energy and courage, and I felt that neither the German nor the Italian choice did so.

In principle, titles should if possible resonate on the content of the work and echo its subject matter and focal point. My choice therefore was *The Golden Harvest*. Like 'land' or 'fruits,' 'harvest' is a noun and therefore inherently less dynamic than a verb. But contrary to the other two, it is what might be called an 'implicit-action' noun, one that connotes an active human involvement rather than a static condition. Without the interven-tion of people, there can be no harvest.

The same circumstances – an unfamiliar geographic allusion in the SL dictating change in *São Jorge dos Ilhéus* – possibly influenced Thomas Colchie to retitle Márcio Souza's rollicking novel *Galvez, Imperador do Acre* a more accessible *Emperor of the Amazon*. Even if recognized as a toponym and not a measure of land, 'Acre' less readily situates the Anglophone reader mentally than does 'Amazon.'

The cardinal rule should be: *change a title only when there is a good reason*. If a literal rendering retains the fundamental meaning, most titles are better left in that form. I saw no cause to call Lima Barreto's satirical short story masterpiece 'O Homem Que Sabia Javanês' anything but 'The Man Who Knew Javanese.' Nor would Rubem Fonseca's 'Corações Solitários' have gained from a name other than 'Lonelyhearts,' for then this delightful comic piece's allusion to Nathanael West's novel – to which it is an informal homage – would have been lost. On the other hand, faced with the title 'Retábulo de Santa Joana Carolina' (Retable of St. Joana Carolina) and discovering that even devout Catholics don't know what a retable is, I felt justified in changing Osman Lins's nostalgic novella to 'The Way of St. Joana Carolina.' This latter is an example of what Phyllis Zatlin referred to in an insightful article, 'Observations on Theatrical Translation,' as an allusive title; though I prefer the term 'thematic,' the concept is the same.

An enigmatic title can be left unchanged if the text itself provides an explanation. At first glance, *Like Water for Chocolate* is both puzzling and intriguing. 'Murder in the Monastery' would have been an execrable alternative for *The Name of the Rose*. Still on the monastic theme, the classic novel by the Chilean Eduardo Barrios, *El hermano asno*, was well

served by a literal rendering, *Brother Ass*, a reference to St. Francis of
Assisi's term for his body. Other provocative titles include Isabel
Allende's *The House of the Spirits*, Gabriel García Márquez's *One Hundred
Years of Solitude*, João Ubaldo Ribeiro's *The Lizard's Smile*, Manuel Puig's
Kiss of the Spider Woman, and Rubem Fonseca's *Bufo & Spallanzani* and
Vast Emotions and Imperfect Thoughts, all of which can prompt curiosity in
a would-be reader. Osman Lins's novel *Avalovara*, translated by Gregory
Rabassa, retained its name and with it the mysterious, musical sonority
of the original.

Where a cultural referent with an immediate resonance in the SL is lacking
in the TL, a change is usually necessary. Puig's *Boquitas pintadas* (Little Painted
Mouths), incorporating the title of a tango reeking with sentimentality, was
adroitly transformed into *Heartbreak Tango* by translator Suzanne Jill Levine.
Edilberto Coutinho's *Maracanã, Adeus* (Farewell, Maracanã) alluded to the
world's largest stadium, a landmark familiar to all in Rio de Janeiro, and was
called *Bye, Bye Soccer* in Wilson Loria's English version.

Here's one man's view of examples of each category of title modification
or adaptation:

- *Optional*: Nobel laureate José Saramago's *Memorial do Convento*
  (Memorial of the Convent). Though this brilliant Portuguese novel
  sank without a trace in its English incarnation (no blame attaches to
  its translator, Giovanni Pontiero), its chances of finding an American
  readership were perhaps improved by the name change: *Baltasar and
  Blimunda*. Autran Dourado's *Ópera dos Mortos* (Opera of the Dead)
  became *The Voices of the Dead* (tr. John M. Parker). Arthur Brakel
  rechristened *O Amanuense Belmiro* (Belmiro the Amanuensis), by
  Cyro dos Anjos, on the well-founded assumption that few people
  have any idea what an amanuensis is; the new title, *Diary of a Civil
  Servant*, while not glamorous, gives an accurate idea of the novel's
  subject matter. J.J. Armas Marcelo's novel *Las naves quemadas* (The
  Burned Ships), published in Spain in 1982, fared well by the rendering
  Ships Afire (tr. Sarah Arvio).

- *Capricious*: Aluísio Azevedo's *O Cortiço* (translated in 1926 by Harry
  W. Brown as *A Brazilian Tenement* and in 2000 by David H. Rosenthal
  as *The Slum*); Machado de Assis's *Quincas Borba* (*Philosopher or Dog?*,
  tr. Clotilde Wilson); Lope de Vega's *Fuenteovejuna* (*The Sheep Well*);
  Quevedo's *El buscón* (*The Scavenger*, tr. Hugh A. Harter). In all these
  cases either a perfectly good alternative title was available (*O Cortiço*
  literally means 'The Beehive') or the SL original would serve
  (*Fuenteovejuna*).

- **Disastrous**: fortunately, this category is smaller than the others. *A Grande Arte*, by Rubem Fonseca and translated by Ellen Watson, was called *High Art* in English, thus guaranteeing its misplacement on library shelves beside works on Michelangelo and Monet. My translation of Fonseca's *Vastas Emoções e Pensamentos Imperfeitos* was dubbed *The Lost Manuscript* in its British version, though luckily restored to its original *Vast Emotions and Imperfect Thoughts* in the American edition.
- **Obligatory**: the title of Ignácio Loyola Brandão's science fiction novel of ecocatastrophe *Não Verás País Nenhum* (No Country Will You See) derives from a poetic allusion obscure even to most Brazilians. Ellen Watson wisely chose *And Still the Earth*, which at least introduces the telluric element. Mariano Azuela's classic novel of the Mexican revolution *Los de abajo* could not of course emerge as 'The People Downstairs,' as a student of mine once translated it! But the translator's long-ago choice of *The Underdogs* was infelicitous and contrary to the theme of the work – after all, even an underdog may have his day – but the thrust of *Los de abajo* is precisely that the peasants, fighting blindly in a revolution they cannot comprehend, are 'like leaves in a hurricane' and have no chance at all. Though it may border on melodrama, I believe a better choice would be 'The Downtrodden.' Another obligatory change: António Lobo Antunes's novel *Os Cus de Judas* – in Portuguese *cu* is etymologically the same as French *cul* or Spanish *culo* – which Elizabeth Lowe was compelled to alter (considering the alternative!) to the excellent *South of Nowhere*. Nor could Guimarães Rosa's *Grande Sertão: Veredas* be left in its original form because *sertão*, unlike *pampas*, needs cultural explanation. Still, *The Devil to Pay in the Backland*, while thematically ingenious, did little to help sales of a translation seriously marred by unresolved problems of tone.

A possible trap for translators is choosing a title based on fads of the moment, for six to 30 months may elapse between delivery of the manuscript and its appearance in print, and nonce terms or transiently popular phrases can quickly become dated. When I was preparing *Memoirs of a Gigolo*, the film *A Soldier's Story* was current and it was tempting to call the translation 'A Gigolo's Story.' I am grateful I resisted, for *Memoirs of a Gigolo* is straightforward, faithful, and descriptive, and who today recalls the movie? Gregory Rabassa once told me that his choice of *In Evil Hour* for García Márquez's *La mala hora* (The Evil Hour), a novel with nothing particularly Miltonic about it, was influenced by his just having taught a seminar on Milton.

An Honor Roll of Ingenious Titles from Latin America	
Luis Rafael Sánchez, *La guaracha del macho Camacho*	Macho Camacho's Beat
Manuel Puig, *Boquitas Pintadas*	Heartbreak Tango
Guillermo Cabrera Infante, *Tres tristes tigres*	Three Trapped Tigers
Machado de Assis, *Memórias Póstumas de Brás Cubas*	Epitaph of a Small Winner*
Ivan Angelo, A Festa	The Celebration
Oswaldo França Júnior, *Jorge, um Brasileiro*	The Long Haul
Ciro Alegría, El mundo es ancho y ajeno	Broad and Alien Is the World*
Dias Gomes, *O Pagador de Promessas*	The Given Word
Julio Cortázar, *Las babas del diablo*	Blow-up*
Carlos Fuentes, *La región más transparente*	Where the Air Is Clear
Augustín Yáñez, *Al filo del agua*	The Edge of the Storm
Euclides da Cunha, *Os Sertoes*	Rebellion in the Backlands
Gabriel García Márquez, *La hojarasca*	Leafstorm

* indicates a title with more impact or more thematically appropriate than the original

Profanity, prurience, pornography

With time, most literary translators run into a situation in which they are called upon to translate words that aren't to be found in family newspapers, even as they are heard more and more on cable television. When translators encounter material that they realize will be disturbing to a portion of the potential readership if translated in all its earthiness, their options are almost self-evident:

(1)   Tell the publisher or author that you are unable or unwilling to translate the text. You are under no obligation to specify the reason.
(2)   Do the same conscientious job of translating as with any other text.

What you cannot do is apply your own standards of decency and morality, or those of any hypothetical audience, to the task. This would be as unjustifiable as 'improving' the SL text. Bowdlerization as a common approach to 'improper' texts may be a thing of the past, thankfully, but the danger of self-censorship still exists. A prissy or sanctimonious translator, or an unscrupulous one, can totally skew the TL reader's perception of a writer; as translators we do not have that right.

Fully aware that I'm repeating a personal mantra, I state once again that the translator who considers any word in either the SL or the TL too offensive or too obscene to translate has chosen the wrong profession. If your sensitivities are assaulted by an author's way of writing, translate someone else. It's that simple.

If you do decide to accept a project involving significant doses of profanity, here are a few guidelines.

Emotional, not literal, equivalents. With the exception of the two top-dog four-letter words in English (one copulative, the other scatological), which seem to occur in every language, trying to translate profanity literally leads to awkward, if not ridiculous, results. Spanish *hijo de puta* is son of a bitch, not son of a whore ('whoreson' may have been fine in Shakespeare's day, but times change). Portuguese *porra*, about as obscene an interjection as the language possesses, means 'sperm' (more or less), but rendering it that way is out of the question. You would translate German *Warmbrüder* as 'warm brothers' at your peril; try 'queers' or something stronger. French *salaud* should probably emerge in English as 'son of a bitch' or 'bastard.'

151

Despite boasting the world's largest vocabulary, English is woefully lacking in socially acceptable terms of opprobrium. Like other Romance languages, however, the Brazilian variant of Portuguese possesses an admirable array of billingsgate – e.g., *canalha, crápula, calhorda, cafajeste* and similar pejoratives – that resists easy translation. 'Rogue,' 'scoundrel,' 'rounder,' and 'cad' are too Victorian, while 'rascal' might better describe Dennis the Menace than a man who has sold his sister into a seraglio; 'bastard' still retains semi-profane undertones absent in the original.

Blasphemy is a special case. As translator you will be hard put to come up with a natural-sounding equivalent of 'goddamn' in the Romance languages. (German, of course, has no such problem.) Hemingwayesque oaths like the Spanish *me cago en la hostia* (I shit in the Host) strike most Americans as more quaint than shocking. In English, the word 'whore' has lost most of its former ability to traumatize, but in some Latin cultures it remains a potent insult.

Selectivity. Not every occurrence of profanity in the SL text has to be translated. At times a zero-translation is the only way to make an utterance sound natural; let your ear and sense of rhythm be your guide. Further, where the SL has a single term and the TL several, don't be afraid of variation.

Correspondence. It's hard to say which is worse: adding profanity where none exists or making scabrous language more decorous for fear of giving offense. Bad as it is to render ¡*Dios mío!* as 'Damn!' or even 'My God!' (in Spanish, its emotional level is closer to 'Good heavens'), it is equally undesirable to make Spanish *follar* or *chingar* into 'screw.' On the subject of correspondence, I have seen translations that render the simple Portuguese word *negro*, which in itself carries no racist overtones in Brazilian usage, into the n-word. Had the author intended to use a pejorative racial term, there is no shortage of verbal resources in Portuguese and most other languages. This is inexcusable and, yes, dishonest if it makes the author appear as prejudiced.

When it comes to out-and-out profanity, our English four-letter expletives can hold their own against any language in the world, but there are still pitfalls. In Rubem Fonseca's short story 'O Cobrador' (literally, 'the collector' but contextually 'the taker' or 'the avenger'), the narrator, a psychopath and mass murderer uses *fodidos* to describe the underclass, the rejects of society with whom he identifies. The past participle of *foder*, it is every bit as obscene as its English counterpart. Since the word occurs frequently, 'those who get fucked over' works only once or twice before growing wearisome. Any substitutes, to maintain the tone, must be terse as well as obscene or bordering on obscenity. English recognizes 'fucker' but not 'fuckee,' except possibly facetiously. (Lysander Kemp, facing this impasse some four decades ago, in Octavio Paz's *The Labyrinth of Solitude*, left *chingado* in Spanish and added a footnote. But what serves in an essay is obtrusive in fiction. I have yet to work out what to do with *fodidos* in 'O Cobrador.')

If the unvarnished language of the above offends you, perhaps it's a sign that you should carefully examine any translation project before agreeing to undertake it. Better safe than #@*&!# sorry.

English is surprisingly deficient in words midway between clinical terms like 'intercourse' and its street equivalents. Brazilian Portuguese suffers no such dearth, and the translator encounters a superabundance, ranging from comical to pornographic: *comer* (lit., 'eat'), *mandar brasa*, *castigar, trepar, faturar* (our 'score'), *passar na cara* (itself a euphemism for *comer*), *ferrar, brincar-de-papai-e-mamãe, picar, rosetar, fazer sacanagem*, etc., etc., etc. Even more than English, Portuguese is replete with street terminology for male and female genitalia, coitus and its variants, and the four major sexes. Mário Souto Maior's famous (or, depending on your point of view, infamous) *Dicionário do Palavrão e Termos Afins* (Dictionary of Dirty Words and Related Terms), now in at least its sixth edition and my indispensable companion when I translated *Cidade de Deus* (literally, City of God) and *House of the Fortunate Buddhas*, fills some 170 pages with sexual and scatological words and phrases missing from most lexicons. The cornucopia of SL alternative terms for the same biological function severely challenges the translator's ability to dredge up synonyms in the TL.

Pornography or 'pornography'?

Should a translator accept a commission for a book that may be pornographic? First, some general observations, followed by a personal experience.

Even the United States Supreme Court has yet to formulate a universally recognized definition of what the term *pornographic* means in practice. Truly, one man's pornography is another man's erotic realism. (I use 'man' advisedly, since – Anaïs Nin notwithstanding – an estimated 99% of all pornography is produced for and consumed by males.) Perhaps Mr. Justice Stewart Potter was right when he said of hard-core pornography that, though he couldn't define it, 'I know it when I see it.'

If, in a translator's view, a text is pornographic, whatever that means, the translator has the same option as with any other translation: not to accept the job. On the other hand, the concept is a slippery one, and accusations of obscenity have at one time or another been leveled against works that include *Catcher in the Rye* (which contains the f-word), *Tropic of Cancer*, and *Sons and Lovers*, along with others recognized today as significant contributions to 20th-century literature.

The question of possible pornography is one in which individual judgment is the only feasible criterion. If translators can turn down a job because its subject matter, the author's style, or the vocabulary is unappealing, then certainly a subjective assessment of obscenity is, for them at least, an equally valid reason. But if you decline on the basis of 'decency,' I caution as one who can recall a time when words like 'ass' and 'screw' were forbidden on American television and movies dared not show married couples in double beds (much less the unclad human form), be prepared to look prudish or just plain silly to future generations.

As for my own walk on the fringes of respectability:

João Ubaldo Ribeiro, the author of *The House of the Fortunate Buddhas* (*A Casa dos Budas Ditosos*) is a respected member of the Brazilian Academy of Letters whose previous novels include the well-received *Sergeant Getúlio* and *An Invincible Memory*, both of which he himself translated into English. *Fortunate Buddhas* purports to be the 'testimony' of a 68-year-old woman, identified only as CLB, who has lived what many would term a sexually profligate life. The usual adjectives – licentious, libidinous, promiscuous, libertine, and the like – seem inadequate to describe the erotic adventures of a person who espouses pansexuality, finds exclusive heterosexuality abnormal, and unabashedly admits to having seduced her brother, her uncle, and more than one of her professors. Further, though she is childless, she baldly states that she probably would have had sex with her son if she had one. Yet the protagonist is an educated, intelligent, well-read woman who quotes, among others, Dante, Shakespeare, Lacan, Robert Graves, Sartre, and Freud. A complex, many-sided individual, she defies easy categorization, however tempting it might be to label her obsessive-compulsive or aberrant.

Is the novel pornographic? Does it pander? Has the author gone slumming, aiming at the lowest common denominator? One of the accusations against the work is that of 'moral pornography' – i.e., the underlying (presumably decadent) philosophy espoused by CLB. As Gabriel Perissé, of the online magazine *Esfera* (www.esfera.net/011/livros-juribeiro.htm), said, writing in Portuguese,

> Throughout…, the character proceeds as if going crazy, creating veritable dogmas, attacking whomever she considers backward and ignorant. The backward and ignorant deserve the hell of virtue, of boredom. But … the narrator-protagonist will still try to convert them to the sexual

fundamentalism that obsesses her. Life is sex. The problem is sex. The solution is sex. But still, she desires to liberate women from a false and inhibited feminism, excite them, open to them the horizon of absolute sexuality: 'I want [with this text] to provoke many lays, I want frightened husbands, boyfriends, and parents to forbid them to read it, I want there to be people ashamed to read it in public or even to ask for it at the bookstore.' Moral pornography wants to punish the hypocrisy of the past, crushed under a superficial puritanism, ... but most of all the hypocrisy of the present, camouflaged by a superficial libertinism....

As with any example of erotic realism, frank depiction of sexual acts in this work runs the risk of overpowering its other aspects. Just as many tend to view a photograph of a nude first for its titillation value and only afterward see it as an aesthetic interplay of light and shadow – in a word, as a *composition* – a novel that incorporates scenes of unromanticized sexuality opens itself up to the accusation of pornography. Passages constituting a minute fraction of the whole become the standard by which the overall work is judged – and are usually the ones quoted in condemnatory reviews. This is both inaccurate and unfair. *The House of the Fortunate Buddhas* is a frank and ground-breaking literary work, not what used to called an 'appeal to prurient interests.'

Taken out of context – as practically all attacks on erotic realism are – excepts such as the following can seem offensive, even pornographic:

A friend of mine was engaged, with a ring on her finger and everything, to a well known young man that everybody liked,... nice as could be... Everybody referred to them as lovebirds; they were always seen together, kissing and hugging. Well, one day they broke up. It caused general consternation, dozens of hypotheses and speculations, and no one knew the real story. Much, much later, the two of us were having a kind of brief affair and she told me, in bed, what had really happened. Unimaginable, but I think that even today it still happens. She told me that she kept her virginity with him but other than that they did a lot of things – things she now knew, she told me, to be mere frottage. And he was her first, the only experience she'd had. So there they are, making out on a deserted balustrade at the Barra as it was getting dark, him sitting down and her leaning back between his legs, when she felt his hard-on brush against her cheek. Then she started rubbing her face back and forth, on top of the cloth of his pants. And then, she told me, and she had no reason whatever to lie and even seemed to need to get it off her chest, she followed the natural course without thinking about what she was doing. She opened his fly and let his cock pop out. It was

the first time she'd seen it like that, face to face, and she was almost
hypnotized, feeling like she'd never felt before, a shortness of breath, an
anxiousness, the desire to grab all of it at once, her body throbbing from
top to bottom. From there to putting his cock in her mouth was only an
instant – and the courtship ended. He suddenly pulled her head away
and punched her. Not a slap, she said, but a punch that left her with a
bruised chin. What was she thinking? In what whorehouse had she
learned that? Did she think that a wife of his was supposed to do that
disgusting thing, which only the cheapest prostitutes do? If he wanted
that, he'd look for some slut in the streets, not his own wife. And where
did that brazenness come from, where had she learned it, who had she
done it with before? He would never kiss her again; he had no desire to
blow some guy by proxy. Yes, he would marry her, because they were
already engaged, but he would never kiss her again. Being a woman of
character, she decided to put an end to everything right then and
there… She never had anything more to do with him, not even after he
was cuckolded by another girlfriend and remorse-ridden came crawling
back to her.

But it must be remembered that this passage occurs in a context.
Although she was able to surmount them, the protagonist is nevertheless a
creature of her times. Growing up in the early 1950s in a country where
strictures on women were far more pronounced than today, she chafed
under the restraints but was obliged to abide by them at least ostensibly.
Even today, outside the urban centers of Brazil, women are still subject to a
double standard all too reminiscent of half a century earlier. In a very real
sense the novel is an emancipatory exercise, and if there is a justifiable criticism to be leveled against it, it is that it should have been written 40 years
earlier and by a woman…

In addition, another context must be considered before tarring *The House
of the Fortunate Buddhas* with the brush of pornography. It was part of a
series on the Seven Deadly Sins, commissioned with leading Brazilian
literary figures by the publishing house Editora Objetiva. Asked to
produce one of the volumes, Ribeiro chose *luxúria* (lust), no doubt a more
appealing assignment than gluttony or sloth. If lust is to be considered a
sin, it must be because of its obsessive nature, its ability to take control of a
person's life to the exclusion of all else – family, fortune, time, reputation,
productivity. The novel is at its core a psychological portrait of an intelligent, free-thinking woman accidentally born into a society that placed
women in a straitjacket of behavior, especially sexually, and her unwillingness to accept those constraints. As she remarks at one point,

... the need to remain technically a virgin.... Even today I'm amazed at that hymenolatry. It was a woman's honor – what a horror.... Pittigrilli, a writer no one reads today but who was once in vogue and whom younger girls couldn't even go near ... [said] it's sad to live in a society where a woman's honor is located between her legs – my God, how stupid.... How many lives have been lost, how many destinies have been ruined, how many tragedies have occurred, how many convents inhumanly filled to overflowing, because of the honor of so many, so many unhappy women?

The tone of *The House of the Fortunate Buddhas* is about as far from Harlequin romances as possible, and virtually the only characteristic it shares with those works is that it's told from the point of view of a woman. Romanticism and glamour play no role, and the narrator has no need for a strong, protective male in her life. Her delivery is straightforward, often earthy, occasionally coarse. She is not afraid of vulgarities and is equally at ease calling an anatomical feature by its scientific name or its street counterpart. The soft-focus veil of fantasy has been ripped away to reveal in the sometimes harsh light of truth how people really act. If she were called a nymphomaniac (what an old-fashioned, sexist word in the 21st century!), she would wear the title proudly. Unapologetic of her sexuality, she revels in it in a way that would cause little adverse comment were she a man – indeed, a male with her sexual history might well be the object of admiring, even envious epithets such as 'stud,' 'swordsman,' and the like.

I have been asked how I felt translating a book that departs so dramatically from the usual fare of literary translators. Although I was not embarrassed by any of the racy passages (I have a high embarrassment threshold), I admit to a degree of self-consciousness when translating some of them. Creating descriptive accounts of sexual practices is never easy, and the task is doubly hard when the voice is purportedly that of a woman. A man writing in the voice of a woman must skirt any hint of affectation and falsity. As self-evident as the notion may be, it is true that men and women see things differently, and sexuality is no exception.

Alongside the inevitable problems that arise in an translation of a substantive piece of literary work, *The House of the Fortunate Buddhas* presented added hurdles. Its choice of words is often frank and uncompromising and so-called dirty words abound. Its graphic descriptions may offend and shock the reader unaccustomed to such candor in detailing physical intimacies between men and women, women and women, and other combinations. In such cases it is advisable to remember what actors say when questioned about their feelings as they perform degrading or demeaning acts on camera or utter the coarsest of four-letter words: 'I wasn't doing it; my character was.' To successfully bring into English a work of this nature, the translator must set aside any squeamishness. The time for objections to a work's content is *before* accepting the job, not afterward. Once it is under way, the conscientious translator is honor-bound to bring to it the same dedication, commitment, and resourcefulness as with any other project. During my career as literary translator I have occasionally had second thoughts about a work in progress, but not based on its rawness or its graphic depiction of violence or sexuality. As I have emphasized many times, this is one of several reasons that a translator should become thoroughly familiar with a work prior to taking it on.

Because the novel is supposedly a transcription of tapes left anonymously for Ribeiro with his doorman, it was important to preserve the orality of the text. Often, I chose marginally less elegant alternatives – e.g., 'like' used as a conjunction instead of the grammatically preferred 'as' – to achieve this end. The narrator is intelligent and college-educated, but like most people speaks more informally than she would write. This necessitated adopting a vaguely 'centrist' approach to the translation, straying neither into overly elevated diction nor into an overly slangy mode of expression. At the same time, she does not mince words when it comes to vulgarisms, so this linguistic freedom also had to be respected.

Various discrete words and phrases were also potential stumbling blocks. They are of interest primarily to Portuguese-to-English translators, but I list a representative few as a reminder that, whatever the language a translator works with, he or she must remain flexible and adaptable when approaching a literary work. *Surra de cama*: bed-lashing (modeled on tongue-lashing); *chove-não-molha*: dillydallying; *naturebas*: granola crowd; *filosofia de botequim*: fortune-cookie philosophy; *casadíssimo*: ver-ry married.

The translation of *The House of the Fortunate Buddhas* presented a unique challenge: the need to respect and reproduce the author's artistic intent in a novel of a directness seldom encountered by translators. Even in an era in which sexuality is more openly expressed in film and literature, it is rare to come upon a work of undeniable literary merit that, however fleetingly, nonetheless enters realms normally associated with hard-core pornography. It is my hope that the translation will emerge with the same power and impact, as well as the careful craftsmanship, that characterize the original.

The crucial role of revision

It is only a slight exaggeration to say that there is no such thing as a well-written manuscript, whether an original or a translation, only well-*revised* manuscripts. It is in the revision stage that words acquire precision, nuances and hues crystallize, and Mark Twain's oft-quoted distinction between lightning and lightning bug (the difference between the right word and the nearly right word) takes shape. In this section I deal with the last, make-or-break stages of a translation. All the earlier effort that goes into creating an English-language version of a work can be negated or at least diminished if this phase is neglected.

How many drafts?

How long is a piece of string? The number of drafts you do is a function of many intangibles related to your work style, your experience as translator (first translation or 15th?), and sometimes to deadlines. Beginning translators should probably count on at least two or three drafts, while some more experienced translators will be able to manage with a single draft that they then revise as if it were an English-language manuscript.

A draft consists of a complete translation of the text, printed on paper; it is difficult to edit any but the shortest passages on a computer screen. As much as some like to think that the 21st century will see the end of paper, for clarity and ease of use there is no substitute for sitting down and making marks on a sheet.

A color-coded system works for me. The initial corrections are made in red ink. The next round, in blue, and the final round in green. As each change is entered into the computer, I mark the amended text, thus providing instant visual verification that the change has been effected. A slower process, perhaps, than some but one that minimizes inadvertent omissions. I print each draft on paper of a different color, e.g., yellow for first draft, light blue for second, white for final.

The first draft, as we have seen, is normally fairly rudimentary, although practitioners vary in how close they come to a semifinished product at this stage. Its purpose is to capture denotative content, with an eye to fine-tuning during the revision phase. In the first draft I mark in square brackets three kinds of dubious lexemes:

(1)   Those I know in Portuguese but for which I can't immediately find the right English. Example: *abarcar o mundo com as pernas* is an informal phrase meaning 'to undertake many things at once' or 'to want everything at the same time.' But neither of these captures the colloquiality of the original.

(2)   Those I don't know in Portuguese and can't find in any dictionary. Example: the phrase *'do conceito'* in Paulo Lins's *Cidade de Deus*, which occurred frequently but always in an ambiguous context (I finally learned from the author that it meant 'respected'). Such sticky items are marked in **bold face** for later examination.

(3)   Those I'm confident I know but have doubts about my choice of English equivalent. So I might write 'there were many idlers [*vadios*] in the area.' This way I remind myself of the option to use 'loafers,' 'vagrants,' 'bums,' etc., in the final version.

This approach allows me to quickly locate on the computer all the problem areas in the translation. Needless to say, before producing the final draft a search-and-replace must be done to find and eradicate the square brackets and their contents lest they somehow make their way into the printed version.

Once a first draft is finished, the revision process entails several steps. Not all of these will be applicable to every project but are nonetheless highly desirable. In all cases, revise from a printed copy of the translation; studies have shown that reading from a monitor screen is some 20% slower than from hard copy, and paper has the added advantage of portability. Even with a laptop, working in a crowded space like bus or subway is still more difficult than with pen and paper.

First read-through (for mechanics). Correct typographical errors and misspellings; it's all too easy to type a *d* when an *s* is intended, which in many cases changes the verb tense from present to past, and no spell checker will catch it. Make sure punctuation and pagination are accurate. Remove any hyphenation occurring at the end of lines; the only hyphens in the manuscript should be of compound words, like 'read-through.' Otherwise, typesetters may be confused about whether a term like 'goal-keeper,' if broken at the end of a line, should have a hyphen; this is especially important where hyphenated foreign names or nicknames come into play. If the author uses blank lines to indicate transitions, ascertain that they do not fall at the end of a sheet; if so, replace them with centered asterisks. Check paragraph division to conform to the SL text, unless you have consciously opted to modify it. Decide which SL terms, if any, should appear in italics.

Second read-through (for content). Fine-tune choice of words ('facetious' or 'jocose'?). Check for inappropriate verbosity ('the book that I read' or 'the book I read'?). Make sure use of character names is consistent throughout. Look for parallelism in sentence construction (for example, you might change 'He was tall, thin, and had red hair' to 'tall, thin, and red-headed' or perhaps 'He was tall and thin, and his hair was red'). Where called for, tighten the colloquial sound of dialogue: 'Do you see what I mean?' is more formal than 'See what I mean?' Make sure any acronyms or abbreviations are explained.

Only now are corrections entered into the computer, and it is notoriously easy to overlook some of them. It is in this step, time-consuming as it is, that in the interests of a 'perfect' manuscript, I scribble a check mark on the paper copy beside each correction as I input it into the PC.

Third read-through (for sonority, rhythm, euphony). If you have any energy left, this is the final phase, the one in which you place emphasis on the way the prose flows. If you're not lucky enough to have someone to read it to, read it aloud to yourself. Only in this way can you detect the tiny cacophonies that would mar an otherwise smooth translation. Unintended resonance (e.g., 'the lone stranger' resonates on 'the Lone Ranger,' calling for recasting, perhaps 'the solitary stranger') shows up in this phase, along with such less-than-inspired constructions as 'whatever you *do* do, be sure to let me know.'

When looking over a translation prior to submitting it, keep in the forefront one cardinal rule: if it sounds strange in English, it's probably wrong.

Final steps

The translation is complete. Or is it? There are still decisions to be made before you call FedEx or hit that SEND button on your e-mail.

Proofreading

It is axiomatic that we are all our own worst proofreaders: we're so familiar with the material that we tend to see what we expect to see, not what's actually on the page. Also, if we misspell a word to begin with (and our spell checker happened to miss it), how likely are we to catch it in the proofreading? I once wrote – and, sad to say, published – a column in which I repeatedly wrote 'ideolect' instead of *idiolect*. Call it a blind spot, but it serves as, uh, proof that four eyes are better than two.

Not everyone will have intimates willing to read the manuscript and point out errors – like the chestnut about a rattlesnake bite in certain parts of the anatomy, this is when you find out who your real friends are. But if at all possible, have a disinterested pair of eyes peruse the translation. Clearly, such a person should be attuned to niceties of expression, but at this stage your focus is less on the turn of a phrase and more on making sure 'recieved' and its ilk won't rear its ugly head. (So okay, in your case that one's a typo, not a misspelling. Whatever.)

If you must do your own proofing, allow the manuscript to get cold. Three days is a minimum cooling-off period, and a week or even a month is better. It's all too easy to overlook an omitted definite article or a dangling participle, and letting the prose sit for a time will decrease the chances of skipping over it a second time. (To cite an example, in the preceding sentence I accidentally wrote 'all to easy,' no doubt thinking ahead to the following words, 'to write.' No spell checker on earth would catch that.)

Proofreading has become more important than ever in an age in which publishers are cutting costs wherever possible, and you can no longer count on professionals to give your manuscript the perusal it deserves. That's why it's paramount to write into the contract a provision guaranteeing that you'll see page- and galley proofs before the book goes to the printers. Luckily, by then enough time will have passed since submission for it to be a fresh text to you.

162

Grammar checkers

These days, most word-processing software includes a grammar checker. How useful are they? In my experience, anyone with the mastery of language at the level of literary translation will find a grammar checker to be more a hindrance than a helper. I use Microsoft Word but have deactivated the grammar checker. (The spell checker, on the other hand, is something I couldn't live without. Although I can spell *vicissitudes*, for instance, I'm the world's worst multifinger typist and am fully capable of producing *teh* on the keyboard, not to mention my invariable typo *transaltion*. Which is why I've put numerous such entries in Word's Autocorrect glossary to be automatically corrected.)

Why not use the grammar checker? Because whatever setting you choose – Casual, Standard, Formal, and Technical are the choices for Word – there are times in literary translation that the software will flag totally acceptable constructions and individual words. *The tourists were kidnapped by rebel guerrillas* has more impact than *Rebel guerrillas kidnapped the tourists*; nevertheless, it will generate an admonition to avoid the passive construction. Especially in translating dialogue, split infinitives should be the least of one's worries, yet they too will be flagged, along with so-called sexist constructions (i.e., failing to use 'his or her') and a host of other 'mistakes.'

Here, from the sardonic short tale 'Be My Valentine,' by Rubem Fonseca, are a few of the less-than-helpful suggestions made by the grammar checker.

Text as translated	Grammar checker suggestions
lay down beside her	'besides her'
He said he didn't have it and telephoned a friend of his and that man there showed up and brought me here and I lost my head, please forgive me. [frenzied tone]	'Comma use (consider revising)'
'Lying! Me?!'	'? or !'
I got my car and headed for Itanhangá, where the upper crust play polo.	'crust plays'
'What about that car?' said the injured cop, in the middle of the confusion.	'confusion?'
Irony or lack of imagination?	'Fragment (consider revising)'
My pockets full of money, a Mercedes at the curb, and what?	'Fragment (consider revising)'

I don't know about you, but I don't need a kibitzer looking over my shoulder as I translate, and certainly not one as literal-minded, naïve, and tin-eared as the typical software grammar checker.

Verifying against the source language

Perhaps one of every twenty translators will have the luxury of a friend or loved one with the *Sitzfleisch* and the literary sensitivity to perform this act of refinement. The interlocutor, a native speaker of the SL, follows line by line as you read the translation aloud. Time-consuming, labor-intensive, draining – it is all these and more. It's also arguably the single most important step in perfecting a translation prior to submission.

There are several pluses to this approach:

- The other person alerts you to skipped words, sentences, and even longer passages. (I have been known to skip entire paragraphs when returning to work after a break.)
- Infelicities or unclear choices in the translation are pointed out, giving you a chance to mark them for later modification.
- The all-important element of sonority is reinforced, allowing you for the first time to hear the translation with your ears rather than your mind's voice. This is where you become aware of unintentional rhymes ('The man who came today was a friend in every way'), inadvertent puns, undesirable connotations, and other lapses that might otherwise slip by.
- You get pre-submission feedback. Just like an earlier step – in which you asked an intelligent, sensitive friend with an appreciation for literature but no knowledge of the SL to read your manuscript – your interlocutor is almost certain to have questions about the translation. Whether or not you agree with these contentions, your final product will be better for having considered them.

If you're privileged enough to have such a collaborator, make the most of it. Few of us could afford to pay for such a service, and the number of individuals qualified to do it is small. Having my wife perform this herculean task with me has been a powerful motivator, and I consider myself among the fortunate few of our profession.

Where to publish

Now that the manuscript is finished, where will it be published? (That's what this is all about, isn't it, making the author's work known to a greater public.) As I've stressed earlier, for a book-length work you should have a contract in hand from a publisher prior to plunging ahead. That said, this section will examine the pros and cons of various publishing outlets for your translation.

Periodicals

Magazines and even occasionally newspapers are often the first place to consider, especially in trying to publish translated poetry, which normally has less popular appeal than fiction. Periodicals have several advantages: accessibility, variety, less dependence on bean-counters always fixated on the bottom line, fast turnaround time (to be sure, more the case with commercial magazines than academic publications), and in some cases visibility.

Don't overlook the fact that English-language publications also exist in locations where the language is other than English. This is especially true in nations whose languages are spoken nowhere else, like several East European countries, Sweden, and India. I recently published English translations from Portuguese in the English-language edition of a Spanish periodical.

Commercial presses

In the world of publishing, this is the big league, the place most aspiring translators hope to break into. Unsurprisingly, it is also the most difficult. Fortunately, however, there are two kinds of publishing houses in this category, large and small, and their criteria differ.

Mergers in the publishing sector during the last decade had shown how prophetic Helen Lane's words were when she stated in 1995: 'I'm convinced the future of publication lies with small presses. I advise [translators] to publish, even if not for money, with small magazines or, if they can arrange it, with small presses. And, if they already have made some reputation, to approach university presses.' As one large house gobbles up its smaller brethren, the number of potential outlets diminishes accordingly, exacerbating an already discouraging situation. For most translators, at least in the beginning, a small commercial press is their best bet, and publishing there in no way precludes their making it later in the rarefied world of major houses.

Small presses

In literary translation, there is no stigma to publishing in even obscure outlets. In fact, many well known translators, especially those doing translation of poetry, continue to rely on small presses even after they have broken through with large commercial houses. 'Small' does not connote lesser quality; in actuality, the prestige of some small presses exceeds that of many larger publishing houses that focus less on literary merit than on potential sales figures.

One important difference of the small presses is that, though naturally they hope to attract significant numbers of readers, their expectations realistically are more limited, and their press runs reflect this. It is the exception for publishers like Sun and Moon or Catbird Press, to name just two, to print more than a couple of thousand copies.

At the same time, books from small presses may be reviewed as often as offerings from their bigger cousins. Publicity is usually less than with larger presses, but as anyone who has published a translation with some of the giants in the field can attest, even there the advertising support more often than not leaves much to be desired. In fact, promotion, or lack of same, is the number one complaint authors, and by extension translators, voice against their publishers.

Academic presses

This sector is less subject to the vagaries of the stock market, interest rates, and other variables of the world economy than are commercial presses, ever obsessed with profit/loss statements. Though academic presses are less numerous than small presses (not all universities have one, and the majority of four-year colleges do not), the annual output of some of the better-funded ones can exceed that of all but a handful of small commercial presses.

Academic presses have one important advantage over any other type of publishing venture: their works tend to stay in print. Whereas typically a large commercial press expects 90% of the return from a book to come within 12 months of publication, if not sooner, a work from an academic press may continue to sell slowly but steadily over a decade or more, often depending on the level of adoption by colleges and universities.

Another plus for academic presses is that they are more inclined to take a chance on a work of undisputed literary merit but limited popular appeal. In addition, academic presses are more disposed to offer the translator a preface or introduction in which to discuss peculiarities of the SL text and some of the accommodations made. Finally, these publishers are all but unique in their willingness – which sometimes takes the form of insistence

– to place the work in historical perspective, usually in the form of a preliminary essay by the translator or a specialist in the field.

On the negative side, it is undeniable that in general academic presses grind exceedingly slow. Vetting of a manuscript may easily take more than a year because it must pass through the hands of several evaluators, some of whom may not be affiliated with the institution in question. Efforts to nudge leisurely readers are hit-and-miss at best, so patience in dealing with these presses is a prerequisite. And did I mention that the prestige of publishing with most academic presses is often felt to be reward enough? (In plain English, they pay next to nothing.)

A word on self-publishing

Having exhausted all other avenues, you may be tempted to lay out the several thousand dollars to publish your translation through a so-called 'subsidy press,' but think twice. The mere fact that only those involved in the business refer to them as subsidy presses should send up a red flag; everyone else calls them vanity presses. The low esteem in which such enterprises are held in the literary world is evidenced by the refusal of the National Endowment for the Arts, which annually funds a handful of translation projects, to even recognize self-published works as qualifying an applicant. Furthermore, self-publishing almost certainly means self-distribution and self-advertising. The most one can expect by way of promotion is a two- or three-line inclusion in an omnibus ad in a couple of journals. In addition, many libraries have policies prohibiting purchase of books from subsidy presses, and such works are almost never reviewed. Given all these drawbacks, is it really worth it?

The ~~Ten~~ Twelve Commandments of Literary Translation

I   Thou shalt honor thine author and thy reader.
II   Thou shalt not 'improve' upon the original.
III Thou shalt read the source text in its entirety before beginning.
IV   Thou shalt not guess.
V   Thou shalt consult thine author and other native speakers.
VI   Thou shalt consult earlier translations only after finishing thine own.
VII Thou shalt possess – and use – a multitude of reference works.
VIII Thou shalt respect other cultures.
IX   Thou shalt perceive and honor register and tone, that thy days as translator may be long.
X   Thou shalt not commit purple prose.
XI   Thou shalt maintain familiarity with the source-language culture.
XII Thou shalt fear no four-letter word where appropriate.

The Working Translator

The translator's tools

Every craft or profession requires tools. Even those activities we often think of as depending solely on the performer's ability need accoutrements: actors and comedians a stage, a psychiatrist an office, a poet paper and pen. Translators too must have certain tools to carry out their function. This section deals with some of the essentials.

References

No one questions the necessity of reference works for the technical translator, especially in rapidly evolving fields where terminology is growing at a dizzying pace – e.g., computers, medicine, molecular biology. But the literary translator's need for a diverse and up-to-date collection of references is sometimes overlooked.

I recall one self-styled literary translator who boasted, if that's the word, that she had exactly one source language dictionary – and it was lent out at the moment! Such an attitude trivializes the most demanding, most challenging area of translation and amounts to an assumption of infallibility that the first brush with hands-on experience quickly belies. If there is anything that translation teaches, it is humility. If we are honest with ourselves, we are constantly reminded how inadequate our final product is, how far from perfection our best efforts leave us. While a library full of reference works will not make one into a translator, a decent respect for our own limitations obliges us to equip ourselves with the best possible tools to exercise our profession.

True, highly specialized technical translators might conceivably get away with limiting their reference resources to a handful of books on air conditioning, say, or metallurgy. (Less likely to be the case in such broad-gauge fields as law or finance, among others.) But literary translators perforce look upon the entire world as their domain; no area of human endeavor is beyond their purview. The natural corollary is that for literary translators a much wider range of reference works is an absolute necessity.

To quote Peter Newmark (in *More Paragraphs on Translation*), 'Reference books are a translator's main tool, [and] the idea of weaning translators away from dictionaries, as though they can do without them, encourages many translators' extraordinary arrogance.' Newmark also condemns the notion that 'dictionaries are not for establishing meaning, but for "refining it" and dictionaries are therefore generally to be mistrusted.'

I tend to be a reference fanatic. In the course of translating over a dozen novels plus numerous shorter works I have encountered the need to display authoritative (or more accurately, authoritative-sounding) knowledge about topics as varied as chess, Ménière's syndrome, cacao production, precious stones, transgenic experimentation, lotteries, tetrodotoxins, costume jewelry, gambling paraphernalia, ichthyology, illegal drugs, tropical plant species, photography, and Sherlock Holmes – to name only a few. My practice has normally been to buy a specialized dictionary, bi- or monolingual, in any subject area that I might conceivably need someday. I'm an especial pushover for anything Brazilian with the word *gíria* (slang) in its title.

Assuming English as the target language, here are a few of any literary translator's minimum needs.

(1)   An *unabridged* SL monolingual dictionary, preferably the acknowl-
       edged authority in its country of origin; 'condensed' or abridged
       general dictionaries are a waste of money. Why a monolingual SL
       dictionary, the one native speakers use? Because bilingual dictio-
       naries, though an essential part of a translator's arsenal, seldom
       provide the nuance and completeness necessary for serious literary
       translation. Compare two definitions, one in James L. Taylor's *A
       Portuguese–English Dictionary*, which though dated is still my nominee
       for best bilingual P–E dictionary, and the other in the *Novo Dicionário
       Aurélio – Século XXI*, universally known in Brazil simply as 'Aurélio'
       and considered the most comprehensive monolingual dictionary for
       Brazilian Portuguese. Both these examples arose when I was trans-
       lating *The House of the Fortunate Buddhas*.

       (a)   ... *faziam uma porção de coisas, na verdade, agora ela sabia, uma porção
       de meras perfumarias*: 'they did a lot of things that in reality, she now
       knew, were mere *perfumarias*.' (The context here is erotic, which
       narrows the possibilities.)

       Taylor: perfumaria (*f.*) perfumery; (*pl., colloquial.*) soft drinks. No help
       there.

       But in Aurélio the final definition reads (in my translation): Braz.
       Vulgar. See *roçado* (6). And sure enough, *roçado* yields the answer: Braz.
       Vulgar. Sexual practice that consists of arriving at orgasm merely
       through rubbing against another person. *Voilà!* Problem solved: *a lot of
       things that she now knew were mere frottage*. (Count on the French to have
       a word for it.)

(b) *dessas mulheres sem queixo que comparecem a toda reunião reivindicatória e fazem colocações*: 'one of those chinless women who show up at every protest rally and make *colocações*.' The key word is obviously *colocações*, the plural of the noun *colocação*. First, Taylor: colocação *f.* act of placing; placement; position, job; place, standing (as of a soccer team). Hmm. Any of those meanings seems a bit of a stretch. Let's continue the search.

Now Aurélio: [From lat. *collocatione*] f. 1. Act or effect of placing 2. Employment (2) 3. Sale, distribution 4. Investment (of funds) 5. Ling. Placement of words in a phrase. *[In Portuguese, for example, the article precedes the noun.]* 6. Braz. House, usually on stilts, of the Amazonian rubber tapper 7. Braz. Pop. Presentation, exposition (of facts or ideas). Aha!

Although Taylor's entries parallel the first two items in Aurélio and include one meaning not found in the latter, it is not until the seventh and final entry in the monolingual reference that we find the one definition that fits the context and makes sense of the sentence: '*who show up at every protest rally and make speeches.*'

(2) An up-to-date unabridged English dictionary such as the *Oxford English Dictionary* or the *Random House Unabridged Dictionary* (both available on CD-ROM). I have already mentioned the immeasurable help the OED provided in assuring me that every word in *A Samba for Sherlock* was vintage 1886 or earlier, and on innumerable occasions I have unearthed in the OED lexemes to be found nowhere else. Thanks to CD-ROM, gone are the days when owning the OED presented two less than optimal choices: investing well in excess of $2000 for the multivolume edition or the constant irritation of having to use a magnifying class (thoughtfully supplied with the purchase) to peruse the flyspeck-sized print in the two volume miniaturization of the work.

(3) Several general SL-to-TL dictionaries (no single work is likely to meet all of your criteria). Some language pairs are better served in this respect than others. German-to-English or French-to-English offers a sizable variety; Farsi-to-English is obviously more limited. One question is whether to discard old dictionaries as new ones are added; my advice is to retain them on the off-chance that they may contain information no longer considered relevant in newer lexicons, as in the case of the aged Viotti dictionary cited below. Given the inevitable lacunae, many translators perforce begin compiling their own glossaries in an

effort to fill some of the gaps. I was fortunate enough to receive from Donna Sandin an invaluable glossary of Brazilian drug terminology shortly before beginning to translate Paulo Lins's *Cidade de Deus*, a novel in which narcotics play a central role. Although no clearing-house exists of specialized glossaries for translators, informal networking can sometimes lead to a fellow translator who has dealt with similar terminology and can provide useful insights – one more reason for not becoming a hermit while translating.

(4)   A comprehensive multivolume encyclopedia in English (the *Encyclopædia Britannica* is now available on CD-ROM as well as online). Why? Because you will need to look up how we write the name of that Byzantine ruler in English, that Greek philosopher you've never heard of, that figure from Roman mythology – something dictionaries are unlikely to tell you. Of course, in case of doubt check with the author, something I wish I had done with Adam Ferguson when translating *Bufo & Spallanzani* (see 'A day in the life of a literary translator').

(5)   A so-called 'visual dictionary' in the SL if one exists. (A bilingual edition is even better.) Instead of providing definitions, these reference works contain numerous illustrations of objects and list their component parts, often in minute detail. For example, a drawing of a schooner might point out its every element from topsail to hull; another might offer the complete vocabulary of shoes. If a picture is worth a thousand words, these dictionaries are the equivalent of several OEDs. There are times when a verbal description leaves uncertainty as to the specific referent; a drawing or photo usually is unambiguous. For French, a good resource is *Le Visuel, Dictionnaire thématique français anglais*. For Spanish, the *Macmillan Visual Dictionary español-inglés* is a worthwhile addition to your shelf. The marvelous series of Oxford-Duden bilingual visual dictionaries are a godsend; they exist for French, German, Italian, Spanish, and Portuguese; their full title is *The Oxford-Duden Pictorial* [Language name] *and English Dictionary*.

(6)   A good English-language thesaurus. Computer-based thesauruses are fine as far as they go, but they should be considered a starting point. If after checking your computer's suggestions the precise word still eludes you, turn to a comprehensive paper version. Of the many good ones (I own at least a dozen), I first go to *The Synonym Finder* (Rodale Press), but every writer develops his or her own favorite over time.

In sum, a good, solid, unabridged SL monolingual dictionary is the point of departure; in time, the translator should supplement this with more specialized dictionaries. In my own work, 90% of which is translating contemporary authors, I have found dictionaries of Brazilian slang and informal speech indispensable and purchase any I can find, however 'outmoded.' The date of publication is unimportant if it happens to coincide with the period of the work being translated. Upon arriving in Brazil in 1965, the very first dictionary I bought, purchased in a *sebo* (used-book store), was a 20-year-old dictionary of slang by Manuel Viotti. Over two decades later, in 1988 when I was translating *The Golden Harvest*, which is set in the 1930s, I came across a phrase that no dictionary or native informant could clarify for me: *'pulo do nove.'* From contextual evidence it was a confidence game of some kind, but details were lacking. To my delight, the obsolete Viotti work had the phrase and a description of its mechanisms, from which (con artists' tricks differing relatively little across cultural lines) I was able to derive an exact English equivalent – 'badger game.'

Does a six- or sixty-foot shelf of reference works guarantee that the literary translator will find every troublesome SL word, phrase, or idiom? No, but it does increase the probability of locating it and in so doing correctly translating it. And a variety of literary tools is called for. Just as you wouldn't drive a nail with pliers, you shouldn't expect a general dictionary to provide an esoteric technical term or a specialized dictionary to explicate idioms.

How to use dictionaries for translation

Should a translator first turn to a bilingual or a source-language monolingual dictionary for the meaning of a word or idiom? This is a question of style and a trade-off; do whatever works best for you. When you have a solid grasp of the meaning of a word but are fumbling for its TL equivalent, a bilingual dictionary will probably save some thumbing through a thesaurus. On the other hand, for vaguer terms where you're less than totally sure of the concept, consulting the monolingual SL dictionary first may be the best approach. The *perfumarias* example above is a good case in point.

Except for abstruse, erudite words the first definition listed under a headword is seldom the one you're looking for. Sometimes it's only the fifth or the tenth meaning that fits the context; sometimes it's none. The more complete the dictionary, the greater the likelihood of breaking the impasse. (As stated earlier, for the serious word-professional the only non-specialized dictionary worth owning is an unabridged dictionary.)

Despite efforts of linguistic purists and national academies, every written language has variant spellings of certain words. In English, *aesthetics* and *esthetics* coexist; in Spanish, *hierba* and *yerba*. A good dictionary will make allowances for such lexical twins, while usually saving space by giving definitions for only one. In literature, especially in dialogue, the translator should be prepared to encounter spellings that, deliberately or inadvertently, differ from standard orthography.

One example is so-called sight dialect, in which, using English as illustration, *women* might be written as *wimmen* to denote the speaker's lack of education. (The same ploy can also be used to make any speaker, however serious, appear ridiculous.) The experienced translator, failing to find a word in a dictionary, always looks for likely alternative spellings. In Portuguese, for instance, a non-tonic *o* is usually pronounced *u*, and on more than one occasion I have read *fudido* or *culhões*, to cite two obscene examples. Similarly, in that language *e* is frequently pronounced like *i* when non-tonic; to indicate hypercorrection (like Americans who mistakenly pronounce Miami as 'Miama') and presumably affectation on the speaker's part, an author may inject a word legitimately written with *i* as if it were *e*. In my maiden effort at translating a novel, *Memoirs of a Gigolo*, immediately on page 1 of the first-person narrative I encountered *rolemã*. There is no such word in Portuguese. Only later, after establishing the narrator's voice (parvenu, arriviste, less intelligent than he supposes), did it occur to me that this was *rolimã*, meaning 'ball bearings' (French *roulement*). At the very outset Marcos Rey had used this device to quickly establish character, an effect that I attempted to replicate in the translation by misspelling Gandhi as 'Ghandi.' While no hypercorrection, it did offer a hint of the protagonist's level of education.

Electronic vs. printed dictionaries

With the exception of translators of poetry, many of whom prefer to use pen and paper, perhaps to maintain contact with the physicality of the written word, most translators of literature in the 21st century have made their peace with the computer age. (In the interest of full disclosure, this book was written on a PC running under Windows 98.) The increasing availability of dictionaries in software form raises the question of which is better for literary translators.

It is beyond dispute that for translators in other fields (e.g., technical, financial, scientific), compilation of a glossary of terms in their area of specialty is a *sine qua non*. Especially in legal or medical translation, where recurrence of entire paragraphs is fairly common, the need for boilerplate dictates computerizing as much of this repetitive material as possible. For translators in such fields, after all, time is money. But these considerations normally do not arise for literary translators, who seldom charge by the word for book-length projects and whose deadlines are usually longer.

If you decide to opt for a software version of a dictionary, which one do you adopt? In English there is a large variety to choose from, including the venerable *Oxford English Dictionary*, which has been my vade-mecum for years. If for no other reason than freeing up precious desk surface in your work area, the OED on CD-ROM is a must, occupying almost no space and obviating the need for wrestling with heavy volumes. In addition, like all software dictionaries, it affords search criteria (for example, all words with a specific ending, or 'reverse search' whereby all headwords containing a specified phrase can be located) that no print dictionary can offer. Also, many monolingual English dictionaries on CD-ROM will pronounce any word on command. One leader in the field is the aforementioned *Random House Unabridged Dictionary* (RHUD), which can be purchased as a print/CD-ROM package. While the RHUD is not as comprehensive as the OED (what is?), it is more than adequate for most definitional tasks in English.

But what about software versions of foreign dictionaries? In some cases they can be found at well-stocked bookstores that specialize in texts in the given language. Even so, the selection is usually limited and they tend to be significantly more expensive than their English-language counterparts. A surer way of acquiring them is by visiting a country where the language is spoken (the trip may even be tax-deductible; see 'Financial matters'). Admittedly, there is no practical way to assess how well software works before taking it home and putting it through its paces; when the purchase is made abroad, it is all but impossible to effect a return or refund, which raises the risk factor in comparison to the print version. Leafing through a book gives a fair idea of its usefulness; reading the blurb on a software box doesn't.

Another caveat about going electronic is the notorious tendency of software to come a cropper at the most inconvenient time. There is little that can go wrong with a book short of physical abuse, and even a broken spine doesn't end a book's usefulness. If you purchase foreign software, make sure it's on CD-ROM rather than diskette; this will allow reinstallation if anything goes awry. Unfortunately, in the so-called developing nations and a few developed countries like Italy, copy protection is still a way of life, so expect the software to ask you to reinsert the CD-ROM in the appropriate drive every few months for verification. That said, I have found the

Aurélio on CD-ROM so helpful and easy to use that for the first time I have not bothered to buy the print version.

A final thought about electronic versions of dictionaries, whether foreign or in English: for the foreseeable future, the range and variety of specialized dictionaries will continue to be limited. And out-of-print books are unlikely candidates for publication on CD-ROM – it's the print version (if you can find it) or nothing. On my own shelf there are at least 20 print dictionaries for each one in software format, for reasons of availability. For example, in book form I boast close to two dozen works on slang but don't know of a single slang dictionary for computers. In short, even the most hard-core techie among us acknowledges that books will be around for a long time

Dictionaries on the Internet

The day will come when on-line dictionaries will replace many if not most of those in use today, whether in book form or as computer software. That day is still far off, and for the time being the working translator will find it more profitable to rely upon existing resources. Nevertheless, there are times when the Internet can bring to bear resources unavailable elsewhere to address a translation problem.

At the outset I must emphasize one overweening precaution: anyone can post anything on the Internet, and the information found there is only as reliable as its source. An even more questionable dictum than 'If it's in print it must be true' is 'I know it's so because I got it off the Internet.' If in doubt, verify from an independent source what you find on the World Wide Web.

Of the many on-line dictionaries, it is my experience that they almost never have anything that can't be found in print or in software. Their major utility seems to be for the casual user; if I wanted to discover how to say 'refrigerator' in Hungarian (a language of which I know only the word *goulash*) that's where I'd look.

With these caveats in mind, the translator can make careful use of the linguistic resources available on the Web. To do so, some familiarity with a search engine is a necessity. Of the scores available (Go, Infoseek, AltaVista, WebCrawler, Yahoo, etc.), I find All the Web (www.alltheweb.com) to be the fastest and more complete. Of course, given the volatility of the dot-com world, by the time this guide is in print one or more of these resources may have gone to the greater server in the sky.

Using All the Web, I searched for a term in a passage from the first chapter of a novel by José Sarney, who besides being a former president of

Brazil is an accomplished writer. The word was *terecô*, which I surmised was a regional term from the author's native state of Maranhão but was not in any dictionary I consulted; queries among numerous Brazilians were equally fruitless. A search on All the Web came up with 19 entries, among which was a folklore-oriented site that solved the riddle. (For those who care, *terecô* refers to an African-Brazilian religion found in Maranhão.)

Given the spottiness of the Web and its often dubious reliability, I prefer to use it as a last resort, but ask me again in five years.

Workspace and work time

Like any endeavor with an aesthetic component, translation is as much perspiration as inspiration. It has been said that in writing, execution is all; translation is a form of writing, so be prepared to exert significant amounts of effort to turn out a polished, literate finished product. While the divine spark must come from within, this section offers some tips on organizing the externalities.

Q. What's a good work plan for a literary translator?
Presumably, you're asking how a translator can most efficiently make use of his or her time. A second assumption is that the translator is not occupied exclusively in this activity, as those who make their living solely from literary translation are the rare exception.

The translator's scarcest resource is time. If, as is likely, you're engaged in other work forty hours a week, translation is perforce restricted to evenings and weekends. Or if you have a family, especially one with young children, and don't work outside the house, you still have the equivalent of (at least) a full-time job; this means your translation hours are equally limited, making a judicious division of time essential. The following tips may be of help, though naturally adjustment must be made to accommodate individual cases.

Establish a regular work routine. If possible, let it be known that 'your' hours are from, say, seven to nine p.m., during which someone else is expected to answer the phone, take messages, etc. (Admittedly, this may entail some retraining of family members.) While two hours a day doesn't seem like much, over weeks and months it adds up. And two highly productive hours is better than four hours of constant interruptions. Nothing derails a train of thought as surely as a phone ringing in the middle of a difficult paragraph. Some translators go as far as turning over the ringer on their phone during those precious couple of hours, leaving the trusty answering machine to field any messages.

Take breaks. Translation is a form of artistic expression, and the muse does not punch a time clock. For the sake of both your physical and mental health, feel free to get up from the computer (does anyone still use a typewriter?) and stretch your legs, go to the fridge for something cool, or just give your eyes, mind, and backside a rest.

Have your materials at hand. Efficient use of time means avoiding unproductive side activities like having to search for a dictionary or suddenly having to go out for more paper for your printer. Try to combine such trips with other shopping, and it's not a bad idea to keep an extra (printer cartridge, fax paper, ream of letterhead, whatever) on hand for just such eventualities. Having all your materials ready to go the moment 'your' time kicks in can save both precious minutes and unnecessary frustration.

Set up a workspace. In even small residences there is probably a corner that can be reserved for translation (a separate office, however cramped, is even better). Keep your materials there, because working off a kitchen table, while doable, is far from ideal. Having your own space both creates an atmosphere free of associations such as housekeeping and avoids distractions from others' television watching and the like.

Q. What kind of workspace is best for translating?

The answer is as varied as are people themselves. Some work uncomplainingly in surroundings that would drive others crazy (think of prison memoirs). There are those who labor with pencil and paper in the computer age. Others manage to produce good writing while juggling young children, a spouse, two dogs, and a cat. It takes all kinds…

Still, it is undeniable that some environments are more conducive to the demands of translation than others. Quiet is a desideratum. Enough space to spread out a few reference materials. A comfortable chair. None of these is a *sine qua non* but as with most mental activities, the fewer distractions the better.

In simplest terms, translators' workspaces fall into two categories: the private and the public. First the private.

The overwhelming majority of literary translators work in their place of residence. Commodious house or cramped apartment, it makes little difference. I am writing this in the same location where I recently completed the translation of a lengthy novel – one corner of a two-room flat. The key ingredient for a workspace is an area in which materials can remain undisturbed for an indefinite period. Most translators are given to bibliographic sprawl, and there are few things worse than not finding a needed item where you left it. For that reason, a kitchen table is not the ideal spot for one's workstation. If you must share space, have a large box in which all materials can be placed at the end of each session, or whenever the area must revert to its primary function.

Public workspaces include locations such as a library or anywhere that a laptop computer or even a notepad can be comfortably used. While a park bench may be stretching it, any place that affords a degree of solitude and allows concentration on the task at hand is at least potentially feasible. Works of art have been created on trains, in bistros, and even in jails; attitude trumps physical surroundings.

Q. As one about to embark on her first translation (a novel), how much time should I allow for the project? Put another way, how many words a day should I expect to produce?

The answer depends on a number of factors. Do you work in a distraction-free environment – which largely equates to no children? Is the novel 'difficult' or 'easy'? (In your case, hard to determine as you have no basis for comparison.) Will you be undertaking other translation tasks simultaneously? Will the translation entail research on your part? Is the author available for consultation? How many revisions (drafts) do you expect to do? These and a myriad of other variables will determine your normal output.

That said, bear in mind that for a translator there are relatively few 'normal' days. Other than the physical setting where the actual work takes place, each day differs from the last, and the translational challenges are seldom the same. This is one thing that makes literary translation both more laborious and more fun than, say, translating birth certificates or foreign college transcripts: boilerplate is all but non-existent. Consequently, output may vary with the complexity of a given passage; paradoxically, a 'good' day may be one in which fewer pages – but polished, virtually final-draft pages – are produced.

Then there is the psychological element. The inevitable mental wear and tear means that even the most seasoned translator cannot crank out pages by the dozen, day after day. Practically speaking, few can sustain such a pace; while exhilarating, literary translation is also exhausting. But seldom is it boring.

There's an additional facet to the psychological component. To be sure, in other areas of translation big stakes may be riding on the accuracy of one's efforts: medical translation, where getting it wrong can be fatal; legal translation, where millions of dollars may be lost if a modifier, or even a comma, is misplaced; technical translation, where the widget may not work if the instructions aren't letter-perfect. But literary translation has its outside stresses too – and I'm not referring solely to deadlines.

For one thing, the conscientious literary translator has an invisible kibitzer looking over his or her shoulder: the author. To a great extent, the SL writer's reputation, at least in the target language, is at the mercy of the translator. If done well, a translation may gain the author acclaim not enjoyed in the SL (the famous 'better-than-the-original' syndrome). When done badly, it may lead critics to ask what all the shouting's about or succumb to the temptation to critique the work solely on its plotting and characterization, ignoring the crucial issue of style. This psychological weight – the awareness that an important writer will be judged through the prism of one's choice of words – can slow down one's output. Unfortunately, it is a factor that cannot be assessed a priori.

Yes, there will be times when everything comes together – a cooperative text, a coinciding of subject matter and translator's expertise – and the words seem to flow directly from one's fingertips as the translation emerges as fast as one can type. Such occasions, alas, are rare. For every day that produces a dozen pages there will many more that result in a meager two or three – not to mention the times when circumstances preclude any output at all. (You do allow for emergencies when negotiating a deadline, don't you?)

It's not side-stepping the issue to say it's impossible to counsel you in the abstract about expected or desirable 'throughput' (odious bizspeak term). Only experience can determine that. But I can assure you that after you've done four or five novels you'll develop a feel for budgeting time. Even so, it's sound policy to err on the side of caution, and when agreeing to a deadline, always allow yourself 10 to 15% leeway. If you finish early, the publisher will be the last to voice any objections.

Financial matters

The point has been made earlier in this guide that money is not the prime motivator for literary translators. Nevertheless, any income deriving from the endeavor is, like all income, subject to taxation and should be part of a coordinated business strategy. This section does not purport to be Business for Dummies but rather an introduction to some of the financial aspects that arise once translation starts to bring in money. Though literary translation is unlikely to provide the major portion of one's income, it is still important to adopt a consistent and systematic approach to this side of the profession, thus avoiding headaches further down the line.

Several things should be borne in mind. First, the following suggestions do not constitute legal advice. Second, they are geared to tax legislation as it exists of this writing in the United States; other countries' laws will differ. Third, tax laws are constantly changing, so in case of doubt consult a financial consultant or an attorney specializing in taxation.

Taxes

Just as it is essential to keep track of manuscript submissions, it is equally vital to maintain an overview of your income and outlay related to translation, as a matter of good business practice generally and specifically for tax purposes. Taxes on the income generated can be offset in part, sometimes *in toto*, by expenses connected to the profession. But in order to qualify for deductions you must be able to document costs, and this is where good record-keeping pays off.

What business expenditures are tax-deductible? As long as your intent is to make a profit, any expenses arising out of the pursuit of your profession are potentially deductible. Under current IRS regulations you are even allowed to show a loss in a given tax year, provided you have offsetting profits in other years. An unbroken sequence of red-ink years, however, increases chances of an audit and might lead the IRS to conclude that rather than a profession you are engaged in a hobby, which is of course not deductible. A non-translation example: you own a boat that you rent out a week or two per year and use the rest of the time for pleasure. Deducting mooring expenses, gasoline, upkeep, etc., might well raise a red flag at Internal Revenue. So the ability to document your expenses is paramount, in case you're ever called upon to prove your seriousness.

For literary translators, typical deductibles might include the following:

- *Dictionaries, reference works, and books, both SL and TL.* Just as the first two are tools of the trade, so works of fiction, poetry, and even non-fiction are important adjuncts to your profession. The typical literary translator is actively engaged in staying *au courant* in the source culture, and that means reading widely in it. Because building an expertise in literary translation signifies possessing a broad range of knowledge, eclectic reading necessitates exposure to a voluminous spectrum of materials from the source culture.

- *Computer equipment and software.* For translators in the 21st century it is a fundamental requisite to be computer literate and to have access to the hardware and software that can maximize output. The wasteful, mind-numbing drudgery of retyping pages is a relic of a bygone age, and skillful use of a computer can turn a 12-month project into one requiring half that time. Naturally you plan to deduct your computer, monitor, and printer, but don't overlook all supplies, from paper to printer cartridges or toner, as well as any repairs. The software you run on the computer, if it ties in with translation, is also deductible, as is a laptop computer to supplement a desktop model, assuming you work while traveling. If you pay for training in using a software program, that too is deductible. If you run a web site dealing with translation, costs such as registration of domain name and hosting fees may be 100% deductible.

- *Office equipment and supplies.* Is a photocopier deductible? A fax? How about an electric stapler, a paper shredder, a scanner, or a set of speakers for your computer? Arguably, even the latter could be deductible if it could be shown that they are intended for aural repro-duction of the SL (for example, tuning in streaming-audio broadcasts from overseas). With both computer equipment and office machines, one consideration is whether equipment should be deducted or 'expensed'; under current US tax regulations, equipment can be expensed (written off in a single year), simplifying bookkeeping and increasing the current year's deductions.

- *Phone and Internet service.* A separate line for business is certainly deductible, and if you have a dedicated line for your computer, it may be wholly or partially deductible. Be prepared to show that you use the Internet principally or exclusively for business-related purposes – e.g., consulting online dictionaries, visiting web sites in the language you translate from, participating in language-related chat rooms, communicating via e-mail with other language professionals, authors, and the like. Naturally, fees for an ISP (Internet service provider) are deductible only if tied to income generation, not if your teenage son is using it for role-playing games. Long-distance charges connected to the business of translating are another deductible, and one more reason for having a phone line exclusively for business purposes is that the separate monthly bill makes it easy to keep track of these expenses.

- *Travel.* Legitimate travel abroad for various business-related ends. A contemporaneous notebook showing mileage serves as documentation of expenses incurred while driving your car for business. It is perfectly kosher to spend a week or two annually in the source culture, where you confer with authors, update your reference materials, learn new terminology, and seek out authors to translate. If an international translation conference takes you to, say, Guadalajara, that too is beyond reproach. One caveat: the IRS and Inland Revenue frown upon disguised vacations, so be ready to document the bona fides of your trip.

- *Periodicals.* Any professional magazines or newsletters you subscribe to, including those from overseas. Newspapers, under certain circumstances. By the way, if you publish a translation periodical or newsletter yourself, any non-reimbursed costs are deductible.

- *Associations.* Membership dues in professional associations like F.I.T., the American Translators Association, the American Literary Translators Association, along with local or regional groups, are deductible, as are costs of attending their meetings (including gasoline expenses and tolls).

- *Conferences.* Registration fees, lodging, car rental, transportation to and from the airport, food, and airfare are all deductible. As always, keeping receipts is a must.

- *Library expenses.* Is there a charge for interlibrary loan usage? How about the library fee itself? Photocopying done there. Transportation to and from.

- *Postage.* A postage meter. Costs of mailing or overnight shipping of manuscripts. A post-office box.

- *Other expenses.* Business cards, stationery, advertising (admittedly, seldom a concern for literary translators, unlike their counterparts in other fields of translation), checking account fees, safe deposit box, entertainment of clients, money paid to assistants (such as a proofreader or editor you hire to look over the manuscript).

- *Office space.* If an area in your place of residence is set aside *exclusively* for income-producing work purposes, a portion of your household expenses equal to that area's percentage of your total floor area is deductible. In a six-room house with one room reserved for translating, you might be eligible to deduct approximately 16% of your heating, electricity, and maintenance costs. A word of caution: this is one of the areas that arouses the attention of the IRS. Also, the home-office provision is intended for the self-employed; if you have a day job and your employer provides you with an office, you're ineligible for the home-office deduction under most circumstances. Again, if in doubt consult a specialist.

Many of the professional expenses will be incurred in a foreign currency, which can cause problems. My advice: at the time of purchase, note on the receipt the equivalent price in your currency. Exchange rates fluctuate, and trying to reconstruct the dollar value at a later date is nettlesome.

Finally, for those working in the United States, a reliable source of up-to-date information is *Tax Guide for Small Business* (Pub. #334), Department of the Treasury, IRS (available free from the US government, online at www.irs.ustreas.gov/prod/forms_pubs/pubs/p334toc.htm). In addition, there are commercial publications such as *J.K. Lasser's Taxes Made Easy for Your Home-Based Business*, which are frequently updated.

Setting a price

The next part of this guide addresses contracts. For now, the issue of determining what to charge for a translation warrants its own discussion. Let me emphasize from the start that every translator is free to charge whatever he or she sees fit, and no rates table exists to influence that decision. What's more, I am speaking as an individual and in no way as representative of any organization in proffering these remarks. (*Pace*, Federal Trade Commission.)

When asked by inexperienced translators how much they should charge for their work, I invariably reply, 'What you think it's worth.' Put another way, you should charge an amount that you feel adequately compensates you for the effort expended on the project, one with which you will be satisfied even if not a penny of royalties ever materializes (which is the case in at least 90% of all translations).

How much you ask for should in some way be a function of your stature as translator. Is this your first book or your 20th? Have you established a track record or are you asking the publisher to go on faith? Have you dealt with this publisher before and are you on good terms with the editors? All of these factors can impact upon the final rate.

A decision early on is whether to go with a per-word or a flat rate. Generally, although practice differs, briefer pieces like short stories, articles, or non-fiction works such as encyclopedia entries or sections of museum catalogs call for a per-word approach. It is less common for book-length projects to quote a per-word rate; usually a flat sum is stipulated for the entire work.

Many factors enter into the determination of price. Among those that, ceteris paribus, would go into the calculation:

- *Tightness of deadline.* Having six months to translate a 300-page novel is not the same as doing it in 10 weeks. Even leaving aside the issue of maintaining quality under such pressure, a short time-frame most likely means suspending any other translational activities for the duration.

- *Research on your part.* Even with the availability of online resources, having to track down obscure references takes time. One frequently encountered example is passages translated from English into the SL, which you then must retranslate verbatim into English. It's axiomatic that you must find the exact quote rather than rely on hoping for the best through a back translation, which never produces a text identical to the original. A quotation from Shakespeare is fairly trivial, but what about one from Ruskin? How do you find it, and how long will it take?

- *Your eagerness to undertake the translation.* On more than one occasion I've been approached to translate works that for one reason or another failed to arouse my enthusiasm initially. I therefore mentioned a figure sufficiently high to appeal to my cupidity if not to my higher instincts. Where the deal was consummated, I soon found myself properly motivated; where no agreement was reached, I was happy to turn to other projects. One observation: whatever your reasons for accepting a commission, professionalism demands that you do your utmost to create a well-crafted final product.

- *Overall difficulty of the text.* Just as in competitive diving more points are awarded for the degree of difficulty of the dive, some texts are inherently harder to translate than others and fees should be set accordingly. Although the assumption here is a work of prose, the inclusion of numerous passages of poetry or of song lyrics increases the challenge and the time involved and must be taken into account.

Other translation-related sources of income

Besides the obvious areas such as commercial, financial, and technical translation, about which readers of this guide presumably need little orientation, there are opportunities for literary translators to earn additional income in fields related to their own.

- *Editing*. Some literary translators, especially those translating out of their mother tongue, can benefit from the input of a well-trained professional in the field. Any contract arrived at is strictly between the translator and outside editor; the publishing house is not a party and will not underwrite any of the extra cost. Unsurprisingly, the best editing is usually that done by a person possessing the same SL/TL skills as the translator. The extent of editing should be agreed upon beforehand and fees set accordingly. Suggesting changes in commas and semicolons is one thing; practically rewriting the work is another. (From experience I can state that rewriting takes longer than translating from scratch.)

- *Proofreading*. After a certain number of read-throughs, typographical errors become all but invisible to the author or translator; knowing what we meant to write blinds us to what we actually wrote. A fresh mind and second pair of eyes can be invaluable, and these days publishers do less and less proofing, with sometimes lamentable results. As a rule, proofreading is less labor-intensive than editing and rates would be commensurately lower.

- *Speaking engagements*. A translator who establishes a reputation is often asked to address translators' groups, sometimes internationally. (I've been fortunate to receive invitations to talk to conferences in Brazil on several occasions.) While any income generated does little more than cover expenses, the opportunity to travel and to interact with intelligent, highly motivated individuals is refreshing – translation, after all, tends to be a solitary activity. On a level closer to home, there are numerous civic organizations – e.g., women's clubs, Jewish Centers, discussion groups, even nursing homes – that invite speakers. While honorariums are modest, it also represents an opportunity to sell some of the extra copies of your translations.

- *Evaluation*. How do publishers decide whether to bring out a translation of an author whose language is unfamiliar to them? Often, an outside reader with command of the SL is hired. Charged with preparing a short report (2–3 pages) of the work, he or she evaluates the book in terms of its literary value, potential commercial appeal, and other elements as specified by the publisher. Theoretically, a potential conflict of interest may exist because in some cases the evaluator may eventually be offered the translation, but this is seldom a problem in real life. Many more are called than are chosen, and if an evaluator gives a work a positive review, it is presumably because he or she feels it's worthy of translation. Personally, I sidestep the issue by accepting only works in Spanish to review, while restricting my translation work to Portuguese.

Contracts

As prices were dealt with – or not – in the preceding section, the discussion here will focus on non-financial aspects of contracts. Most laymen in any field mistakenly assume that a contract is carved in stone and that like-it-or-lump-it prevails. That is far from accurate, and this part of the guide is intended to alert you to your room for maneuvering when negotiating a contract.

Faced with his or her first contract, a formidable-looking document, it may be difficult for a translator to accept that a contract is first and foremost an *agreement* between two or more parties. As one of the signatories you have the right to ask for modifications in the contract before affixing your name to it. Whether they will be granted is another question, but it's a truism that unrequested emoluments are seldom offered. The old squeaky-wheel metaphor applies here as in most cases.

I won't insult your intelligence by saying it is imperative to read *any* contract before signing it, but I do want to point out that it is easier than most people believe to effect a change in a contract. All that's necessary is to cross out provisions that you disagree with and/or add paragraphs that you feel should be in the document, then write your initials next to each modification; this is done on each copy of the contract, including the one you keep.

What to include

Now, what to add to a translation contract?

Credit. Under any but the most unusual circumstances, it is current practice for the translator's name to appear on the title page, directly below the author's. (The exceptions include photo books, large 'coffee table' books, and museum catalogs, where the translator's name normally appears in the so-called 'back matter' at the very end. In some non-fiction works, it is printed on the copyright page, a regrettable custom that we translators should labor to expunge.) In my recent translations I have also incorporated a stipulation that following any biographical data on the author, a blurb about the translator will appear. I'll spare you the details, but suffice it to say that I limit my self-promotion to no more than the number of lines about the author. The added cost to a publisher of accommodating you in this fashion is exactly zero. I prefer to look upon this not as ego-aggrandizement but as a tiny contribution to the professionalization of literary translation, a reminder that without the translation there would not exist the physical object that the reader now holds.

After you have a few published translations under your belt, you might want to add a clause specifying that your name will appear on the cover – either front or back. I didn't venture to ask for this until my fourth novel; you may want to be bolder.

Can you specify that the translation be published under a pseudonym or anonymously? Yes, although that would seem to defeat the purpose. That said, I can imagine a situation in which a translator might need the shield of anonymity – e.g., one of the courageous men and women who translated Salman Rushdie's *The Satanic Verses*. Similarly, if one wishes to avoid identification with the contents of a work (translation of *Mein Kampf* comes to mind), a pseudonym might be insisted upon in the contract. Along these lines, I was once approached to do a 'ghost translation,' which would have been an uncredited translation of the memoirs of a Cuban defector that were to pass as an English-language original. The project never came to fruition.

Translator's copies. In the US, most publishers will provide the translator with 10–12 free copies of the finished work. Since the marginal (extra) cost to the publisher is next to nothing, I normally ask for 20 and have been turned down only on a couple of occasions. Bear in mind that with expensive books on art or photography different standards apply, and one copy of each of the hardcover and paperback editions is probably all you can expect.

An important addendum you should place in the contract is this: the translator reserves the right to purchase at deep discount *x* copies of the book when it is about to be remaindered or (shudder) pulped. Just as extinction is forever, so too once a book goes out of print, that's probably the last it will ever hear of itself. I bought 100 hardcover copies of João Ubaldo Ribeiro's *The Lizard's Smile* from the publisher for a song and donated them to major libraries throughout the country, thus saving the work from total oblivion. (Did I mention that the expense is tax-deductible?) And they make nice Christmas gifts.

Payment terms. In the States, the most frequent method of payment is one-half of the advance (see the Glossary) at the time the contract is signed, one-half upon delivery of a satisfactory manuscript. Any departure from this should be nipped in the bud. The only publisher that sent me a contract outlining payment in thirds quickly relented when I struck that clause out and substituted the customary half-and-half arrangement.

Proofreading. This task should not be looked upon as onerous but as a

privilege. Monolingual Anglo-Saxon typesetters (and even in this comput-
erized age there are still publishers that rekeyboard the manuscript *ab
initio*) are prone to making *beaucoup* mistakes when transcribing words of
foreign origin, especially names. Only you can prevent their appearing in
print, and in the contract you should insist on having the opportunity to vet
the manuscript in both galleys and page proofs. By that time the translation
will have become cold enough that it's almost like new material to you, and
you'll be able to catch typos that would have eluded you before. Don't let
happen to you what befell me in my first translation of a novel, *Memoirs of a
Gigolo*. I was sent galleys but not, it later turned out, page proofs. On the
galleys I saw that 'Sigsmund' Freud (an indication that the protagonist's
imperfect grasp of things extended to psychology) had erroneously been
'corrected' by an editor to 'Sigmund.' So I changed it back to Sigsmund and
added [*sic!*] to make sure the typesetters understood. You guessed it: when
the book hit print, it read: 'Sigsmund [*sic!*] Freud.'

The © question

Copyright law is an exceedingly complex area fraught with complica-
tions and therefore one into which only a specialist should venture.
Though international agreements may apply, the specifics of copyright
provisions vary from country to country, making this definitely no area for
amateurs. Fortunately, for most translators the matter can safely be left in
the hands of the publishers, whether of periodicals or books. In cases where
the project originates with the publisher (i.e., you're commissioned to do
the translation), fortunately the translator has no responsibility for
assuring availability of copyright.

One exception worth mentioning: most publishers include a protective
clause in their contracts by which the translator guarantees the originality
of the translation – in other words, that it is not plagiarized. Copyright
infringement might well be alleged if significant portions of a preexisting
translation found their way into a new version (retranslation) of the work.
For ethical translators, a category comprising every practitioner I have
known, this does not constitute a problem.

There are times, however, when having unearthed a novel, poem, or
short story that cries out be translated you want to start the process rolling.
Where do copyrights come in? The holder of the foreign rights has absolute
control over the conditions under which the work can be translated into
other languages. Depending on how the original contract was worded, this
means either the author or, more frequently, the publisher. When in doubt,
write or fax the publisher first. If, as is sometimes the case, you already

enjoy a relationship with the author, he or she will know how to go about obtaining foreign rights. In case of doubt, protection under copyright should be assumed.

As copyright can raise some pretty tricky issues, you owe it to yourself to achieve at least a cursory acquaintance with the field. As of this writing, the non-signatory nations to the Berne Convention for the Protection of Literary and Artistic Works (and consequently having no copyright relations with the United States) were Afghanistan, Bhutan, Ethiopia, Iran, Iraq, Nepal, Oman, San Marino, Tonga, and Yemen. The remaining 96.6% of the world's population is covered, making for rather small odds of finding literary works free of copyright. In case you're interested, a work under copyright 'is automatically protected from the moment of its creation and is ordinarily given a term enduring for the author's life plus an additional 70 years after the author's death' (US Copyright Office data).

For those treading the unfamiliar terrain of contracts, I strongly recommend visiting the web site of PEN American Center (www.pen.org) and downloading the translator's Model Contract found there. It addresses many of the doubts facing translators at all levels of experience. As for copyright *per se*, the best place for obtaining information is from the copyright office of the United States government, at:

   http://www.loc.gov/copyright/circs/circ1.html.

This site, from which numerous documents can be downloaded, has all the data necessary to pursue a copyright and reflects the latest US laws. It should be noted that there is no such thing as an 'international copyright,' given the differing laws of various countries, but the overwhelming majority of nations are signatories to copyright-protection agreements of various kinds.

When contracts aren't honored

Let's suppose your contract specifies that your name will appear on both the title page and the front cover. But you end up buried in the middle of a long list of acknowledgments. You contact the publishers and they express deep regrets for the 'oversight.' What to do?

It depends on how miffed you are. In this litigious society of ours, the possibility always exists of suing over a perceived or actual wrong. Is this the way you want to go? Sure, it seems like an open-and-shut breach-of-contract case, but unless you hire Johnny Cochran your chances of proving damages are slim. Was your professional reputation besmirched? Did it cost you other jobs? Was sexual harassment involved?

(That's usually a good one these days.) The publisher's apology would seem to indicate an honest error. Furthermore, if you sue you'll burn your bridges with that press ('You'll never publish in this town again!'), and the publishing world is smaller than you might think. Do you want the word getting around that you're the type who goes to court at the drop of a byline? All things considered, it's probably best to write it off. By that I do *not* mean 'chalk it up to experience,' for there's no useful experiential lesson to be learned. On the other hand, if the same thing should occur again with the same publisher...

Short of the alternative of seeking legal redress, in the US you could refer the case to the Translation Committee of PEN American Center, which serves as a kind of watchdog to protect translators' interests. While the committee does not act as legal representative, it may, depending on the individual merits, contact the publisher on your behalf or choose to publicize the case.

One of the more notorious disputes in recent times concerning possible failure to live up to contract obligations was that involving translator Helen Lane and a major New York-based publishing house. In the mid-1990s she agreed to translate a non-fiction work by Mario Vargas Llosa. Upon submitting the finished manuscript, she found that almost $2000 had been deducted from the agreed-upon honorarium. Alleging that the manuscript was 'unsuitable,' despite its approval by Vargas Llosa himself, the publisher had sent it an outside editor who did copyediting and added paragraphs to the text without authorization. After her protests, the matter was finally settled in the translator's favor, but her experience serves as a reminder that not everyone adheres religiously to the dictum *pacta sunt servanda* (treaties should be honored).

In concluding this section, and as a way of demonstrating that my thoughts throughout this guide are intended as stimuli to thought and action, not as immutable dictates of how to conduct the aesthetic and financial aspects of translation, here's a flow chart created by Peter Theroux, translator of the 1988 Nobel laureate Naguib Mahfouz and other Arabic-language authors. Though I hold fast to my admonition that a book-length work should only be translated under contract, his approach merits consideration.

ONE WAY OF TRANSLATING A BOOK

Peter Theroux

READ WIDELY IN SL for pleasure as well as business. (Publishers and agents never do this; they only know best-selling, controversial, or already translated foreign books.)

→

SELECT A BOOK using your own taste and judgment. (You may be the sole possessor of these qualities.)

→

CONTACT (by fax, phone, or whatever) **THE AUTHOR OR PUBLISHER** offering résumé, publication, or sample. **DEMAND THIS AGREEMENT OR VARIATION ON IT:**

1. Translator gets one-year option on rights; he/she contributes own time, funds, etc., to translate the book.

2. No money changes hands (yet)—i.e., option is given for no fee.

3. Translator will find a publisher (with or without an agent).

4. All income from the published book split 50-50 between author and translator. Agents get 10%.

5. Author given three vetoes: over the translation, the choice of publisher, and the deal. His/her approval NOT TO BE WITHHELD UNREASONABLY.

6. If the translator does not meet obligations, his/her rights in the project after one year will automatically terminate (but extension may be given).

FIRST SERIAL RIGHTS income belongs to translator

+

'DOWNSTREAM' TRANSLATIONS into non-SL, non-TL languages (esp. if SL is non-European) have provision for translator percentage.

(TRANSLATOR PAYS THE RENT!)

→

IF THIS WORKS...

IF THIS FAILS...

A final word on literary translation

This guide began with an exquisitely wrought and harrowing short story that proffered a disquieting glimpse into the Other. I want to end it with an equally compact, well honed tale from the opposite end of the spectrum, as amusing as it is, er, insightful. Both of these brief tales by talented Brazilian writers constitute the best possible illustration of why I translate. It is my hope that this short journey into the realm of literary translation has whetted your appetite to go and do likewise.

BLIND JUSTICE
by Moacyr Scliar

'The one that just went by was a 1962 Volkswagen, wasn't it, Gedeão?' said the blind man.

'No, it was a Simca Tufão.'

'A Simca Tufão? ... Ah, yes, that's right. A powerful Simca. And very economical. I know the Simca Tufão from a long way off. I can tell any make of car by the sound of its engine. – Wasn't the one that just went by a Ford?'

'No. It was a Mercedes truck.'

'A Mercedes truck! Who would've thought it! It's been a long time since a Mercedes truck came by here. A great truck. Rugged. Holds the curves well. I can tell the Mercedes from a long way off ... I can tell any car. Know how long I've been sitting here by the highway listening to motors, my friend Gedeão? Twelve years, my friend. Twelve years.

'That's a long time, isn't it, my friend? Long enough to learn a few things. About cars, I mean. Wasn't that a Gordini Teimoso that just went by?'

'No, it was a motor scooter.'

'A scooter ... They fool you, those scooters. Especially when they leave their exhaust open.

'But as I was saying, if there's one thing I can do it's recognize automobiles by the sound of their motor. After all, I should: years and years of listening!

'This ability came in very handy on a certain occasion ... Wasn't the one that just went by a small Mercedes?'

'No, it was the bus.'

'I knew it: two Mercedes in a row never come by here. I was just kidding. But where was I? Ah yes.

'My ability once came in handy. Want me to tell you about it, Gedeão? Then I'll tell you. It helps kill the time, doesn't it? That way the day goes by faster. I like night better: it's cool this time of year. But as I was saying: a few years ago a man was killed about 120 miles from here, a very rich rancher. He was killed by 15 bullets. Was that a Galaxie just then?'

'No, it was a '64 Volkswagen.'

'Ah, a Volkswagen ... A good car. Very economical. And a very good transmission. But, anyway, the rancher was killed. Didn't you hear about it? It was a widely discussed case. Fifteen bullets! And they took all the rancher's money. At the time I was already in the habit of sitting here by the side of the road, and I heard of the crime, which had been committed on a Sunday. On Friday the radio said the police didn't know where to begin. Wasn't the one that just passed by a Candango?'

'No, it wasn't a Candango.'

'I was sure it was a Candango ... As I was saying, by Friday they didn't know where to begin.

'I sat here, in this very chair, thinking, thinking ... I do a lot of thinking. So I formed a line of thought. I felt I should help the police. I asked my neighbor to let the police detective know I had some information for him. That one has to be a Candango!'

'No, it was a Gordini Teimoso.'

'I could have sworn it was a Candango. The detective look a long time to come talk to me. He must have thought: "A blind man? What can a blind man have seen?" That sort of foolishness, you know how it is, my friend. Even so, he showed up, because they were so confused that they'd even go talk to a stone. The detective came and sat right where you are now, Gedeão. Was that the bus?'

'No, it was a Chevrolet station wagon.'

'An old station wagon, but a good one. Where was I? Oh yes. The detective came by. I asked:

'"Detective, at what time was the crime committed?"'

'"About three p.m.," he replied. "Then," I said, "you should look for a 1927 Oldsmobile. The car has a hole in its muffler. One spark plug is misfiring. In the front seat there was a very fat man. In back, I'm certain, there were two or three people." The detective was astounded. "How do you know all this?" was all he asked. Wasn't that a DKW that just went by?'

'No. It was a Volkswagen.'

'Right. The detective was astounded. "How do you know all this?" "Look, detective," I answered, "for years I've been sitting here beside the road listening to cars go by. I know every make of car. I know more than that:

when the motor's bad, when there's a lot of weight in front, when there are people in the back seat. That car came by here at a quarter to three and returned to the city at 3:15." "How did you know what time it was?" the detective asked. "See here, detective," I replied, "if there's one thing I know – besides recognizing cars by the sound of their engines – it's how to calculate the time by the height of the sun." For all his doubts the detective went along ... Did an Aero Willys just go by?'

'No, it was a Chevrolet.'

'The detective found the 1927 Oldsmobile with the entire gang inside. They were so astonished that they gave up without resistance. The detective recovered all the rancher's money, and the family gave me a large chunk as reward. Was that a Toyota just now?'

'No, it was a '56 Ford.'

Bibliography

Author/translator relations

Mordecai Richler, 'Who or What Is 'Liz Smith'?' *GQ*, October 1991.
Isabelle Vanderschelden, 'Authority in Literary Translation: Collaborating with the Author.' *Translation Review* 56 (1998).
Kurt Vonnegut, Jr., *Fates Worse Than Death*. G.P. Putnam's Sons, 1991.

Business aspects of literary translation

Gary W. Carter, *J.K. Lasser's Taxes Made Easy for Your Home-Based Business*. John Wiley & Sons, 2000.
Jennifer Lyons, 'An Agent's View.' *ATA Chronicle*, January 1994.
Marilyn Gaddis Rose, 'Literary Translation Is an Equation of Love.' *ATA Chronicle*, January 1994.

Culture in literary translation

Alexandra V. Belenkaya, 'Culture-bound Concepts in Russian Translations of American and British Literary Texts.' *Proceedings of the 40th Annual Conference of the American Translators Association*, 1999.
John Bester, 'The Other Art of the Possible.' *Japan Quarterly*, January-March, 1991.
Sanford Budick and Wolfgang Aser, eds *The Translatability of Cultures: Figurations of the Space Between*. Stanford University Press, 1996.
Peter Glassgold, 'Translation: Culture's Driving Wedge.' *Translation Review*, 1987.
Nidra Poller, 'Don't Call Me Nègre, Toubab: Humanism vs. Political Correctness as a Guiding Principle in the Translation of an African Novel/Round 2.' *ATA Chronicle*, June 1999.
Jean Ouédraogo, 'Translating the Politically and Culturally Sensitive.' *ATA Chronicle*, May 1988.
Jean Ouédraogo, 'Rescuing the Human in Poller's Humanism.' *ATA Chronicle*, June 1999.

Euphemism

John Ayto, *Euphemisms*. Bloomsbury, 1993.
Hugh Rawson, *A Dictionary of Euphemisms and Other Doubletalk*. Crown, 1981.
Richard A. Spears, *Slang and Euphemism*, 2nd revised edition. Signet, 1991.

General reference

David Crystal, *Cambridge Encyclopedia of Language*, 2nd edition. Cambridge University Press, 1997.
Tom McArthur, ed., *The Oxford Companion to the English Language*. Oxford University Press, 1992.

Getting started

ALTA Guides to Literary Translation. *Breaking into Print.* American Literary Translators Association, 2000.
Gertrud Graubart Champe, 'Letter to a Young Translator.' *ATA Chronicle,* August 1996.
Keith Goldsmith, 'How Badly Do You Want to Be a Literary Translator?' *ATA Chronicle,* January 1994.

Literary translation: general

Eugene Eoyang, 'Speaking in Tongues: Translating Chinese Literature in a Post-Babelian Age.' In Eugene Eoyang and Lin Yao-fu, eds, *Translating Chinese Literature.* Indiana University Press, 1995.
Clifford Landers, 'An Interview with Helen Lane.' *Translation Review* 47 (1995).
Cees Nooteboom, 'Lost and Found in Translation.' *The Washington Post,* July 17, 1999.
Gregory Rabassa, 'The Ear in Translation.' In *The World of Translation.* PEN American Center, 1971.
Gregory Rabassa, 'No Two Snowflakes Are Alike: Translation as Metaphor.' In John Biguenet and Rainer Schulte, eds, *The Craft of Translation.* University of Chicago Press, 1989.
Theodore H. Savory, *The Art of Translation.* Dufour Editions, 1960.
Robert Wechsler, *Performing Without a Stage: The Art of Literary Translation.* Catbird Press, 1998.
George Woodcock, 'More Than an Echo: Notes on the Craft of Translation.' *Canadian Literature,* Summer 1988.
The World of Translation. PEN American Center, 1971.

Poetic translation

Willis Barnstone, *The Poetics of Translation: History, Theory, Practice.* Yale University Press, 1993.
Robert Bly, *The Eight Stages of Translation.* Ally Press and Rowan Tree Press, 1986.
John Du Val, 'Where the Bee Sucks: Translation Failure #34.' *Delos,* No. 17 (October 1995).
John Felstiner, 'A Double Decalogue: Translating Paul Celan.' *ATA Source,* Spring 1999.
Anselm Hollo, 'On Translation.' *Talisman, a Journal of Contemporary Poetry and Poetics,* Spring 1991.
Edwin Honig, *The Poet's Other Voice: Conversations on Literary Translation.* University of Massachusetts Press, 1985.
André Lefevere, *Translating Poetry: Seven Strategies and a Blueprint.* Van Gorcum, 1978.
Alexis Levitin, 'Translator at Work: Apologia of a Pragmatist.' *Proceedings of the 31st Annual Conference of the American Translators Association,* 1990.
Jean Longland, 'World World Vast World of Poetic Translation.' *Latin American Research Review,* Vol. 12 (1977).
Margaret Sayers Peden, 'Building a Translation, the Reconstruction Business: Poem 145 of Sor Juana Inés de la Cruz.' In *The Craft of Translation.* University of Chicago Press, 1989.

Lia Purpura, 'Where Language Lives: Notes on Poetic Translation.' *ATA Source*, Spring 2000 (originally appeared in *Willow Springs*).

Burton Raffel, *The Art of Translating Poetry*. The Pennsylvania State University Press, 1988.

Daniel Weissbort, ed., *Translating Poetry: The Double Labyrinth*. University of Iowa Press, 1989.

Clement Wood, ed. *The Complete Rhyming Dictionary*. Dell, 1994.

Portuguese-language references

Bobby Chamberlain, *A Dictionary of Informal Brazilian Portuguese*. Georgetown University Press, 1983.

Aurélio Buarque de Hollanda Ferreira, *Novo Dicionário Aurélio Século XXI*. Editora Nova Fronteira, 1999.

Hamilcar de Garcia and Antenor Nascentes, *Caldas Aulete Dicionário Contemporâneo da Língua Portuguesa*, 5th edition, Editora Delta, 1964.

Antônio Houaiss and Ismael Cardim, *Webster's Dicionário Inglês-Português*. Editora Record, 1982.

Mário Souto Maior, *Dicionário do Palavrão e Termos Afins*. Editora Record, 1988.

Novo Dicionário Melhoramentos, 5th edition. Editora Melhoramentos, 1969.

Maria Chaves de Mello, *Dicionário Jurídico Português–Inglês, Inglês–Português*, 2nd edition. Barrister's Editora, 1985.

Gumercindo Saraiva, *A Gíria Brasileira dos Marginais às Classes de Elite*. Editora Itatiaia, 1988.

Felisberto da Silva, *Dicionário de Gíria*. Papelivros, n.d.

Ariel Tacla, *Dicionário dos Marginais*. Forense-Universitária, 1981.

James L. Taylor, *A Portuguese–English Dictionary*. Stanford University Press, 1970.

Manuel Viotti, *Novo Dicionário da Gíria Brasileira*, 3rd edition. N.p., 1957.

Profanity and obscenity

David Burke, *Bleep! A Guide to Popular American Obscenities*. Optima Books, 1993.

Jeremy R. Ellis, *Talking Dirty: Slang, Expletives, and Curses from around the World*. Citadel Press, 1996.

Sterling Johnson, *English as a Second F*cking Language*. St. Martin's Griffin, 1995.

Christina Kunitskaya-Peterson, *International Dictionary of Obscenities: A Guide to Dirty Words and Indecent Expressions in Spanish, Italian, French, German, Russian*. Scythian Books, 1981.

James McDonald, *The Wordsworth Dictionary of Obscenity & Taboo*. Wordsworth Editions, 1996.

Lawrence Paros, *The Erotic Tongue: A Sexual Lexicon*. Henry Holt and Company, 1984.

Jesse Sheidlower, ed., *The F-word*. Random House, 1995.

Richard A. Spears, *Forbidden American English: A Serious Compilation of Taboo American English*. Passport Books, 1990.

Puns and word play

Cait Murphy, '"Ulysses"' in Chinese.' *Atlantic Monthly*, September 1995.

Special problems in literary translation

Carrol F. Coates, 'Problems of "Translating" Bi-/Multilingual Texts: The Haitian French of Jacques Stephen Alexis.' *ATA Chronicle*, June 1999.
Marlene Dolitsky, 'The Translation of Nonsense.' *Babel*, Vol. 34, No. 2 (1988).
Robert N. Sebastian, 'On Translating French Occurring in English into Spanish.' *Hispania*, Volume 72, No. 3 (1989).

Slang

John Ayto and John Simpson, *The Oxford Dictionary of Modern Slang*. Oxford University Press, 1992.
Robert L. Chapman, *Thesaurus of American Slang*. Harper & Row, 1989.
Tom Dalzell, *The Slang of Sin*. Merriam-Webster, 1998.
Jonathon Green, *The Dictionary of Contemporary Slang*. Stein and Day, 1984.
Jonathon Green, *The Slang Thesaurus*. Penguin, 1988.
Esther Lewin and Albert E. Lewin, *The Random House Thesaurus of Slang*. Random House, 1988.
J.E. Lighter, *Historical Dictionary of American Slang*. Random House, 3 volumes, 1994–2000.
Clarence Major, *Juba to Jive: A Dictionary of African-American Slang*. Penguin Books, 1994.
Alan Richter, *Dictionary of Sexual Slang*. John Wiley & Sons, 1993.
Richard A. Spears, *Slang American Style: More than 10,000 Ways to Talk the Talk*. NTC Publishing Group, 1997.
Richard A. Spears, *Slang and Euphemism*, 2nd revised edition. Signet, 1991.
Tony Thorne, *The Dictionary of Contemporary Slang*. Pantheon Books, 1990.
Karen Watts, compiler. *21st Century Dictionary of Slang*. Laurel, 1994.
Harold Wentworth and Stuart Berg Flexner, *Dictionary of American Slang*. Thomas Y. Crowell Company, 1960.

Specialized dictionaries

Benét's Reader's Encyclopedia, 4th edition. HarperCollins, 1996.
John H. Dirckx, ed., *Stedman's Concise Medical and Allied Health Dictionary*, 3rd edition. Williams & Wilkins, 1997.
Adrian Room, *Dictionary of Translated Names and Titles*. Routledge, 1986.
Clayton L. Thomas, ed., *Taber's Cyclopedic Medical Dictionary*, 18th edition. F.A. Davis, 1997.

Translating for the theater

Eric Bentley, *Thinking about the Playwright*. Northwestern University Press, 1987.
Victor Dixon, 'On Translating the Duke's First Soliloquy in Lope de Vega's *El castigo sin venganza*.' In Malcolm Coulthard and Patricia Anne Odber de Baubeta, eds, *The Knowledges of the Translator: From Literary Interpretation to Machine Classification*. The Edwin Mellen Press, 1996.
David Johnston, 'Text and Ideotext: Translation and Adaptation for the Stage.' In Malcolm Coulthard and Patricia Anne Odber de Baubeta, eds, *The Knowledges of the Translator: From Literary Interpretation to Machine Classification*. The Edwin Mellen Press, 1996.

David Johnston, ed., _Stages of Translation_. Absolute Press, 1996.
Phyllis Zatlin, Observations on Theatrical Translation,' _Translation Review_ 46 (1994).
Phyllis Zatlin, 'Translating for the Stage: Getting Past the Title.' _ATA Chronicle_, June 1999.

Translating titles

Michael S. Doyle, 'Contemporary Spanish and Spanish American Fiction in English: Tropes of Fidelity in the Translation of Titles.' _Translation Review_ 30/31 (1989).
Clifford E. Landers, 'The All-Important Title.' _Proceedings of the 31st Annual Conference of the American Translators Association_, 1990, edited by A. Leslie Willson.
Gregory Rabassa, 'A Book by Its Cover: The Translation of Titles.' _ATA Chronicle_, January 1994.

Translation techniques

Susan Bassnett-McGuire, _Translating Literature_. Boydell & Brewer, 1997.
John Biguenet and Rainer Schulte, eds, _The Craft of Translation_. University of Chicago Press, 1989.
Geoffrey Samuelsson-Brown. _A Practical Guide for Translators_. Multilingual Matters, 1998.
William H. Gass, _Reading Rilke: Reflections on the Problems of Translation_. Knopf, 1999.
James S. Holmes, _Translated! Papers on Literary Translation and Translation Studies_. With an introduction by Raymond van den Broeck (Approaches to Translation Studies 7). Rodopi-USA/Canada, 1988.
André Lefevere, _Translating Literature: Practice and Theory in a Comparative Context_. Modern Language Association of America, 1992.
André Lefevere and Susan Bassnett, _Constructing Cultures: Essays on Literary Translation_. Multilingual Matters, 1997.
Suzanne Jill Levine, _The Subversive Scribe: Translating Latin American Fiction_. Graywolf Press, 1991.
Breon Mitchell, 'The Trial and the Sentence.' _ATA Source_, Winter 1994.
Murat Nemet-Nejat, 'Translation and Style.' _Talisman, a Journal of Contemporary Poetry and Poetics_, Spring 1991.
Peter Newmark, _About Translation_. Multilingual Matters, 1991.
Peter Newmark, _Paragraphs on Translation_. Multilingual Matters, 1993.
Peter Newmark, _More Paragraphs on Translation_. Multilingual Matters, 1998.
Burton Raffel, _The Art of Translating Prose_. The Pennsylvania State University Press, 1994.
Paulo Rónai, _A Tradução Vivida_, 2nd edition. Editora Nova Fronteira, 1981.
Kurt Mueller-Vollmer and Michael Irmscher, eds, _Translating Literatures, Translating Cultures: New Vistas and Approaches in Literary Studies_. Stanford University Press, 1999.
Rosanna Warren, ed., _The Art of Translation: Voices from the Field_. Northeastern University Press, 1989.
The World of Translation. PEN American Center, 1987.

Translation theory

Ben Belitt, *Adam's Dream: A Preface to Translation*. Grove, 1978.
Leo Hickey, *The Pragmatics of Translation*. Multilingual Matters, 1998.
Douglas Hofstadter, *Le Ton Beau de Marot: In Praise of the Music of Language*. Basic Books, 1998.
Rainer Nagele, *Echoes of Translation: Reading Between Texts*. Johns Hopkins University Press, 1997.
Douglas Robinson, *Translation & Taboo*. Northern Illinois University Press, 1996.
Douglas Robinson, *The Translator's Turn (Parallax: Re-visions of Culture and Society)*. Johns Hopkins University Press, 1991.
Douglas Robinson, *What Is Translation?: Centrifugal Theories, Critical Interventions*. Kent State University Press, 1997.
George Steiner, *After Babel: Aspects of Language and Translation*. Oxford University Press, revised edition 1993.
Lawrence Venuti, *The Translator's Invisibility: A History of Translation*. Routledge, 1995.
Lawrence Venuti, *The Scandals of Translation: Towards an Ethics of Difference*. Routledge, 1998.

Glossary

advance: money paid to an author or translator prior to publication and in anticipation of revenue generated by sales. The advance is discounted from ROYALTIES.

archaicism: in literary translation, use of a deliberately outmoded LEXEME to achieve the sensation of remoteness in time, nostalgia, or quaintness, among other effects. Examples would include *thou, hath, fain would I, methinks, feather merchant,* or *23 skidoo.* When the use is unintentional, 'archaicism' applied to a translation is pejorative.

authorial voice: the tone or tenor in which the narrative is presented: objective, detached, involved, intimate, jocular, informal, professorial, pedantic, etc. It may encompass first- or third-person narration, colloquialisms and slang, various levels of intelligence or education, social position, ethnicity, and other variables. It is usually but not always independent of the speech of characters in the work. It is the translator's duty to determine and reproduce as far as possible the authorial voice.

back-translation: translation into Language A of a text translated from that language into Language B. Example: a citation from Mark Twain is quoted in a German *Bildungsroman* and the translator of that novel must put it into English. If the original quotation can be located, the practice is best avoided.

cliché: a hackneyed expression showing little thought or originality–e.g., 'out of the blue,' 'a meteoric rise.' When the SL uses a cliché, an equivalent cliché in the TL is called for. See also DEAD METAPHOR.

connotation: a secondary meaning associated with the denotative sense of a word or expression. In some cases, especially those related to sexuality, the connotation is strong enough to exclude the primary meaning, as in *intercourse* or *gay.* Translators must be constantly on the alert to avoid unintended connotations of their word-choices. See also DENOTATION.

copyright: the legal right to control who may print a published (or sometimes unpublished) work. Material under copyright is normally indicated by the symbol © or by the words 'Copyright [date]' plus the name of the copyright holder.

crib: see TROT.

dead metaphor: closely related to the CLICHÉ, a dead metaphor (e.g., 'a tower of strength,' 'the heart of a lion') has through usage lost its originality and emotional impact. A dead metaphor in the SL calls for an equally shopworn equivalent in the TL.

denotation: the principal or semantic meaning associated with a word or phrase, usually the first entry under the headword in a dictionary. Example: the denotation of *gay* for centuries was *happy, joyous* but in the 20th century its CONNOTATION made the use of the word problematic. Translators must be aware of connotations attached to even the most seemingly innocuous words.

dialect: a speech pattern characteristic of a given group, often regional but sometimes ethnic, that includes grammar and vocabulary differing from the generally accepted mode. It should be remembered that the so-called 'standard' variant of any language is merely the prestige dialect that through historical happenstance became associated with the political, economic, and social elite. Although accent can play a part in dialect, the two should not be confused. For the translator, efforts to reproduce dialect are risky at best and disastrous at worst. See also REGIONALISM.

discourse, level of: the overall impression created by description, dialogue, or exposition. Levels of discourse include, *inter alia*, formal, conversational, profane, erudite, illiterate, and so-called street talk. Certain usages can automatically trigger a perceived discourse level: the word *epistaxis* for *nosebleed* marks the discourse level as very high (medical); *she ain't got none* sets an entirely different level. In a given text, level of discourse may vary widely, and it would be a mistake to translate the speech of an illiterate peasant at a discourse level appropriate for an educated speaker. See also REGISTER.

gloss: an explanation inserted interlinearly or in the margins of a text; generally restricted in translation of fiction or poetry to scholarly or sacred texts in which preservation of meaning is paramount.

hypercorrection: a non-standard or deviant form, spoken or written, originating from the desire to avoid a perceived substandard usage. Example: because they believe the pronunciation **Alabammi* for *Alabama* to be semi-illiterate, some speakers generalize and pronounce *Miami* as **Miama*. Similarly, an intrusive *-g* at the end of *chicken* would be a hypercorrection.

idiomatic: in literary translation, a style that takes full advantage of the structure of the target language to produce a natural-sounding product. 'Idiomatic' as applied to a translation is normally considered praise, though advocates of RESISTANCE might disagree.

indirect translation: a translation made from other than the source language, as for example, a translation of the Tibetan *Book of the Dead* into Basque via French, bypassing the original language. In the present era the 'middle language' is most often English.

interpolation: in literary translation, a short, unobtrusive, explanatory word or phrase incorporated into the text to afford target-language readers information already known to source-language readers.

lexeme: a linguistic term referring to any lexical unit, whether a phrase, word, or stem. Examples: *go for broke, sandwich, -pose.*

loose sentence: as opposed to PERIODIC SENTENCE. A sentence in which the main clause precedes the dependent clause: 'The butler entered the room, first knocking discreetly at the door.'

metalanguage: when a text becomes self-referential, as in discussion of its grammar (He said, 'In English we can say *in* the boat or *on* the boat') or in the use of puns or wordplays, it is language talking about itself (metalanguage). For obvious reasons, this is one of the most difficult elements for the translator to deal with.

mimesis: the artificial effect based on tacit agreement between writer and reader that creates a simulation of reality. Any departure from this convention, such as the author or a character directly addressing the reader, destroys the effect, as does the introduction of footnotes, asterisks, and the like.

mimetic effect: see MIMESIS.

model contract: a contract designed to serve as template or point of departure for other contracts. The PEN American Center Model Contract provides helpful suggestions for literary translators.

periodic sentence: as opposed to LOOSE SENTENCE. A sentence in which the main clause follows the dependent clause(s): 'After knocking discreetly at the door, the butler entered the room,'

pony: see TROT.

regionalism: see also DIALECT. A lexeme distinguishing native speakers of a language in a given geographical area from others that share the same language. Example: in the southern United States, the term *croaker sack* for standard *burlap bag*. In literary translation, it is usually counterproductive to attempt to reproduce regionalisms. See also DIALECT.

register: a culturally defined variant of language employed in a specific setting: academic, medical, engineering, military, financial, etc. While vague, the terms 'higher' and 'lower' register serve to alert translators to the need to adjust their choice of vocabulary and syntax to reflect the given register.

resistance: as viewed by its proponents, the term refers to the conscious effort to indicate the non-native origins of a work through close adherence to the source language and source culture in the translation, deliberately promoting its 'otherness.' The result is often perceived as strange or even bizarre by many readers. 'Foreignizing' is considered desirable because, in the words of Lawrence Venuti, one of its chief advocates, it 'can provoke new thinking about culture, new ways of writing cultural history, and, eventually, new translation strategies.' Most translators, however, will encounter difficulties enough in achieving a readable text without actively striving to introduce such elements into the translation.

royalties: a percentage of gross sales of a book, usually based on cover price, to author and/or translator. Normally, royalties begin to accrue once the total equals the amount of the ADVANCE.

'third language': similar to TRANSLATIONESE, it emerges as neither source language nor target language and betrays the text as not originating in English.

tone: a somewhat vague term relating to the overall feeling conveyed by an utterance, a passage, or an entire work, including both conscious and unconscious resonance. Tone can comprise humor, irony, sincerity, earnestness, naïveté, or virtually any sentiment.

'translationese': an awkward, often stilted style of language characterized by unidiomatic usages and strained constructions. Frequently it is the result of undue adherence to grammatical norms of the source language. Similar to 'THIRD LANGUAGE.'

undertranslation: translation of a LEXEME that omits parts of its SL meaning, usually in the interests of readability. For example, after translating the initial occurrence of the Portuguese *sobrado* as 'two-story house,' subsequent appearances of the word would be rendered simply as 'house.' Undertranslation may also take place in order to avoid complicated explanations of a term, provided the approximation is sufficient to convey the necessary contextual information. *Delegado* in Portuguese is not exactly the same as a police precinct captain but is close enough for practical purposes.

trot: originally a schoolboy term denoting a literal translation used for purposes of cheating or cramming for an exam, in literary translation it refers to an interlinear translation designed to provide the semantic content without regard to aesthetics or style.

zero translation: translation by omission. It is recommended when translation of a term would lead to a misunderstanding of the SL utterance or the SL culture. For a fuller discussion, see 'Change of address: problems of the English vocative.'

Appendix: Ethical questions in literary translation

There are no right or wrong answers to these questions. The opinions of the author of this guide, based solely on his own experience, should be taken as suggestions rather than as absolutes.

(1) In translating a recent novel, you discover that the author, now deceased, made a factual error in the order of geological epochs, reversing the Jurassic and the Cretaceous periods. Would you rectify this oversight in your translation?
Yes ☐ No ☐

A. Would you act any differently if the author were living?
Yes ☐ No ☐

B. Would it make a difference if the error appeared to be the mistake on the part of a character in the novel?
Yes ☐ No ☐

C. Would deadline considerations have any effect on your decision?
Yes ☐ No ☐

(2) You understand perfectly the meaning of a given SL phrase in a short story, recognizing also its strangeness in the original. If you translate it faithfully, you will achieve one of two results, neither especially desirable: either the author will sound awkward in English or the reader will think you're a poor translator. Do you retain the strange construction in your translation?
Yes ☐ No ☐

(3) In a possibly corrupted text of a 19th-century novel, in a crucial passage you encounter a grammatical construction that can be interpreted two distinct ways, depending on the presence or absence of a diacritical marking. You are almost certain, based on internal evidence, that your interpretation is correct but have no way to verify the original SL text. Would you point out to the editor or publisher the doubtful passage?
Yes ☐ No ☐

(4) In selecting a title for your translation of a short story you have two choices. One is straightforward but uninspiring; the other is thematically less apropos but is catchy and more likely to increase the salability of the piece and attract readers. Which do you choose?

The inventive title □ The straightforward title □

(5) An earlier translation of the text you are now translating, which has become part of the 20th-century canon, became a best seller despite the mistranslation of the title. Should you give it a new title or stick to the old, less-than-optimal one?

New title □ Old title □

(6) Either of two words will satisfactorily render the SL term, but one of them achieves a subtle foreshadowing effect related to events that occur later in the work. Unfortunately, there was no such effect in the original. Should you use it anyway?

Yes □ No □

(7) A particular pun in the novel you are dealing with is untranslatable, but in the same passage there is an opportunity to create a pun based on a different sentence uttered by the same speaker, a pun that did not occur in the original. Are you justified in 'transferring' the pun?

Yes □ No □

(8) Would you read an earlier translation of a novel or short story before beginning your own translation?

Yes □ No □

of a poem?

Yes □ No □

(9) For full understanding by the TL reader, a certain cultural referent requires explanation beyond that found in the SL text. But introducing a footnote will destroy the mimetic effect. The item in question is a one-time reference of no importance to the development of plot and the theme. An approximate translation renders the term in a way that, while comprehensible and unobtrusive to the TL reader, does not convey its full sense. Do you use a footnote?

Yes □ No □

(10) In a passage ostensibly in a language that is neither SL nor TL, the author has erroneously placed non-existent grammatical construc-

tions in the mouths of supposedly native speakers. The third language is sufficiently close to the SL so that readers of the original text could easily make out the meaning, but this is not the case in the TL into which you are translating.

A.   Do you translate the third language into the TL?
       Yes □ No □

B.   Do you leave it in the third language and correct the grammatical errors?
       Yes □ No □

(1) *No.* The author presumably had the opportunity to correct such errors of fact during his or her lifetime, whether in a subsequent SL printing or through an errata insert. It is also possible that the mistake was intentional; only a close examination of the text, based on internal evidence, can determine that. Finally, a check of translations of the work into other languages will reveal if any change was made, which might be a clue to the author's intention. Finally, there is the possibility that the author left instructions for future translators that may include mention of this anomaly. All in all, in the absence of any clear probative evidence, the tendency should be to leave the passage as it is.

A.   *Yes,* because then it would be a simple matter to ask the author.

B.   *Yes.* Leave it as is; many people of all levels of education could easily make the same mistake.

C.   *Conceivably.* If time pressure were a significant factor, you would probably have to base your decision on the considerations enumerated above.

(2) There is no clear-cut answer. Your chosen solution depends on where you stand on the author-translator-reader continuum. (See 'Decisions at the outset.') Obviously, your feelings about the desirability of 'resistance' also play a part.

(3) *Yes.* Usually the publisher or editor will defer to the translator's judgment in such cases, and you have met your ethical duty by reporting the problem.

(4) *The inventive title.* (See 'The all-important title.') Your goal is to maximize the potential audience for the work in the TL, and the bibliographical equivalent of 'curb appeal' – the title and the dust jacket

material – is crucial. Most authors accept retitling as a way of life and do not take umbrage at the practice; to the typical TL reader, of course, the act is invisible

(5) *Indeterminate.* More often than not, the choice is not in your hands; the publisher will make the final decision. If, however, it's left up to you, here are the practical dimensions of the dilemma: if you go with a more accurate title, some unsophisticated members of the larger public may take it to be a new (or newly discovered) work by the same author; contrariwise, if you use the existing less-than-accurate title many will be unaware that this is a new translation. All told, it's not an easy nut to crack. I lean about 60% toward the former, based on the idea that people who read translations are a cut above the reading public in general and will not be seriously misled by the new title.

(6) *Yes,* provided there does not exist in the source language a term that would adequately convey such foreshadowing. If there is such a term, we must assume the author considered and rejected it, and we have no right to 'improve' the original. As in similar cases, when in doubt, run it past the author.

(7) *Yes.* Note that this is not an instance of 'improving' the original. The authorial intent was to convey a personality trait of a specific character, namely the type who makes puns, and by having the same individual make a different play on words in another part of dialogue you effectively convey that impression.

(8) *No* (whether short story, novel, or poem). In all three genres the same danger lurks: your perception of meaning – that is, how you interpret ambiguous items – as well as your choice of vocabulary and even syntax may be influenced unconsciously by exposure to previous translations. While this is not plagiarism, why subject yourself to second-guessing? Note that there is no ethical constraint against checking your own translation against previous ones upon completion of your first draft. The fact that the ideal word or turn of phrase has already appeared in an earlier translation should not preclude your own use of it; isolated words can't be copyrighted, and there are only so many ways to express, say, 'She turned heads wherever she went.'

(9) *No,* in fiction or poetry. *Yes,* in non-fiction. (See 'Other areas of literary translation.') The mimetic effect in fiction and the need for succinctness in poetry trump fine semantic distinctions. Given a single

non-crucial occurrence of a problem word, an undertranslation is acceptable.

(10) **Indeterminate**. Either approach is justifiable. If opting to translate the passage into English, an interpolation might be used, such as 'he said, in Spanish.' If leaving it in the third language, grammatical errors should be corrected. (See 'Care and feeding of authors.')